DRAMA FOR A
NEW SOUTH AFRICA

DRAMA
FOR A NEW

SEVEN
PLAYS

SOUTH AFRICA

Edited by
David Graver

INDIANA UNIVERSITY PRESS   BLOOMINGTON & INDIANAPOLIS

This book is a publication of

Indiana University Press
601 North Morton Street
Bloomington, Indiana 47404-3797 USA

www.indiana.edu/~iupress

Telephone orders   800-842-6796
Fax orders   812-855-7931
Orders by email   iuporder@indiana.edu

The following three plays are being used with permission of Witwatersrand University Press:

Mooi Street Moves, previously published in *Mooi Street and Other Moves* by Paul Slabolepszy (1994)

And the Girls in Their Sunday Dresses, previously published in *And the Girls in Their Sunday Dresses: Four Works by Zakes Mda* (1993)

Sophiatown, originally appearing in *Sophiatown by the Junction Avenue Theatre Company* (1993), and subsequently in *At the Junction: Four Plays by the Junction Avenue Theatre Company* (1995)

Any public performance (including a public reading) of *Mooi Street Moves, And the Girls in Their Sunday Dresses*, and *Sophiatown* is subject to clearance of performance rights and payment of royalties. Applications for performance rights must be directed to:

DALRO (Pty) Limited, P.O. Box 31627, Braamfontein 2017, South Africa

Permission to perform any other play in this collection must be obtained from the playwright.

The paper used in this publication meets the minimum
requirements of American National Standard for Information
Sciences—Permanence of Paper for Printed Library
Materials, ANSI Z39.48-1984.

Manufactured in the United States of America

Library of Congress Cataloging-in-Publication Data

Drama for a new South Africa : seven plays / edited by David Graver.
   p.   cm. — (Drama and performance studies)
   ISBN 0-253-33570-1 (Cloth : alk. paper). — ISBN 0-253-21326-6 (pbk. : alk. paper)
   1. South African drama—20th century. 2. South Africa—Social conditions—Drama. 3. Apartheid—South
Africa—Drama.   I. Graver, David, date.   II. Series.
PL8014.S62D73   1999
822—dc21   99-25444

   1   2   3   4   5   04   03   02   01   00   99

DEDICATED TO

BARNEY SIMON

1933–1996

DATE DUE

CONTENTS

ACKNOWLEDGMENTS

In the initial research for this collection, I am indebted to Anna Mabitsela for giving me access to the Market Theatre archives and to Peter Midgley and his staff at the National English Literary Museum for their efficient and thorough bibliographical assistance. Heather Inge and Shelagh Blackman in the press office for the Grahamstown Festival also provided invaluable assistance in gaining access to the most recent theatrical performances. For their help in assembling the plays and background material for this collection, I would like to thank Pat Tucker at Witwatersrand University Press, Regina Sebright at the Market Theatre, Elizabeth Ellenbogen, Malcolm Purkey, Ismail Mahomed, Reza de Wet, and Brett Bailey. I am also grateful to my research assistant at Columbia University, Lisa Silberman-Brenner, for her help in formatting, typing, and proofreading the manuscript, and to the editors at Indiana University Press, Robert Sloan and Timothy Wiles, for their advice, assistance, and patience. For advice and support throughout the work on this project, as well as for translations of Afrikaans and Zulu phrases, I have relied repeatedly on Loren Kruger. Without her assistance, I would not have dared undertake this project.

DRAMA FOR A
NEW SOUTH AFRICA

Introduction

South African theatre captured world attention with its vivid protests against apartheid. Now that apartheid has passed, South African theatre deserves continued attention for its innovative variety of hybrid dramatic forms rich in vivid language, forceful performance styles, and incisive social functions. With its confluence of African and European aesthetic values and its response to a social milieu that combines elements of industrialized and developing countries, South African theatre has relevance to and resonances with drama in many parts of the world. Now that apartheid has been abolished, South Africa is no longer so much unique in as it is emblematic of many of the world's abiding tensions and promises: bitter historical memories, uneven social development, impoverishment and greed, diversity, resourcefulness, and cooperation. The eloquence with which these tensions and promises are played out in South African theatre has universal lessons and appeal. This collection of plays is the first devoted to drama aimed at a post-apartheid South Africa. The plays do not ignore the apartheid era, but look beyond the narrow concerns of the anti-apartheid struggle to more abiding cultural realities. Here is both a selection of recent plays and a sampling of dramatic themes and forms likely to occupy South African theatre for many years to come.

THE LIMITS OF RESISTANCE THEATRE

During the 1970s and 1980s, as the struggle against apartheid gathered strength, the performative power of theatre in South Africa seemed to increase as its thematic range shrank. Although the variety of dramatic forms and theatrical occasions was and remains diverse, the physically oriented theatre of resistance was the only kind to gain widespread acclaim and financial success.[1] Productions such as *Survival!* and *Asinimali!* combined extraordinary displays of physical prowess in mime, dance, song, and quick-change character portrayal with a rivetingly direct contact between actors and audience—a contact anchored vividly and courageously to the present moment's social injustice. The defiance of the actors and the complicity in resistance they offered the audience made the more purely aesthetic pleasures of conventional drama seem tepid and irrelevant.

Unfortunately, away from the townships where the struggle against apartheid was being fought, the politically engaged social function of resistance theatre became less an assault upon injustice than a marketing ploy. On international tour, performances designed to participate in resistance and revolt were reduced to images of resistance and revolt served up for the audiences' inconsequential pleasure. The reduction of revolt to an image of itself is confirmed most strikingly in the BBC film version of *Woza Albert!* At the end of their play, the performers Percy Mtwa and Mbongeni Ngema call upon members of the audience to "rise up" as resurrected heroes of the struggle against apartheid. The gesture was powerfully subversive in apartheid South Africa, but meaningless elsewhere. The producers of the BBC film seem aware of this problem, for in response to the actors' calls of "Woza!" (rise up), they show film clips of the anti-apartheid struggle. Here we see clearly how the social function of protest and resistance plays can become nothing but an aesthetic spectacle. The sense of community and commitment the play tries to generate in the theatre in South Africa becomes a ghostly image of itself in international venues, a dream of rebellion rather than the act.

The co-optation of protest and resistance drama by entertainment-oriented theatre institutions abroad, was in many ways a good thing. It gave the violation of human rights in South Africa international attention; it demonstrated the power of a theatre oriented toward political engagement and pedagogy (even if this demonstration itself was not strongly political or pedagogical); and it rewarded some very talented, hard-working artists. A vicarious alternative to the monotonous domination of commercial theatre at least suggests the possibility of other cultural functions for theatre.

An overemphasis on resistance plays can, however, have debilitating effects. The forceful plots become formulaic. The short vignettes, which make possible a quick pace and broad thematic reach, can excuse incoherence. The keenly observed character-types can become stock figures. The forceful opposition of oppressor and oppressed can become a simpleminded division between good and evil. In the townships today, too many young theatre troupes place their hopes for success upon overused resistance theatre conventions.

As South Africa begins to redress the inequities of apartheid, the theatre has begun to experience material difficulties. Some theatre practitioners have blamed themselves for this decline, wondering if the lack of audiences is due to their inability to generate compelling new themes,[2] but other debilitating forces are more obviously at work. Given the broad range of social problems the government must address, it has been reluctant to commit large funds to theatre. The end of apartheid has reduced interest in South African theatre abroad, while the continuing high crime rate in the country makes audiences reluctant to risk attending evening performances, especially since television now offers an alternative, uncensored source of entertainment. The end of the cultural boycott means that South

African theatre must now also compete with a more daunting array of cheap and attractive foreign imports, from which it has long been inadvertently shielded.

As the plays in this collection demonstrate, the crisis in South African drama is not due to a depletion of themes or formal ingenuity. The theatre is certainly facing some difficulties, but one can hope the vitality and variety of its artistic reserves will see it through this transitional period.

THE ROOTS OF SOUTH AFRICAN THEATRE

To understand what South African theatre is drawing from as it moves out of a period dominated by protest and resistance drama,[3] we should look briefly at its performance traditions. These traditions have contributed significantly to the character of resistance theatre, but have also spawned other forms of theatrical expression that have been obscured by resistance theatre's heroism and glamour.

South African theatre incorporates both indigenous performance forms and the European dramatic tradition. Developments in twentieth-century European drama (e.g., the innovations of Meyerhold, Brecht, Artaud, and Grotowski) have brought it closer to African performance forms, but before this century, the two were far apart, offering fundamentally distinct approaches to theatre. Indigenous African performance is communal, drawing performers and audience together and often obscuring the boundary between them. The performance is used to mark a particular occasion in social life (birth, wedding, death, planting, harvest, coronation, etc.) rather than marking off a time separate from the rest of social life and devoted solely to the theatrical performance (as in European drama).[4]

African Theatrical Aesthetics

By European standards, African performance seems eclectic and hybrid. It combines dramatic and narrative elements and fuses song, dance, and mimicry. One performer might take on all the parts in a play (as in the Zulu *inganekwane* and the Xhosa *intsomi*) thus emphasizing the varied mimetic skills of the actor as much as the course of the dramatic action. The forms of performance commonly called praise poetry (*izibongo* among the amaZulu and *dithoko* among the Basotho) serve to theatricalize social occasions by flattering leaders with eloquent encomia or prodding them to react with finely barbed satirical thrusts.[5] African performance forms are typically very fluid in mood and tenor, running easily from the sacred to the profane, the solemn to the ludicrous. The protean transformations and multiple identities of the performers are accepted, often highlighted, elements of the theatrical experience. Moreover, because performances are parts of larger social events, they do not create dominating spectacles that sharply divide spectators from actors. Cooperation and exchange, rather than passivity and domination, mark the relationship between audience and performers. Spectators may mingle in or even become a dominant element in the spectacle, and performers may watch and react to the audience as much as to their intended performative script.

European Theatrical Aesthetics

European theatre, in contrast, relies on rigid conventions of representation and performance. Theatre is a place and occasion separated from other cultural activities. Its overt function is dramatic representation but a frequent implicit function is social legitimation. Theatre is attended and supported primarily by educated elites (not necessarily the most wealthy or powerful sections of society, but generally the most educated). Going to the theatre is a way of establishing one's membership in a particular group. Decorum and submission to the theatrical spectacle are required. The spectators are carefully separated from the stage; they sit quietly in the dark. On stage, characters are also carefully separated from each other. Although minor parts may be doubled, the actors take care to make each character distinct and consistent as an individual with a rich inner life. This stress on character allows for more complex and varied forms of interaction between characters, although the plots of European plays are not necessarily more complex or imaginative than Africa's theatrical storytelling.

The sharp division between stage and audience in European theatre facilitates the creation of a detailed imagined world behind the proscenium arch. While the spectators are expected to admire the technical expertise with which this world is constructed, they are encouraged to engage with it primarily through their emotions. The audience becomes sentimentally attached to the characters and events represented on stage and judges the quality of the performance by the intensity of the emotional experience prompted by the dramatic representation. In contrast, African theatrical performance does not create a detailed imagined world and does not encourage the audience to attach itself emotionally to the representational aspects of the performance. The African audience is more interested in the performative expertise of the actors than in the emotional flux of the represented events. African spectators look for and respond to virtuosity more than sentiment, and their judgment of the represented events depends more on the ideas and arguments made than on the emotions portrayed.

European Theatre in Africa

Africans began to use European dramatic forms to tell their own stories in mission schools and then in urban cultural clubs. Although these efforts began as a means of mastering English and the cultural values and rituals of the colonizers, they quickly evolved into a means of responding to colonial values and forging a modern, detribalized African national identity. Herbert Dhlomo's plays from the 1930s and 1940s are the most important early example of this work in South Africa. While working in a dramatic form similar to Galsworthy and Shaw, Dhlomo fills his plays with important historical and contemporary African themes and sometimes includes songs and dances that draw upon indigenous forms to create an African tradition of (hybrid) performative spectacle.[6]

The fusion of African aesthetic norms with European ones was facilitated by one other major influence: African-American theatre. Beginning with the visit of Orpheus McAdoo and the Virginia Jubilee Singers in the 1890s[7] and nurtured by college attendance in the United States and subscriptions to African American magazines such as *Opportunity*, South African Blacks borrowed heavily from African American cultural forms as they forged their own urban culture. Jazz was certainly important, but so was musical theatre, put together at first by small groups in the 1920s and 1930s[8] and giving rise to larger productions, some with international renown, in the late 1950s and onward. The most important of these early musicals was *King Kong* (1959), about a Black prizefighter and life among urban Blacks. The production helped launch the international career of Miriam Makeba and provided an important early stimulus to Gibson Kente, who went on to forge a distinctive, influential popular musical theatre for township audiences.

DIVERGING THEATRICAL STYLES

From the early 1960s, other influences added to the growing variety and richness of South African drama. Improvisational workshop techniques—which allowed the ensemble of actors, rather than the playwright, to dominate the creation of the performance—came to South Africa with Barney Simon when he returned from working with Joan Littlewood in Britain and Joseph Chaikin in the U.S. Other experimental techniques, particularly Brecht's and Grotowski's, were taken up, most noticeably by Percy Mtwa and Mbongeni Ngema in *Woza Albert!* (1980). Building on a tradition of educational theatre established in West Africa during the colonial era, strategies of the Workers' Theatre Movement of the 1920s in Europe and the U.S. were combined with recent innovations by Augusto Boal in Brazil and Ngugi wa Mirii in Kenya to enliven both trade union theatre and theatre for development.[9]

Athol Fugard's work from 1958 to 1980, although dominated by the concerns of traditional European dramatic realism, does give some indication of the rich variety of theatrical forms in use in South Africa. Even when Fugard's dramatic form is entirely European, the situations and characters he creates are distinctly South African. Some of his plays belong to the protest school in critically representing situations created by the apartheid regime (e.g., *Statements After an Arrest under the Immorality Act*, 1974), while others deal with issues of poverty that, although exacerbated by apartheid, are not completely dependent upon it (see *Nongogo*, 1959, and *Boseman and Lena*, 1969). He has experimented with non-verbal performance in the European avant-garde tradition of directors such as Peter Brook in *Orestes* (1978—a meditation in gestures on the motivations behind terrorism) and used the elaborate narrative framing and presentational comedy of township performance forms in collaboration with John Kani and Winston

Ntshona in *Sizwe Bansi is Dead* (1972). In *The Coat* (1966), he even cultivated a confrontational, problem-presenting style drawn from Brecht's learning plays and similar to the Workers' Theatre Movement and theatre for development. From the 1980s forward, however, Fugard held to the tradition of a detailed, naturalistic imagined world with predominantly sentimental attachments to the audience. Although he works skillfully within the realistic European tradition, his work reflects less and less the variety of approaches to drama and theatre practiced in South Africa.

By 1980, a number of distinct forms of drama existed in South Africa. Naturalistic drama played frequently for Afrikaner, English-speaking, mixed-race "Coloured," and Indian communities with content varying from support for through avoidance of to dissent from the policies of the racist government. Gibson Kente led in the development of a distinct form of township theatre, which combined song, dance, melodrama, and clowning in extravagant displays of talent and energy. As the government clamped down on dissident performance, smaller performing units (perhaps only one or two actors) found ways of expressing dissatisfaction through satire and farce. Black performers dissatisfied with Kente's excessively sentimental plots and avoidance of controversial themes developed the resistance theatre with which the rest of the world is most familiar. Non-commercial forms of theater also arose in trade unions to aid with organization, education, and motivation, in cultural centers dedicated to giving oppressed communities a sense of their worth and a place to develop their skills and find shelter from the grim realities of township life, and in traveling shows designed to educate impoverished communities about issues of development, health, and citizenship.

Holding these disparate forms of theatre together and providing an invaluable venue for cross-fertilization has been a responsibility shouldered mainly by Johannesburg's Market Theatre, where Barney Simon was artistic director until his death in 1996. While other independent theatres in Durban and Cape Town, as well as several university theatre programs, have had important roles in fostering South Africa's unique mix of theatrical forms, the Market is both the longest-enduring independent theatrical institution and the most ecumenical in its support of theatre's many aesthetic forms and social functions. Besides providing the educated elite with a venue for plays critical of apartheid, the Market has made serious efforts to train people interested in all forms of theatre, offer cultural outreach to sectors of the population unfamiliar with theatre, and support the development of theatre for non-traditional audiences (rural settlements, townships, students, union members, etc.). That township music and dance, recent British drama, Broadway hits, European avant-garde performances, and labor activists' skits can all be seen within the same complex of theatres and galleries has been instrumental in establishing a distinctively South African theatrical vocabulary and allowing the separate forms of South African drama to borrow from each other to enrich their particular modes of expression.[10]

The selections for this volume were made to bring together some of the very best theatrical texts of recent years and to highlight texts whose social and aesthetic commentary is relevant to the evolving post-apartheid world. As a group, the plays exhibit three important concerns of post-apartheid theatre: the recovery of the past, abiding social injustices, and hybrid theatrical forms.

NEW USES FOR THE PAST

Much recent drama seeks to reconstruct a national historical narrative untainted by the ideology of apartheid. Of great interest in this endeavor is the interracial, urban culture of the 1940s and 1950s (which the National Party government moved quickly to dismantle after they came to power in 1948). Sophiatown (an outlying district of Johannesburg) in particular has become a major object of nostalgic celebration due to the large number of intellectuals, artists, and national figures who lived there or frequented its nightclubs and unlicensed bars.

Junction Avenue's *Sophiatown* was the first major play to take up the theme of this fertile and dangerous district. It eschews lighthearted reverie and nostalgic idealization for a keen and detailed examination of the pleasures and blights of urban life before all attempts at an improvised, imaginative community of cultures were smothered under the order of apartheid. The play aims both to condemn the racist policies that separated South Africa's ethnic groups and to take note of the barriers that stand in the way of these groups reapproaching one another. It constructs a new, progressive historical narrative and explores the ways in which various individual lives might exist within (but not always in harmony with) this narrative.

Reza de Wet also delves into the past, but rather than constructing a new national narrative, she searches for places where narrative breaks down into obsessive individual longings. As an Afrikaans writer, she is recovering the past from the grand narrative of her people for the sake of broader human interests. *Crossing* transforms 1910, the year of the Act of Union when South Africa became a self-governing colony of the British Commonwealth, from a milestone in the development of Afrikaner nationalism to a meeting place for gothic romance, Puritan repression, and spirit possession.

Brett Bailey is more interested in cultural heritage than in historical narrative. His play, *Ipi Zombi?*, draws upon the power of sacred Xhosa performance forms such as church hymns and the trance chants and dances of sangomas (traditional diviners and healers). He demonstrates both the power of these cultural resources and the stresses placed on them by the modern world. He neither dismisses nor idealizes the past, but, rather, shows how it both haunts the present with atavistic prejudices and offers psychological solace and communal ties to a fragmented, stress-laden society.

ABIDING SOCIAL PROBLEMS

Besides recovering the past, South African drama shows a keen interest in contemporary social inequities. Most of the problems from which people suffered during the National Party's reign (low wages, high unemployment, inadequate housing, crime) remain pressing issues, but without an obvious target for accusations. Dramatizing current problems requires many approaches because the dominating problem of apartheid has disappeared. The plays by Mda, Ellenbogen, Slabolepszy, Mahomed, and Bailey all offer distinct treatments of injustice after apartheid.

Zakes Mda's *And the Girls in Their Sunday Dresses*, although written when apartheid still ruled South Africa, is set in Lesotho, where issues of poverty, corruption, dependency, and self-assertion are not over-written with the social and psychological dynamics of racial bigotry and discrimination. Although intended for the same township venues and audiences as resistance drama, Mda's play does not turn on the opposition between oppressor and oppressed. He eschews resistance-theatre for theatre-for-development motifs that examine the experience of dependency and the resources of the disenfranchised rather than the causes of poverty. Mda's inquiries move in the same direction as the post-apartheid South African government: both suggest the historical causes of inequity are not as important as the paths to improvement. Mda's play examines the motivations and responsibilities of the poor. His dramaturgy implicitly suggests that the period of resistance, when affixing blame and making demands was most important, has passed and a period of reconstruction, when personal empowerment and cooperation are paramount, has begun.

Of all the playwrights in this collection, Nicholas Ellenbogen borrows most extensively from the protest and resistance theatre tradition. His plays focus on concrete examples of injustice and exploitation and make generalized denunciations of systems of inequity and degradation using athletic and imaginative physical mimicry, tour-de-force multiple roles and quick changes, song, dance, narrative, and clowning in a distinctive South African style first developed in the Black townships. His work is unique for its attempts to draw together the interests of poor Black communities and privileged White communities around the interrelationships between poverty and environmental degradation. He balances an interest in the fate of endangered species with an interest in the pressures on the lives of South Africa's rural, poor populations.

Paul Slabolepszy's *Mooi Street Moves* treats the issue of urban decay through a favorite South African plot device: a naively trusting young man from the country comes to the big city to make his fortune but falls victim to the temptations and brutality of urban life. This basic plot-line, identified familiarly in South Africa as "Jim Comes to Jo'burg" after the eponymous 1951 film by Donald Swanson, has been told repeatedly in novels, films, and plays as diverse as *Cry the Beloved Country, Come Back Africa, Sizwe Bansi Is Dead, Ipi Tombi, Too Late!,* and *Pula*.[11] Slabolepszy's witty innovation on this perennial theme is a surprising reversal of roles. In all previous versions of the story, the rural-born protagonist is Black, but Slabolepszy makes him an Afrikaner and contrasts his naive country manners with the streetwise operations of a thoroughly urban Black man who befriends him. This alteration in the storyline is pointed, because rural Afrikaners were one of the chief beneficiaries of the apartheid system and are likely to experience one of the most wrenching changes in lifestyle under the new dispensation. The urban Black character throws light on the many years of appalling living conditions in the cities and dismisses the apartheid myth that all Blacks have ties to a rural homeland. The humorous and poignant interactions of the Black and White characters measure cultural differences against shared social situations.

Ismail Mahomed's play *Purdah* takes up the international issue of Muslim fundamentalism and deals with the particularities of its manifestations in the Indian community of South Africa. This one-woman monologue is both about and for the Islamic Indian community. Although it has played in South Africa's major theatrical venues, some of its most powerful and pointed performances have been for all-women audiences in suburban living rooms. The Spartan stage properties and single actress were conceived with such mobility and adaptability in mind. The play takes advantage of the diverse nature of South Africa's Muslims to pointedly juxtapose some of the more egregiously repressive trends in rigidly orthodox circles with more humanistic and egalitarian interpretations of the faith.

Bailey's *Ipi Zombi?* deals with witchcraft paranoia and an array of related post-apartheid problems in poor Black communities. Although his play is set in a rural Xhosa township, the fear of witches and the ravages of poverty and social disintegration he highlights are widespread problems. Bailey shows how an array of practical problems for poor rural communities have led to disturbing results. The unregulated and overworked taxi service upon which rural communities depend often puts the lives of poor commuters at risk. In 1995, the township of Kokstad was wracked with grief when twelve boys died in a crash of one of these taxis. The police in such communities, although no longer the ministers of apartheid, remain notoriously incapable of adequate investigations. Communal authority often falls on the shoulders of teenagers because adults must leave the area to find work and because the role of teenagers in the resistance to apartheid was of well-acknowledged importance. Unfortunately, without the clear enemy offered by the racist National Party, teenage vigilantes are now persecuting those whom they take to be witches. The victims tend to be older women whom the adolescents resent or fear either because they are eccentric or because they seem inexplicably better off than the rest of the community. Thus, grandmothers who live in relative comfort because their children send them money from their jobs in the big cities are condemned as witches who have grown rich by enslaving the souls of the community's untimely dead.

In a bold move beyond the protest-play tradition, Bailey does not offer a simplistic condemnation of witchcraft paranoia (elements of which are tied to traditional beliefs held by a large segment of South Africa's population) but seeks to show the audience the social pressures that lead to witch killings as well as the brutality and uselessness of this behavior for solving the community's problems. None of the characters in the play serve as a moral compass for the audience, and none act out of evil intentions. Bailey's play shows how evil can steal upon a community despite the goodwill of all the residents. It asks the audience to understand and confront this danger.

FORMAL FUSIONS

The variety of hybridized theatrical forms in South African drama is well represented in this collection. Slabolepszy's play is the only example of purely realistic drama in the European tradition, but even his play distinguishes itself from anything produced in Europe or the U.S. by virtue of the playful verbal invention prompted by the mixing of languages on the city streets. Mda's and De Wet's plays are still fundamentally dramatic in that they tell their stories exclusively through the interaction of characters in a particular setting, but the form of this drama is no longer entirely realistic. Mda mixes the empowerment rhetoric and pedagogical thrust of theatre for development with the playful minimalism and implausibility of absurdist drama. He harnesses the powerful allegorical potentials of the absurd to the cause of human rights without succumbing to the numbing solemnity often associated with pedagogical theatre. His play teaches, but it cannot be reduced to a lesson; it portrays vivid characters in conflict but does not become absorbed in the sentiments of the dramatic situation.

De Wet's *Crossing*, part of a trilogy that deals with characters wrapped up in various forms of theatricality, bears a distant resemblance to plays by Wole Soyinka that deal with sacred African performance forms (cf. *The Road* and *Death and the King's Horseman*). Like Soyinka, De Wet portrays the powers of theatricality in everyday life where transitional states develop that blend mimesis with spirit possession. Where Soyinka deploys the figure of the *egugun,* a god or ancestor inhabiting a costumed and masked human body, De Wet deploys the seance and hypnotism. Thus, while her methods of creating a haunted theatricality are thoroughly Western, the results resonate as much with African spirit-possession rituals as with European dramatic representation. The characters in her plays commune with the dead and the unconscious more passionately than with other living beings. The central scenes of *Crossing* are not so much set in the past as inhabited by ghosts from the past. A gothic night of the living dead attempts a reverential dance of the ancestors, mixing repulsion and attraction and turning the stage into an uneasily sacred space.

Bailey's *Ipi Zombi?* mixes sacred and profane forms of theatricality even more pointedly than *Crossing.* The stage is designed to resemble an African ceremonial ground. A church choir sings sacred hymns, sangomas perform divination rituals, and the actors occasionally work themselves into trance-like states designed to suffuse the theatre with a palpable spirituality. As in *Crossing,* the restless dead haunt the stage space. In contrast to this strong spiritual element, Bailey also includes humorous burlesque moments involving men in comical drag and sober moments of reflection on social problems. *Ipi Zombi?* also makes use of strong visual elements, which Bailey often clashes against the performative elements. A character that we expect to speak turns out to be an inanimate cadaver; a lifeless mask opens its mouth to intone an elaborate monologue. Eerie transformations are constantly at play. The actors portray actors portraying characters who suddenly turn back into actors. A comically campy drag queen portrays an eleven-year-old girl with creepy accuracy and conviction. Umbrellas become the wings of birds. Birds become unquiet ghosts.

DRAMA AND NARRATIVE

Three of the plays mix narrative elements with drama in a variety of ways. *Purdah's* one-woman monologue tells its story primarily with narrative, but Mahomed creates theatrical tension by shifting frequently between the cool, precise rhetoric of the narrative and the emotional outbursts from the young woman and the characters she impersonates. Her monologue is not realistic, because such a young, poorly educated, traumatized woman could not describe her experiences with such measured reasonableness, but the gap between her verbal lucidity and her benighted life helps highlight the social issues of the piece. The actress's sudden shifts from a dispassionate narrative to the impersonation of her imperious relatives or to her own pained cries turn the story into experience that demands a moral perspective to contain its anguish. The judicious use of the minimal stage props also helps anchor the narrative to the theatrical spectacle on the stage.

Sophiatown is built upon an extensive exercise in cultural archaeology that goes far beyond what appears on the page or stage. For Junction Avenue, theatre is not just a venue for presenting a play but a place where conflicting or isolated historical and cultural currents can meet for dialogue and exchange. After a long discovery process involving library research, interviews, and workshop improvisations, the group has constructed a play that uses historical narrative to create a precise frame for a series of dramatic vignettes that highlight the social tensions in urban South Africa and a series of song and dance numbers that revive the vibrant performance forms of the 1950s. Because the play developed collectively, it does not make a point so much as present a series of problems and encounters. It grapples with historical tensions that have a moral urgency but no easy solutions. Because the play begins with extensive background research, it is unusually well-informed on political and cultural points. Because the text arose from the actors' improvisational workshops, the social issues have been translated into engaging dramatic vignettes.

Horn of Sorrow offers the most elaborate mix of theatrical traditions. Some of the clowning and stage business clearly belongs to the British panto and variety theatre traditions with their jocular audience engagement and shamelessly infantile humor. Much of the song, dance, character-types, and street-corner scenes borrow from Gibson Kente's township musicals. The witty and dexterous imitation of animals, which is a hallmark of Ellenbogen's work, draws both from the European tradition of pantomime, which Ellenbogen studied in London and Paris, and a southern African tradition of physical mimicry traceable to 6000 B.C.E. among the Bushmen and made famous recently by the Soyinkwa African Theatre group. The South African interest in elaborate narrative structures, which springs from indigenous storytelling traditions and is used frequently in theatrical performance, can be found in this play's use of the comic vulture, Zulu and Portuguese characters, and elegiac chorus as alternating narrative voices.

THEATRICAL PERFORMANCE AND SOCIAL ACTION

The richness and power of theatre springs from the innovations and impact it can make in three distinct spheres of expression: dramatic mimesis, theatrical performance, and social action. An anthology of plays necessarily highlights dramatic mimesis because the structure of the dialogue and the words spoken are the primary medium for this form of expression. Theatrical performance and social action can be strongly suggested in the structure and focus of a play script, as they are in several of the texts in this anthology, but they lack a vivid presence on the page.

In many South African plays, the absence of performance from the printed text is a particularly acute problem. Where European drama usually subordinates performance to the playwright's text, South African theatrical works often make the playwright's text ancillary to performance. In some cases, the text is dispensed with entirely; in others, it provides only a loose schema that is fixed and filled with purely performative elements such as song, dance, mimicry, and other forms of what Antonin Artaud calls "affective athleticism."

It is clearly impossible to include in a printed anthology the many forms of South African theatre that exist only in performance. Indeed, this collection necessarily favors more literary forms of theatre, since these offer the reader the most satisfaction and the greatest amount of information about possible performances. But I have included plays with strong performative elements (e.g., *Sophiatown, Horn of Sorrow,* and *Ipi Zombi?*) when the text that supports the performance still offers significant pleasures of its own and gives some indication of the missing performance dynamics. To a certain extent, the printed text can compensate for its lack of a vivid performative element by simultaneously suggesting a number of performance possibilities. Readers can never have full access to all the affective athleticism displayed by the creators of these texts, but they are free to contemplate potentials for affective athleticism not yet realized. Hopefully, these texts can stimulate such contemplation.

The varied institutional parameters and cultural functions of theatre in South Africa are harder to indicate in a collection of plays than are performative elements because South African theatre so often moves decisively in a variety of directions away from theatre's conventional social function as an elite form of aesthetic recreation. Plays are presented everywhere from private homes to state-sponsored theatres. The venues include private non-profit theatres, universities, township halls, union meetings, village squares, and shopping malls. Financial support for shows comes from government agencies, private donors, arts organizations, religious, professional, and neighborhood groups, labor unions, political parties, and commercial investors—all of whom influence the tenor of a production by the prominence of their association with it. The places, occasions, and sponsors of theatre lead to cultural functions for the plays ranging over entertainment and education, distraction from and engagement with social issues, and the affirmation of high, popular, and minority cultures. Plays can aim at enhancing group solidarity or promoting individual empowerment. They can expose political corruption or criticize cultural prejudices. They can offer lessons in history or manifestos for the future. They can encourage a sentimental attachment to the spectacle or a critical distance from it.

THEATRICAL SOCIAL FUNCTIONS BEYOND THE TEXT

The social functions theatre serves in South Africa are too diverse and often lie too far from the realm of literature to be captured in print and too far from the typical circumstances of North American theatrical production to serve a similar social function here. The Sibikwa Community Theatre Project, for example, produced an internationally popular song and dance revue called *Kwela Bafana* in the early 1990s. On international tour, the production offered entertainment through and education concerning the song and dance styles of South Africa in the 1950s. These are noteworthy traits of the show, but its most important social functions were visible only in the East Rand township community where Sibikwa is located. There the show provided work for older performers from the 1950s who had been forced to give up their entertainment careers when the apartheid government closed down multiracial nightclubs in places like Sophiatown. (Only the few superstars of the era, such as Miriam Makeba and Dollar Brand, had the option of pursuing a career abroad.) At the Sibikwa Community Centre, these older musicians trained young high school dropouts in the dance and singing styles of the 1950s, thereby providing employment for old and young and redressing the fragmentation and degradation of urban Black culture perpetrated by apartheid. The international tour brought hard currency back to the community so that their cultural programs could be expanded. This use of performance for community rejuvenation is the least visible social function served by *Kwela Bafana* (from an academic, literary, or theatrical perspective) but arguably its most important one.

Trade union plays are another example of theatre in which the social function is more important than the literary or performance text attached to it. Indeed, union plays often have no fixed text. Their power lies not in what might be written down from any individual performance, but from the way the plays constantly evolve and are improvised upon to meet the needs of a particular place and occasion.[12] They make no claims to an autonomous theatrical or dramatic value, but establish their worth by contributing to the education and mobilization of workers and by adding a thematic focus, celebratory spark, or militant impulse to particular public events.

These skits and spectacles are pointedly non-literary. They are protean outlines in the service of workers and their unions. They take on a specific life and form only in the actions of people in a particular time and place. During the apartheid years, it was an advantage that they could not be captured in print. During the shifting circumstances of the new transitional regime, there is no interest in freezing union skits in a literary form that would instantly become irrelevant to the changing goals and strategies of the union.

The plays written by eminent township cultural workers such as Matsemela Manaka and Peter Ngwenya have a more fully literary existence than labor union skits, but they would seem slight and schematic if separated from their intended performative circumstances. Some of South Africa's most effective playwrights fuse their work to specific social situations. Their plays are valuable not for what a reader might glean from the text, but for the way they intervene in and shape particular communities. Manaka is famous for the cultural pride and social cooperation he promoted in Soweto until his death in 1998. In the 1990s, he moved away from the arresting performative tableaux that made his troupe Soyinkwa African Theatre popular on tours and devoted his energies to productions designed to develop the cultural identity of urban Black South Africans in general and his own neighborhood in Soweto in particular. The power of his work could not be easily separated from the museum-like surroundings of the cultural center he established and the home-brewed beer he ritualistically offered to theatre-goers and visitors.

Ngwenya has won acclaim for his work with children and for his voter education skits. His fine sense of dramatic tableaux is dedicated entirely to educating marginalized sectors of the population about important elements of daily life. His skits have, perhaps, reached more people and had a greater positive effect on society than any play included in this anthology, but the lack of a significant autonomous aesthetic appeal in them makes them inappropriate for an audience far removed from the social circumstances of his work. Reproducing the texts that Manaka and Ngwenya use in their cultural work in an international anthology would not give a very clear indication of the strength of their work.

Another group worth noting despite their absence from this anthology is Bachaki.[13] Since 1988, they have been producing highly mobile, small-cast plays on specific social problems for particular audiences. Their *Top Down* (1988) looked at the educational system in the waning days of apartheid and was performed principally for teachers, students, and parents. Another play took up the problem of contaminated water in the townships, and more recently, *Weemen* (1996) looked at the issue of domestic abuse. Their work is striking for the detailed analysis they make of social problems and the efficacy with which their performance poses questions to the audience. They rigorously eschew simplifying dichotomies between good and evil or tyrant and victim in favor of highlighting the variety of forces at play in a social problem.

Wife abuse has become a popular topic lately in South Africa, but whereas another production (*On My Birthday,* which toured to Lincoln Center, New York in 1997) exploits the spectacle of physical violence and the emotional catharsis of vicarious victimization, *Weemen* offers a levelheaded analysis of the problem. In place of physical violence (which township audiences tend to read as slapstick), *Weemen* begins by showing the devastating effects of emotional abuse (a less well-acknowledged form of maltreatment). In place of an escalating victimization, *Weemen* portrays a woman who takes control of her own life and eventually learns to stand up to her husband. The husband is not portrayed as a one-dimensional ogre but as a rather weak, pathetic individual with a drinking problem who resents being dominated by women superiors at work and tries to enhance his self-image by denigrating his wife and shirking his responsibilities to the family. The play's action builds repeatedly to a series of questions for the woman: Should she run away? Should she murder her husband as he sleeps? When he asks for forgiveness and promises to stop drinking, should she give him another chance? Is his sudden commitment to religion a genuine reform or another means of manipulation? When he steals the money she was saving for her daughter's education, should she throw him out for good?

The systematic muting of emotional appeals and the avoidance of lurid spectacles would make this play very puzzling to a North American audience. Its emphasis on what the characters do, rather than on what they feel or how they express themselves, makes the scenes seem crude and schematic by European standards of dramaturgy. For this reason, I did not include it in this anthology. The power of Bachaki's work is that it portrays social problems in ways designed to vividly engage a Black South African audience. South African Blacks often display marked discomfort with the obsessively emotional appeals of drama in the European tradition. They prefer plays that present moral and social issues. During the performance of *Weemen* that I attended, the predominantly Black, well-educated audience constantly whispered advice or conferred quietly among themselves as each issue in the play came to a head. At the end, many seemed more inclined to start a general discussion of the issues than to end the gathering with the traditional applause. Such an astonishing theatrical event deserves scrutiny, but placing the script in this anthology would not give it the kind of attention it deserves. The value of Bachaki's work is hard to understand when it is separated from the audience for which it is crafted.

PSYCHIC AND SOCIAL FUNCTIONS WITHIN THEATRICAL TEXTS

A collection of South African plays for a North American audience will inevitably neglect some of the social functions theatre serves in South Africa and distort the importance of others. The pages of an anthology opened to the eyes of a single reader encourage a quiet, individual delectation similar to that of a passive spectator sitting in the dark auditorium of a proscenium arch theatre. Plot, character, and spectacle loom large on the page while the place and occasion of South African theatre is less easily imagined and appreciated. Nevertheless, this anthology does contain plays with social functions that both disrupt and move beyond the private aesthetic pleasures of conventional Western theatre. Although larger institutional functions such as those served by the Sibikwa Community Theatre Project are not readily discernible in the printed texts of plays, the texts can give a good indication of how the plays work upon the audience. They reveal some innovative and unusual cultural functions intended for the theatre event.

PERFORMATIVE DISPLAY

The prominent display of performative prowess in dance, song, and athletic mimicry found in *Sophiatown*, *Horn of Sorrow*, and *Ipi Zombi?* encourage an audience engagement closer to that of a sporting event or music concert than to that of the Western stage. Rather than sink into the emotional life of the characters, the audience stands back in judgment of the technical proficiency of the performance or engages somatically, rather than sentimentally, with it. Enthusiasm for the performative work in which the actors are engaged is often encouraged more than a vicarious identification with the characters the actors portray. But, of course, rather than reduce theatre to an athletic performance, these plays actually blend performative and representational elements, shifting the emphasis back and forth from one to the other. While allowing the cathartic payoffs of sentimental identification, these plays also encourage the more immediate critical pleasures of witnessing and assessing expert performances. The spectators feel the performance in their bones and muscles as much as they feel it in their hearts.

THE SPECTACLE OF SOCIAL ISSUES

Another important social function that many of the plays are designed to perform is a combination of pedagogy and the encouragement of public debate. This function has two distinct forms. In *Sophiatown*, *Horn of Sorrow*, and *Ipi Zombi?*, which have relatively large casts and production requirements and can only realistically be performed for fairly large audiences, pedagogy becomes a kind of spectacle that the spectators take in but cannot immediately react to. *Sophiatown* offers a lesson in history and urban culture. *Horn of Sorrow* lays out social and ecological issues. *Ipi Zombi?* discusses social tensions and psychological strains in a rural township. The bold and overwhelming gestures of the play are meant to impress the audience with facts that need to be remembered and problems that need to be solved. While the pleasures experienced during performance are predominantly aesthetic ones, these pleasures produce a pedagogical afterglow designed to encourage discussion and action by the audience after they leave the theatre.

INTIMATE ISSUE THEATRE

And The Girls in Their Sunday Dresses and *Purdah* have more modest production requirements that allow them to be performed before smaller audiences. In these more intimate circumstances, the pedagogical function becomes more immediate and interactive. The audience can respond to the social issues presented on the stage with comments that the whole audience can hear. These plays can work in a way similar to *Weemen*, creating an immediate debate on controversial topics and forging a strong sense of community in the small audience. While there certainly are many aesthetic pleasures to be had from these plays, their focus on clear social problems and the possibility of performing them for small, focused audiences allow the pedagogical interactions with the audience to become a much more powerful force in the performance itself. The prominent feminist issues of both plays invite performances before predominantly female audiences to forge interest-group solidarity or before audiences of men and women when the goal is to foster debate over cultural norms and women's rights. Mda's play might also be performed for small groups of social workers, community activists, or a particular impoverished community, with distinct pedagogical effects for each audience. Mahomed's play could create a heightened interactive pedagogic function for either an Islamic audience or an Indian audience, because these are the communities in which the issues the play handles are most volatile.

ELEMENTS OF COMMUNITY THEATRE

Three of the plays in this collection also function as forms of community theatre. Anne Jellicoe developed the concept of community theatre in England from the 1960s onward. Through her promotion, the form developed a number of features that distinguish it from conventional theatre. First, it represents the local milieu and a story or social issues rooted in the locale. Second, it uses a great deal of local talent in the creation of the performance. People from the community help make costumes and sets, appear as extras, or offer cameo displays of their own performative talents (juggling, singing, acrobatics, etc.). And, third, the production creates a special occasion at which the entire community comes together to witness the combined efforts of neighbors and outside professionals in portraying unique features of the audience's world.

Sophiatown could be seen as an archeological form of community theatre. The community in question was destroyed thirty years before the play was created, but the Junction Avenue collective searched out and gathered together the pieces of this community. Some of the work was purely archival—looking at old films, photos, and written accounts of Sophiatown in the 1950s—but much of the work involved interviewing people who had lived in Sophiatown. By asking a wide range of people to remember their lives in Sophiatown and weaving together these accounts, Junction Avenue created something like community theatre for the scattered remnants and descendants of an urban world before apartheid.

Purdah often functions, at least in part, as a kind of community theatre for Islamic and Indian groupings in South Africa. Its narrow topic, which is not rooted in a particular place, and modest production requirements, which do not allow for significant local contributions, differentiate it from the standard form of community theatre. Nevertheless, the play does serve a role similar to community theatre in drawing together an Islamic or Indian community to view a play on an issue of great importance to the community. The extent to which *Purdah* functions fully as community theatre depends on the extent to which it is integrated into broader community activities. If it is part of a cultural festival in which many people take part or is used to spark debate as part of a symposium on social values, then it is more fully a form of community theatre. *Purdah* does not function in itself as community theatre, but it turns itself toward and offers itself as an element of such a theatrical form.

Ipi Zombi? was first conceived primarily as community theatre. When it premiered in Grahamstown under the title *Zombie* in 1996, it featured a cast of sixty residents from Grahamstown townships, including a twenty-voice choir and five sangomas. The story enacted took place in a township not far from Grahamstown and involved issues of great importance to the community. Unfortunately, the community producing the play was not well represented in the audience, given the constraints of the theatre's location and the ticket prices. Nevertheless, one of the most compelling elements of the play was the enthusiasm and sincerity of the amateur performers in portraying social tensions close to their lives.

Bailey remounted the play in Cape Town with local actors and this time successfully drew a local audience to the production in Nyanga, a predominantly Xhosa township. This urban audience, however, laughed so much at the witchcraft theme that it failed to appreciate the seriousness and danger these beliefs hold for rural communities.[14] *Ipi Zombi?* uses a smaller, more professional cast than *Zombie* did, but Bailey has plans to continue to work on the community aspects of the play by translating it into Xhosa and taking it on tour to rural communities.

ANTI-THEATRE

Ipi Zombi? stands out from the other plays in this collection because of its strong anti-theatrical elements. No matter what functions the other plays are serving, they all welcome the eyes of the spectators. *Ipi Zombi?,* however, seeks to make at least certain audiences uncomfortable about the privileges of theatrical voyeurism. The title *Ipi Zombi?* (Where are the Zombies?) makes reference to the musical and dance extravaganza *Ipi Tombi* (Where the Girls Are, 1974), which popularized Black South African music for White audiences but also presented a debased and distorted version of Black culture tailored to White condescension and prejudice.[15] The largely White audiences for *Ipi Zombi?* must cringe slightly at the reference to the apartheid era *Ipi Tombi,* especially since, as in the earlier play, *Ipi Zombi?* offers a representation of rural Black life for urban White entertainment.

Bailey adds to the self-consciousness of the theatrical event by highlighting the artificiality of the performance. The actors play actors portraying various characters, often in drag. Comic and tragic elements are mixed together or juxtaposed in jarring succession. The invisible wall between audience and actors is breached frequently through the performance but the most conventionally accepted breach, when the actors bow in acceptance of the audience's applause at the end, is not allowed. The actors abandon the theatre before the audience and stand outside caught up in a trance-like song, oblivious to whether the spectators applaud or not as they file out.

In contrast to these derisive swipes at conventional theatricality, Bailey also includes equally anti-theatrical ritual elements in the play. In theatre, an audience watches the performance, but in ritual, everyone participates. The power and privilege accorded the spectator's eye in theatre is shifted to the spiritual energy that suffuses the ritual event. At several points in the play, the performers point to the presence of this spiritual energy. It is something invisible that creeps into the performance space and tingles the nerves of actors and audience. It might be a healing or destructive force. The ritual is broken and filled with sacrilegious elements that will not allow it to contain and channel the spiritual force. The audience feels out of its element and must search with the performers for solid ground somewhere beyond the standard conventions of theatre. A curtain call would not be appropriate. The audience must follow the actors into the outside world, where the spiritual energy of the ritual elements still reverberates in the actors' song.

PLAYS IN PRINT

South African drama demonstrates well the variety of social functions plays can fulfill in performance. A collection of plays fulfills its social function if it brings drama to an audience beyond the theatre and preserves some information about performance. I am confident that this collection tells us as much as the printed page can about current South African drama. For a fuller sense of the powers of theatre implicit in these texts, one must turn away from literature to production and performance.[16] The high quality of the texts collected here can be measured both by what they explicitly express and by the challenging avenues of production and performance they open up to theatrical collaborators.

In moving beyond the concerns of anti-apartheid theatre, this collection offers a broader sampling of theatrical forms and subject matter than any previous anthology. The playwrights come from Afrikaner, Anglo, African, and Indian communities. Their plays are set in the countryside and the city, the past and the present. They involve wealthy and destitute characters, educated elites, struggling artists, lower-middle-class entrepreneurs, and criminals. The dramas portrayed aim to delight, excite, entrance, absorb, provoke, educate, and mobilize. In these texts, one can see many sides of South African society and many versions of South African drama.

A WORD ABOUT LANGUAGE

South African English is at least as distinct from English in the United States as are the dialects of Britain and Australia. The unique vocabulary arising from the country's geographic isolation is enriched further by the influence of ten other (now official) languages in the country. Although English is the language of power and commerce and the de facto lingua franca, it is the mother tongue of only 10 percent of the population—more people speak Zulu, Xhosa, and Afrikaans as a first language. Many of the plays in this anthology reflect this linguistic diversity by borrowing liberally from other languages and by lapsing into them on occasion. Although I wanted to make the vocabulary accessible to North American readers, I did not want to unduly disrupt the flow of the dialogue or completely destroy the occasional verbal opacity that is intended in the plays for the South African audience. My solution to this dilemma was to translate long foreign phrases parenthetically within each play and to provide a glossary of single words and historical or cultural references in an appendix. Occasionally, when the characters shift between several languages, I have identified the language with an abbreviation: *A* = Afrikaans; *S* = Setswana; *T* = Tsotsitaal; *Z* = isiZulu.

NOTES

1. Athol Fugard's naturalistic drama of marginalized characters actually enjoyed more frequent productions abroad and more scholarly attention than the resistance theatre pieces conceived and executed primarily by his Black compatriots, but Fugard's success was primarily that of the dramatic text, whereas the international recognition of South African theatre came predominantly through the tours of productions such as *Survival!*, *Woza Albert!*, *Gangsters,* and *Asinimali!*

2. For renditions of the theme "Whither South African theatre?" by critics and practitioners, see Mark Gevisser, "Truth and Consequences in Post-Apartheid Theater," and Carol Steinberg and Malcolm Purkey, "South African Theater in Crisis," both in *Theater* 25, no. 3 (1995): 9–18, 24–37.

3. I use the terms "protest" and "resistance" to refer to the array of theatre that used township performance forms to voice some measure of discontent with the apartheid regime. The two employ similar theatrical techniques, but for different ends. At his most politically engaged, in plays such as *Too Late!*, Gibson Kente (the most successful producer and director of township plays) never did more than protest the miseries caused by apartheid. In other words, his theatre complained about social injustices but was not actively involved in trying to overcome them. Fugard's anti-apartheid plays also protest, rather than resist, the actions of the racist regime. Plays produced by the Black Consciousness movement are clearly instances of resistance theatre, because they were part of an organized campaign against apartheid. Plays such as *Woza Albert!* are more difficult to categorize. The extent to which they merely protest or engage in resisting apartheid depends on the circumstances of their production. If they are raising money for the ANC or calling upon the audience to fight against racist laws, they are resistance theatre. If they are demonstrating the injustices of apartheid to an audience not likely to become directly involved in a concerted resistance themselves (even if seeing the play makes them more sympathetic to the cause and likely to offer some token of support), then they are protest drama.

4. For a schematic, tabular comparison of European and African aesthetic values, see E. Quita Craig, *Black Drama of the Federal Theatre Era: Beyond the Formal Horizons* (Amherst: University of Massachusetts Press, 1980), pp. 95–96. For an overview of traditional African

drama and the conceptual prejudices that have long made it difficult to define, see Christopher Kamlongera, *Theatre for Development in Africa with Case Studies from Malawi and Zambia* (Bonn: German Foundation for International Development, 1989), pp. 13–29. For a discussion of various developing forms of theatre in Africa, see Michael Etherton, *The Development of African Drama* (London: Hutchinson University Library for Africa, 1982).

5. For further comment on these and other forms of African performance, see Zakes Mda, "Theater and Reconciliation in South Africa," *Theater* 25, no. 3 (1995): 38–39, and Temple Hauptfleisch, "Post-Colonial Criticism, Performance Theory and the Evolving Forms of South African Theatre," *South African Theatre Journal* 2, no. 2 (September 1992): 66–69.

6. For more on Dhlomo's drama, see Loren Kruger, "An 'African National Dramatic Movement': New African Drama and National Representation in South Africa," in *Crucible of Crisis: Performance and Social Change,* ed. Janelle Reinelt (Ann Arbor: University of Michigan Press, 1996), pp. 123–41.

7. For an account of this group's activities in South Africa, see Veit Erlmann, *African Stars* (Chicago: University of Chicago Press, 1991), pp. 21–53.

8. For information on performance in the 1920s and 1930s, see Erlman, pp. 54–94; David Coplan, *In Township Tonight!* (Johannesburg: Ravan Press, 1985), pp. 90–139; and Loren Kruger, "Placing the 'New African' in the 'Old' South Africa: Drama, Modernity, and Racial Identities in Johannesburg, circa 1935," *Modernism/Modernity* 1, no. 3 (1994): 113–131.

9. For short accounts of theatre for development in Africa, see Etherton, pp. 314–357, and Zakes Mda, *When People Play People* (Johannesburg: Witwatersrand University Press, 1993), pp. 6–13. For a longer treatment, see Kamlongera.

10. For a more detailed discussion of South African drama to the end of the apartheid era, see Martin Orkin, *Drama and the South African State* (Manchester: Manchester University Press, 1991), which focuses more on published plays than on theatrical performance; and Loren Kruger, *The Drama of South Africa* (London: Routledge, 1999), which devotes considerable attention to theatrical performances.

11. The references are to the novel *Cry the Beloved Country* by Alan Paton (1947); the film *Come Back Africa,* directed by Lionel Rogosin (1958); the play *Sizwe Bansi Is Dead* by Fugard, Kani, and Ntshona; the musical extravaganza *Ipi Tombi,* produced by Bertha Egnos (1974); the township musical *Too Late!* by Gibson Kente (1975); and the Soyinkwa African Theatre group's *Pula* by Matsemela Manaka (1982).

12. For an account of labor theatre and sample texts, see Astrid von Kotze, *Organise and Act: The Natal Workers Theatre Movement 1983–1987* (Durban: Culture and Working Life Publications, 1988).

13. For a discussion of the differences between purely theatrical performances and community cultural work that focuses on Bachaki's first play, see David Graver and Loren Kruger, "South Africa's National Theatre: The Market or the Street?" *New Theatre Quarterly* 5, no. 19 (August 1989): 272–281. For a summary of their first play, see Graver and Kruger, "Synopsis of *Top Down* at the Market Theatre, Johannesburg," *Maske und Kothurn* 35, no. 1 (1989): 77–85.

14. For an account of the Nyanga performance, see Donna Marshall, "Voices of the Dead," *Weekly Mail and Guardian,* 17 January 1997.

15. For a discussion of the place of *Ipi Tombi* in South African theatre, see Loren Kruger, "So What's New? Women and Theater in the 'New South Africa,'" *Theater* 25, no. 3 (1995): 46–54, esp. 47–50.

16. For reviews of South African theatre in recent years, see David Graver, "Theatre in the New South Africa," *Performing Arts Journal,* no. 49 (1995): 103–109; Michael Carklin and David Alcock, "Standard Bank National Arts Festival," *Theatre Journal* 49, no. 1 (March 1997): 53–56; and David Graver "Standard Bank National Arts Festival," *Theatre Journal* 49, no. 1 (March 1997): 56–59. The Grahamstown Festival, held every July, offers the largest sampling of current South African drama and music.

Sophiatown
(1986)

Junction Avenue Theatre Company

The Junction Avenue Theatre Company was formed in 1976 by a group of White students at the University of the Witwatersrand interested in creating historically informed plays about South African society. Their first project, The Fantastical History of a Useless Man, *responded to the Soweto uprisings of 1976 by comparing White, English-speaking South African ideology to historical realities from 1652 to 1976. The group became nonracial when Blacks from the seasoned Workshop '71 joined. The core of the company has been constant since this merger, but each production has involved a different combination of people and talents. Their historical dramas include* Randlords and Rotgut *(1978), which examines labor relations and liquor sales in the gold mines at the turn of the century;* Will of a Rebel *(1979), about the life of dissident Afrikaans poet Brey-ten Breytenbach; and* Marabi *(1982), about urban culture and removals in the 1930s and 1940s. From 1979 to 1982, the company produced a series of short plays on contemporary social issues that toured both the Black townships and the White suburbs, and some of its members collaborated with the labor union move-ment Ilanga Lizo Phumela Abasebenzi in creating workers' theatre. The company was awarded the 1985/86 AA Life Vita Award for Playwright of the Year for* Sophiatown. *In 1989, the company produced* Tooth and Nail, *a fragmented series of vignettes dealing with the hopes and fears rife at the end of the apartheid era.* Sophiatown *was revived in 1993 to celebrate the end of apartheid.*

This play was conceived and developed when the struggle between the National Party government and advocates of democracy was at its most extreme. In 1985, a state of emergency was declared and the army occupied the townships, killing more than 1,000 people demonstrating against apartheid. In 1986, the state of emergency was renewed, newspapers and magazines were heavily censored, and the police were given a free hand to arrest anyone suspected of opposing the gov-

ernment. Although major statutory emblems of the apartheid era, such as the Immorality Act and pass laws, were repealed, the White minority government refused to entertain any notion of sharing power with the Black majority. Mandela refused to renounce the armed struggle. Foreign countries and international banks began to sharply increase economic sanctions.

In the heated atmosphere of the moment, Sophiatown *served a function similar to earlier plays of protest and resistance. Rather than expose current injustices, it looked back at the beginning of the apartheid era to give some sense of the immense legacy of destruction for which the National Party was responsible. The main point, from a protest-drama perspective, was to condemn the vision of order upon which apartheid was built and (somewhat more circumspectly) to note how ineffectual the era of nonviolent, passive resistance had been in opposing National Party policies. But* Sophiatown *is more than protest drama.*

The escalating belligerence in 1986 brought with it an increasing hope that the days of apartheid were strictly numbered. In looking back at urban culture before the full institution of apartheid (but not before racial prejudice and discrimination), the play also contemplates the possibilities of a world after apartheid. The agon between the People and the Government so central to protest and resistance plays is pushed to the background of Sophiatown's *vignettes in favor of an exploration of the differences among the People and the extent to which people from very different cultural backgrounds can forge a common social order.* Sophiatown *and other urban areas like it are important not simply because they were unjustly de-stroyed, but because in them a vibrant hybrid culture was being formed. They offered the beginnings of a nonracialist urban culture that had been interrupted by apartheid and could be continued now. So, in using* Sophiatown *to oppose the apartheid regime, Junction Avenue was also using it to look beyond the apartheid regime at the difficuties and promises of a democratic South Africa. The director's comments on the creation of the play precede it.*

Sophiatown *premiered at the Market Theatre Upstairs, Johannesburg, 19 February 1986 with the following cast:*

JAKES: Patrick Shai

MINGUS: Arthur Molepo

MR. FAHFEE: Ramolao Makhene

LULU: Doreen Mazibuko

MAMARITI: Gladys Mothlale

PRINCESS: Madidi Maphoto

RUTH: Minky Schlesinger

CHARLIE: Siphiwe Khumalo

The play was created in workshops by Angus Gibson, Ruth Jacobson, Liz Johannson, William Kentridge, Siphiwe Khumalo, Doreen Mazibuko, Arthur

Molepo, Gladys Mothlale, Ramolao Makhene, Malcolm Purkey, Sarah Roberts, Minky Schlesinger, Tessa Spargo, and Pippa Stein

Additional material by Jane Dakile, Deborah James, Madidi Maphoto, Colin Purkey, and Patrick Shai

Directed by Malcolm Purkey

Designed by Sarah Roberts and William Kentridge

Lighting design by Gerry Coughlan

Choreography by Jill Waterman

Produced in association with the Market Theatre Company

Lengthy interviews and invaluable information graciously given to the company by Jane Dakile, Don Mattera, Nadine Gordimer, Es'kia Mphahlele, Baruch Hirson, Theo Mthembu, Father Trevor Huddleston, Anthony Sampson, Kort Boy, Phillip Stein, and Arthur Maimane.

SOPHIATOWN: THE PLAY

An obsession to reclaim and popularise the hidden history of struggle in our country is part of Junction Avenue Theatre Company's self-appointed task. This history has been wiped off the map by the state in its oppression of the majority of South Africans. The powerful flourishing of the contemporary theatre in South Africa, against all the odds, indicates the hunger that all South Africans have, to have their world interpreted. We need an informed and articulate new generation, steeped in the past and carefully theorising about the future, who have shaken off the blanket of silence and are committed in the deepest way to liberation. We believe that one of the most effective ways to communicate ideas, information, and feelings is through the living theatrical encounter.

[...]

Marabi [based on the popular novel by Modikwe Dikobe, *The Marabi Dance* (1982)] was an unfinished piece of work. Dealing as it did with the State's destruction of Marabi culture and the removal by force of the black working-class from the urban areas, it provided a model for further investigation. The issue of forced removals was certainly not exhausted. The destruction of Sophiatown, an urban community of the fifties, seemed a possible next area of research. The current struggle, with its roots firmly in the Freedom Charter, had its first seeds in the momentous political events of the fifties, events which the official culture and history have attempted to hide.

Our concern to explore these issues remained an abstraction, however, until we chanced upon the following story about two well-known journalists in Jim Bailey's account of the spectacular rise of the popular fifties magazine *Drum*:

Nat [Nakasa] and Lewis [Nkosi] set up house together [in Sophiatown] and adver-

tised for a Jewish girl to come and live with them. Despite all the legislation of South
Africa, they obtained one. I met the sporting lass. She was good enough looking but
very tall and thin—I could not banish the impression that she was originally constructed by being drawn through a hole, like a wire.

What an extraordinary story! And what a spark for us! We were immediately
intrigued. Who could she possibly have been? Why did she take up the challenge?

In the workshops, we deliberately refrained from pursuing too far the actual
facts of that event, attempting, rather, an imaginative reconstruction. We were
nonetheless aware of our enormous responsibility to the people of Sophiatown—
we had to strive to remain true to the spirit of the times. And so we started a series
of interviews with representative figures from the period.

We were fortunate to witness, in a workshop, four hours of the most revelatory
storytelling from Don Mattera, sometime Sophiatown gangster and poet. We
became awed at the scope of our task. From Mattera we learned that we had to
reflect a whole network of vital subcultures, and immediately we became immersed
in Tsotsitaal, an explosive articulation of street culture.

Kort Boy, leader of the American Gang, provided another challenge: how to
capture the language and gesture of the rival gangs . . . how to capture the peculiar
mixture of politeness and extreme violence, the obsession with dress and fancy
shoes, the power of the American movies, the attitude to women. . . .

Schoolteacher and Sophiatown property owner Jane Dakile told of the brutal
destruction of her home, an unbearably moving story which set the emotional tone
of the play's climax. Anthony Sampson and Nadine Gordimer, amongst others,
shared their experiences of the intellectual life of Sophiatown interwoven with the
pursuit of pleasure—the Softown shebeens were great meeting places for black
and white bohemians.

One day we set off in four cars to Pretoria, to the film archives to study the films
of the fifties, *African Jim* and *The Magic Garden*. There we learned of the vital
importance of a particular style of music played in the Sophiatown and Johannesburg nightclubs. We also spent hours paging through *Drum* magazines from
the period to establish aspects of the design style, and we read as much of the
literature of the time as we could get our hands on.

As the play began to take shape, there were central questions to answer: what
does the Jewish girl do on the first day she arrives, unannounced, into the already
established Sophiatown household? Under what conditions is she accepted? How
does a sixteen-year-old schoolgirl respond to the call for a school boycott in 1955,
when Bantu Education is first implemented? Where does an American gangster
store his goods? What was the role of a journalist from *Drum* magazine at the
height of its popularity? What was the role of the resistance movement and to what
extent did it affect the life of our Sophiatown household? Countless questions,
researches, and workshops were needed to find answers; the answers not always to
be found.

One night we were exploring what happens the day Ruth arrives in Sophiatown.
Suddenly Ramolao Makhene burst into our imaginary house and launched into a

tirade of words with such a powerful guiding rhythm, it was almost like an opera. 1 is for King, 2 is for Monkey, 3 is for Seawater. . . . We had encountered fahfee before but never like this. A numbers system with almost mystical connotations unfolded before my eyes. This improvisation gave us the key to the character that became Mr Fahfee, fahfee runner and political activist, and opened up a whole structuring principle for the play.

Meeting at night, three times a week for six months, we attempted in the workshop to confront each other creatively across the apartheid divide. In the workshop we wished, as if by magic, to forge a collective vision of the future. Through the workshop, we found a meeting ground and a way to explore our common life experiences. One of our most important workshops centred on rites of passage: each member of the group had to enact or describe a crucial ritual of transformation in his or her life. It could be private or formal.

The fascinating stories included William Kentridge's detailed description of his preparations for his Bar Mitzvah, how, in a cracked voice, he learned to sing parts of the Scriptures, written without vowels, in a language he didn't understand, in a flat in Hillbrow, at seven o'clock in the morning, his teacher refusing even to get out of bed! We listened to Siphiwe Khumalo's account of the ritual slaughter of a goat, how its bile is carefully stored, then smeared onto a motorcar's engine to protect the car from being stolen. . . . What extraordinary reports for the uninitiated among us!

We spent hours in narrative workshops, examining the different structures for our story, weighing up the effects of different beginnings and endings, constantly reminding ourselves, when the seductions of a particular character's story threatened to overwhelm our story, that our central concern was to tell the story of the destruction of Sophiatown.

After six months of work, the tapes and files of recorded material became burdensomely large. I was sent off for six weeks to shape the material into a working script. After six weeks of intensive daily rehearsal and rewriting, we were ready to open. [. . .] The play has had many seasons since, and each season demands some kind of re-evaluation of the script. What you have before you is as close to the finished script as we are likely to get.

MALCOLM PURKEY
16 May 1988

SOPHIATOWN

CHARACTERS

JAKES: a *Drum* magazine journalist and intellectual. In his late twenties.
MINGUS: a member of the American Gang. In his late twenties.
MR FAHFEE: Fahfee runner and Congress activist. In his forties.
LULU: a sixteen-year-old schoolgirl.

MAMARITI: a Shebeen Queen and owner of a house in Sophiatown. She is the mother of MINGUS and LULU.
PRINCESS: lover of MINGUS and good-time girl. In her twenties.
RUTH: a Jewish girl from the white suburb of Yeoville. In her twenties.
CHARLIE: MINGUS's sidekick. Barely articulate. He is obsessed with shoes.

THE SET

The play is set in the 1950s and takes place in MAMARITI's freehold Sophiatown house. The living area is cramped but comfortable, suggesting care and warmth. Each character, particularly, has a corner defined by his or her things. JAKES, a table, chair, typewriter, books; CHARLIE, a broken car seat and a steering wheel; LULU, school books, pencils and pens; MAMARITI, a comfortable armchair and a side table covered with photographs. There are other assorted chairs and a kitchen table. There is a kitchen recess and exits to various parts of the house. The front door is located through the kitchen recess and out of sight. Three telegraph poles are placed at intervals on the set. These poles are attached to telegraph wires which run out over the audience. The action is played against a backdrop of painted images deriving from newspapers, magazines and photographs from Sophiatown and the period.

ACT ONE

SCENE I

Shafts of light slowly reveal the Cast as they sing "Kofifi Sophia." MINGUS is centre stage, his hat pulled low over his eyes.

Kofifi Sophia, Kofifi Sophia
Kofifi Sophia, Kofifi Sophia
Ons pola hier in Sophia
Ons pola hier in Sophia
Moegoes nou moet nou gaan
Moegoes nou moet voetsak
Daar's nie plek vir al the G-men
Daar's nie plek vir al die gatas
Ons wietie met die wiebits, majietas en mataras
Ons wietie met die wiebits, majietas en mataras
(Sophiatown, Sophiatown
Sophiatown, Sophiatown
We are staying here in Sophiatown
We are staying here in Sophiatown
All the fools must move now
All the fools must bugger off now
There's no room for the G-men
There's no room for the cops

We're talking to the girls, the guys and the ladies
We're talking to the girls, the guys and the ladies *T*)

> *MINGUS returns to his seat, the song quietens to a murmur,*
> *and JAKES rises to speak.*

JAKES: Sophiatown, Softown, Kofifi, Kasbah, Sophia . . . Place of Freedom Square, and the Back of the Moon. Place of Can Themba's House of Truth. Place of the G-men and Father Huddleston's Mission. Place of Balansky's and the Odin Cinema. And let's never forget Kort Boy and Jazz Boy and the Manhattan Brothers, and Dolly Rathebe singing her heart out—here in Sophia . . .

> [*The song swells momentarily.*]

The Americans, the Berliners, the Gestapo, the Vultures—they fought here and blood ran in the streets of Sophia.

Can Themba, Nat Nakasa, Lewis Nkosi, Bloke Modisane wrote their best, here in Sophiatown. Tambo and Mandela walked here. Luthuli stood, and a city's people walked past, here in Sophia.

Sophiatown, named after one Tobiansky's wife. Gerty Street, Ray Street, Edith Street, Bertha Street, named after Tobiansky's daughters. Did he know what he was making, I wonder, here in Sophia?

65 Gerty Street, that's where I found myself, in a shack at the back of a Softown cottage. Live-in at Mamariti's Diamond Shebeen. One pound a month! I say an exorbitant price to pay for a room hardly big enough to hold a bed. Tap in the yard, toilet in the corner—but it was grand because it was Softown. Freehold! It was ours! Not mine exactly, but it was ours. And it was close by to the big city—that is the why-for we wanted to stay. This! This is what made the Boere mad. I wanted to stay—they wanted me to go. Too much freedom, too much meeting, too much fantasy, too much easy access. White bohemians and black intellectuals—that meant trouble for the Boere's dream of a whites-only world.

I was banging out a living at *Drum* magazine. Boxing was my beat, but I wanted to cover the Softown lifestyle. Anything could happen here, and if it did I wanted to be there. I needed stories—anything to get off the boxing beat. My brain was working overtime. I had to find something new, something different . . .

> *As JAKES seats himself in front of his typewriter, the song builds up again.*
> *FAHFEE, MAMARITI, RUTH, PRINCESS and LULU exit, jiving to the*
> *music. Lights change.*

MINGUS: Jakes!
JAKES: Mingus!
MINGUS: 'n Bla van 'n man! (buddy! *T*) [*Catching CHARLIE's eye.*] Charlie!
JAKES: Whe've you been, Mingus? Been making trouble again?
MINGUS: Jakes, I'm in love, man. I've just been to a wonderful funeral.
JAKES: A funeral? Is there a story there?
MINGUS: Ja, skryf daar, (yeah, write there,) "I went so nobody could say I killed him."

[*CHARLIE has crept up to MINGUS and begins to shine his shoes while he is wearing them.*]

Hey Charlie—leave off! Leave off! Go and sleep in the car. We've a job tonight. I want you wide awake. Hey Charlie—move!

[*CHARLIE persists in trying to clean the shoes.*]

Go on! [*MINGUS pushes CHARLIE away.*] Jakes, ek will 'n brief hê—'n letter van love. (Jakes, I want a letter—a love letter.)

JAKES: A love letter for you?

MINGUS: Ja, ek's in love, met 'n real tjerrie, 'n matara, a real ding, 'n princess (yeah, I'm in love, with a real chick, a lady, a real thing, a princess) . . . That's her name—Princess!

JAKES: Why don't you write it yourself, Mingus? I'm working.

MINGUS: Ag man Jakes, ek kan nie skryf nie. You know that—ek kan wietie, maar ek kan nie skryf nie. (I can talk, but I can't write.)

JAKES: Well, that's too bad, man. I'm busy.

MINGUS: Listen, I'll give you a story, a story for a love letter.

JAKES: A story?

MINGUS: The Americans.

JAKES: Come off it, Mingus. Everybody's got an angle on the gangsters. Mr Drum, Casey Motsitsi—everybody.

MINGUS: My personal story, Jakes. How I pull the jobs. How I met Kort Boy. How I get rid of the stuff. I'll tell you everything.

JAKES: I want names, details, the good yards, the whole lot.

MINGUS: A story for a love letter?

JAKES: It's a deal.

MINGUS: Start writing! Write the address—I want her here tonight at six o'clock.

JAKES: Oh boy, Mingus!

CHARLIE *is trying to clean MINGUS's shoes again.*

MINGUS [*taking off his shoes*]: Hey, Charlie, for God's sake, take them away!

CHARLIE *retires and squats in a corner. JAKES types the address.*

JAKES: How do I start?

MINGUS: Ag man, skryf man. Jy's die B.A.—intellectual. Ek is net 'n outie. (Ah man, write man. You're the B.A.—intellectual. I'm only a gangster.)

JAKES: You want me to waste my talents on a mere love letter!

MINGUS: That's your business, Jakes. Every day jy sit daar en tik-tik . . .

JAKES: Yes but that's boxing . . .

MINGUS: . . . and this is love, Jakes . . . Skryf!

JAKES [*typing*]: My dear darling beloved Princess! Right! The Americans.

MINGUS: Ag, skryf man, Jakes. And she must love that letter.

JAKES: First the Americans.

MINGUS: All right! All right! You want to know about the Americans, I'll tell you about the Americans! We want to hit the yards, the railway yards in Braamfontein, so we park the Chrysler, Charlie checks out the place. Hey Charlie, there's a guard but it's cool, it's okay. I jump out—I check for my thing, it's there. I feel for my gonee—it's there. The guard's half asleep—we throw a stone into the far corner. It's clear. We move in. We only go for the best. Jakes?

JAKES: Ja?

MINGUS: Tell her I only go for the best.

JAKES: How do you know it's the best?

MINGUS: Easy, man—check the labels! Only genuine English or American imports, "Can't-gets"—Florsheims, Winthrops, Bostonians, Saxone and Manfield, Arrow shirts, suits from Simpson's, Hector Powe, Robert Hall, Dobbs, Woodrow, Borsalino hats. You tell her I'm a smart guy—no messing around, and I want her here tonight at six o'clock!

JAKES [*typing*]: Oh boy, Mingus!

MINGUS: So we load up the cars and we're ready to go. And who the hell arrives? The Berliners—in our own territory, man! These Berliners—real bastards. Only rob the local people, man—no respect. Jakes?

JAKES: Ja?

MINGUS: Tell her I'm an honest gangster! Only rob die town, ek. (I only rob the town) So we tell them just split, man . . . Fok off! Get out, gee pad, man! (hit the road, man!) Go back to Edward Road. Then this one Berliner takes out his jungle and it's war, man—Second World War all over again. Jakes?

JAKES: Ja?

MINGUS: Tell her I fought in the war, man—tell her I'm a war hero.

JAKES: You fought in the war?

MINGUS: Yes man—I fought in the planes, in the tanks, just like Clark Gable in that . . . that . . . "Gone With the Wind."

JAKES: I'll tell her you'll take her to the Odin Cinema.

MINGUS: Ja man! And the Ritz—for long-arm dancing. So it's the Second World War, man. All over again. The Americans and the Berliners, but we're gonna win, man. We got the edge. I smile. I smile and move back. Jakes?

JAKES: Ja?

MINGUS: Tell her I've got a lovely smile, man. Now the thing's in my hand, man. Hey guys, gee pad, gee pad! They don't move. My thing's itching man, it's talking to me, my special Baby Brownie. Hey man, gee jy die pad, man—dis onse town. (Hey man, get outta here, man—this is our town.) Jakes?

JAKES: Ja?

MINGUS: Tell her I own the town.

Enter MR FAHFEE

FAHFEE: Hey, hey, hey, hey, hey! Bo Resha says the Boere own the town and we must never forget that.

JAKES: Hey, Fahfee, that smells like a story.

FAHFEE: News of the Day! Dikgang tsa gompieno! Dolly Rathebe is singing in "African Jazz and Variety" for Alf Herbert at the Windmill Theatre in Johannesburg and guess in what language she's singing?

JAKES: What?

FAHFEE: Yiddish! What's the number today, gentlemen, what's the dream?

MINGUS: Hey Fahfee—we're busy—Jake's writing me a masterpiece.

FAHFEE: Words again, Mr Jakes?

JAKES: A love letter, Fahfee.

FAHFEE: A love letter! Let me see—love . . . That's number 35—Katpan. Or 36—Nonkwayi. Male and female anatomicals—35 or 36 it is!

JAKES: Love! It's just quarrels all the way.

FAHFEE: Quarrels—number 5—the Tiger.

MINGUS: Ag man, Jakes, what do you know of love? Waar's you ousie? (Where's your girl?)

JAKES: Ek het nie. (I don't have one.)

MINGUS: Daar's die main trouble, man. (That's the main trouble, man.)

FAHFEE: So what's the love letter?

MINGUS: Read it Jakes, read it! Fahfee here is a man with an ear for numbers. Tell me this is not my number!

JAKES: It's not finished.

MINGUS: [*threatening*] Read it out, Jakes.

JAKES: Okay. 65 Gerty Street, Sophiatown, Johannesburg. 21st November 1954. My dear darling beloved Princess. I saw you at the funeral and I think you're smashing. I only go for the best. Winthrops, Bostonians, Simpsons, Borsalinos, and you. I'm the best dresser in town. American straights. I'm a smart guy and I don't get messed around. Be here at six o'clock tonight. I'm an honest gangster. I only go for the town centre—I don't touch Sophia. I fought in the war, in planes and tankers and I love the Odin Cinema. Balansky's is not for me—too much shouting.

MINGUS: Ja and tell her I don't like it when they piss off the balcony and throw bottles down.

JAKES: Okay, Mingus! [*Reading.*] I've got a lovely smile . . . and that's as far as we got when Mr Fahfee came in.

MINGUS: So what you think, Fahfee?

FAHFEE: Well. Is she a Diamond Lady? That's number 17. Or a Young Girl—that's number 19. I think the letter must be a romance, like: "I spend sleepless nights dreaming of you. My heart goes put-put. I see you everywhere . . ."

MINGUS: Rubbish! It must flow like music.

FAHFEE: All right. All right! [*Improvising a rhythm.*] You know—you know—you know—I love you—full stop. You know—you know—you know—I want you—full stop. You know—you know—you know—I'm yours—full stop. Your most passionate American Admirer, "Clark Mingus Gable."

He concludes by miming a punctuation mark in the air.

MINGUS: Rubbish passionate! Jakes, just put, "I won't wait after six!"

JAKES: Okay Mingus . . . Mr Fahfee, what's in the news today?

FAHFEE: Ah. Father Huddleston has started a Western Areas protest committee. Congress has called for five thousand volunteers. Bo Resha says, "The time has come."

JAKES: Did you bring those books for Lulu?

MINGUS: Politics! You leave my sister alone. She's at school and she's got a bloody lot of work. An' you, Fahfee, don't come here with your own troubles.

FAHFEE [*sidestepping the issue*]: Just tell me your dreams and I'll give you the right number.

JAKES: I'm dreaming up a scheme that'll floor the lot of you. Just wait—I've got a story up my sleeve that'll move me right to the top.

FAHFEE: The top? That's number 1!

JAKES: The king?

FAHFEE: Yes . . . We need help from you, Mr Drum. You must write about Sophiatown. We're not going to move, and you must tell the whole world.

JAKES: At the moment all I'm gonna tell the world about is boxing, but just you wait—promotion is just around the corner.

MINGUS: Ouens, ouens, we must finish this love letter and get it off. Charlie!

FAHFEE: So how's it gonna end?

MINGUS: How about "Yours in loving memory"?

JAKES: That's for the dead, Mingus.

FAHFEE breaks into uncontrollable laughter.

MINGUS: Ag . . . skryf daar about die moon, man, Jakes! Charlie!

JAKES [*largely romantic*]: Ours is a night time love, ours is a silver light love, ours is a love as full as the moon.

FAHFEE: Your voice is like moonrays, like the silver rays it calls to me . . .

JAKES: . . . and my letter calls to you.

MINGUS: . . . to be here at six o'clock sharp! Charlie! [*CHARLIE responds.*] I want this letter to be there and back in quicker than two flaps of a dove's tail!

The four men break into a close harmony quartet about PRINCESS, love, Sophia-town, and moonlight.

SCENE 2

The scene opens with PRINCESS sitting on the table painting her nails.
MAMARITI is asleep in her chair. LULU is preparing for school.

LULU: I wandered lonely as a cloud . . .
that floats on high, above vales and hills.
When all at once I saw a crowd,
a host of golden daffodils.
Besides the lakes, beneath the trees,
fluttering and dancing in the breeze.

There is a knock on the door. Silence. PRINCESS doesn't move. Another knock.

MAMARITI awakes with a start.

MAMARITI: Kom in! [*Knock.*] Kom binne! [*Knock.*] Hey kom in, come in! [*Knock.*] Jislaaik. Well if you don't want to come in, fok off man! [*She is now fully awake.*] Princess, go and open the door.

PRINCESS: I'm busy.

MAMARITI: How my son can live with you I don't know. Lulu, open the door.

LULU: I'm busy, Ma. I'm studying.

MAMARITI: For crying out loud! Stand up and go and open the door! What is going on in this house?

LULU [*going to the door*]: I wandered lonely as a cloud . . . [*bangs her head*] . . . I wandered lonesome like a cloud . . . I'll never learn this thing.

Enter RUTH, the Jewish girl from Yeoville. She is carrying two suitcases and seems prepared to move in. LULU, PRINCESS and MAMARITI draw back in surprise.

RUTH: Hullo! I'm Ruth. [*Silence.*] Ruth Golden. [*Silence.*] I'm the Jewish girl. [*Silence.*] I wonder if this is the right address? [*She scratches in her clutch bag.*] 65 Gerty Street?

LULU: Yes?

RUTH: Well, I came in response to the advertisement . . . Where shall I put my things?

LULU: Look, who are you?

PRINCESS: Yes, this is Sophiatown you know.

RUTH: Yes, I know. I've come in response to the advertisement.

Enter MINGUS and CHARLIE.

MINGUS: Hey, hey what's going on? What's happening?

LULU: This lady seems to think she's moving in.

RUTH: Yes, well . . .

MINGUS: Listen, lady, who are you and what do you want?

CHARLIE who has followed MINGUS in, begins to paw at RUTH's shoes. She pretends not to notice.

RUTH: I'm Ruth Golden, the Jewish girl from Yeoville. I came in response to the advertisement.

CHARLIE's advances have become overpowering.

RUTH: Aaaah!

MINGUS: Charlie! Off!

LULU: Which advertisement?

RUTH: Here it is. [*She attempts to show it to MINGUS who stares at it, and turns away.*] "Wanted: one Jewish girl to live in Sophiatown for study purposes. Come to 65 Gerty Street, or phone 46-7894."

LULU: Well?

RUTH: Well, I'm Jewish.

MINGUS: So?

RUTH: So here I am . . . [*CHARLIE is at it again.*] Please!

MINGUS: Charlie, off! [*CHARLIE retreats.*] Look lady, is this some kind of joke?

RUTH: I assure you it's not.

PRINCESS: We don't want European girls here. European girls mean trouble.

MINGUS: Where did you see this advertisement?

RUTH: In *Drum* magazine.

MINGUS: *Drum* magazine!

RUTH: I do read it, you know!

MINGUS: This is Jakes's business!

RUTH: Jakes!

MINGUS: Charlie! Go fetch Jakes. This is all Jakes's nonsense again. Hey look here lady, what kind of person are you? Do you know this is Sophiatown?

RUTH: Yes! I read all about it before I came.

PRINCESS: This is a native township.

LULU: Father Huddleston says it's a freehold suburb.

Enter MR FAHFEE.

FAHFEE: Hey, hey, hey, hey, hey. News of the day! Dikgang tsa gompieno! Albert Luthuli has been banned. All houses to be sold to the Resettlement Board. (i.e., homeowners in Sophiatown must sell their property to the government.) [*FAHFEE turns and sees RUTH.*] O Mang? (Who are you? *S*)

RUTH: I beg your pardon?

FAHFEE: Wie's jy? (Who are you? *A*)

RUTH: Sorry?

FAHFEE: Give me a number.

RUTH: What?

MINGUS: Give him a number.

RUTH: Any number?

LULU: Yes, any number.

RUTH: [*bewildered*] Number 17.

FAHFEE: Number 17! Diamond Lady. I knew it—that's the one for the day!

RUTH: What?

FAHFEE: 1 is for King, 2 is for Monkey, 3 is for Sea Water, 4 is for Dead Man, 5 is for Tiger, 6 is for Ox, 7 is for Skelm, 8 is for Pig, 9 is for Moon, 10 is for Egg, 11 is for Car, 12 is for Granny, 13 is for Big Fish, 14 is for Dead Woman, 15 is for Slegte Vrou, 16 is for Pigeon—Amajuba, 17 . . . Diamond Lady!

Enter JAKES.

JAKES: You are the Diamond Lady and I'm Jakes!

RUTH: Thank God! I was beginning to think I was at the wrong place.

MINGUS: How do you know you're at the right place?

JAKES: I'd like you to meet Mingus . . .
RUTH: How do you do?
JAKES: Mingus's lady friend, Princess . . .
RUTH: Hullo.
JAKES: This is Mr Fahfee . . .
RUTH: Hullo.
JAKES: Lulu over there . . .
RUTH: Hullo.
JAKES: This is the Mama of the house . . .
RUTH: Hullo.
JAKES: And Charlie I believe you've met.

CHARLIE has been pawing at RUTH's shoes right through the introductions.

RUTH: Yes!
MINGUS: Com'on Charlie, back off! Listen Jakes—if you're making trouble again . . .
JAKES: There's going to be no trouble. This young lady has bravely stepped into the unknown. Jumped in where angels even fear to tread. Answered an unusual advert—and here she is. We are going to do everything we can to make life easy for her. I assure you, Ruth—you have the best protection in the neighbourhood. Mingus here is an American.
RUTH: An American!
MINGUS: An American. Nobody troubles an American's friends. But I choose my friends very very carefully!
MAMARITI: Lulu!

LULU crosses to her mother, who whispers in her ear, gesticulating furiously.

LULU: My mother wants to know if you can pay a good rent.
RUTH: A good rent? I'm sure I can.

Whispered exchange.

LULU: My mother wants to know if you can pay £2.5s a month?
RUTH: It's a bit steep.
LULU: So?
RUTH: Well, I can do it . . .

Whispered exchange.

LULU: My mother says you can stay.
RUTH: Thank you.
MINGUS: Hold it! Hold it! I'll decide. [*He takes a long walk around her, evaluating her.*] All right, she can stay.
LULU: Yay!
JAKES: I knew it would work out. You'll stay with me of course. I've got a room at the back.

RUTH: I beg your pardon?

PRINCESS bursts out laughing, long and loud.

MINGUS: What you laughing at? I didn't bring you here to laugh at our guests.
PRINCESS: Ha! This Jewish is going to stay in the back with the situation.
This I want to see.
MINGUS: Luister—watch out . . . watch out!
RUTH: 'Scuse me—I really don't think its's such a good idea to share a room—
I hardly know you.
JAKES: It's quite all right. There's a curtain I'll put up.
RUTH: On the telephone you said I could have a room all to myself.
PRINCESS: A room all to yourself! Are you some kind of a moegoe?
RUTH: I beg your pardon!
PRINCESS: No one lives in a room to themselves here. You think this is Yeo-
ville?
RUTH: But I can't just move in with a man I've hardly met. Look, I can pay a
reasonable rent.
MAMARITI: Ja . . . Lulu.

LULU crosses over to her.

LULU [*after whispered exchanges*]: My mother wants to know if you can bring
spirits from town.
RUTH: Spirits from town?
LULU: Ja, spirits . . . whiskey, brandy, gin . . .
RUTH: Oh yes, I can do that.
JAKES: Hey, Fahfee!
LULU: My mother wants to know if you can help me with my homework.
RUTH: Yes!
LULU: Yay! My mother says you can sleep in her room.
RUTH: Thank you.
MINGUS: Ja, you can sleep in Lulu's bed.
LULU: Hey!
RUTH: Where will Lulu sleep?
MAMARITI: With me!
LULU: Ag Ma!
JAKES: There we are. No problems—I told you. It's simple. Spirits for the front
room. Rent for the bedroom. Homework for the kitchen and stories for the back-
room.
PRINCESS: And Mingus, perfume for the Princess!
MINGUS: Ag my sweetie, anything for you.
RUTH: I'll bring you perfume from John Orr's, if you want.
MINGUS: There you are, everything's gonna be just fine. Dis khuvet onder die
korset. (Everything's fine.)
RUTH: See, I'm the easiest person in the world to please. I'm happy with the

simplest things. All I need is a light to read by, somewhere to sleep and a place to bath.

Everyone exclaims incredulously.

MINGUS: Charlie! Go out there and find me a bath!

Lights change. The cast set up a rhythm of typewriters with body and sound as the following song is chanted by JAKES.

I said to Dam-Dam, Hoozit ou Dam-Dam?
I said to Dam-Dam, What's been going on?

He said to me, Oh, Jackie Boy, Jackie Boy,
He said to me, I'm looking for my dream girl.

I said to Dam-Dam, Come on ou Dam-Dam,
Whatever happened to the dazzling Boksburg blonde?

He said to me, Oh Jackie Boy, Jackie Boy,
He said to me, I'm a sucker, I've been conned.

My love's not for sale—she's been messing me around,
Showbiz is my biz, not no lover's hunting-ground.

I said to Dam-Dam, Come on ou Dam-Dam,
Whatever happened to the nut-brown from Softown?

He said to me, Oh Jackie Boy, Jackie Boy,
You know a juicy berry when she's hanging on your neck.

I said to Dam-Dam, Come on ou Dam-Dam,
Dam-Dam is the biggest playboy in the plek.

He said to me, Oh Jackie Boy, Jackie Boy,
If she's not in town, she's just coaldust off my feet.

I said to Dam-Dam, Come on ou Dam-Dam,
Have you seen the Jewish girl who's living down the street?

Blackout.

SCENE 3

LULU is sitting on the floor trying to learn "The Daffodils" by Wordsworth. JAKES watches as MINGUS and PRINCESS quarrel. MAMARITI sits quietly in a corner. FAHFEE sits at the kitchen table working on his gambling numbers.

PRINCESS: Ek soek haar nie hier nie. Mingus, hoe kan jy so maak? (I'm not looking for her here. Mingus, how can you do this?) Let this Jewish girl just move in? As jou my like (if you like me), Mingus, you'll get rid of her.

MINGUS: Listen my angel, my princess, ek mnca you (I'm hot for you), okay, but you're driving me mad. If you don't shaddup I'll have to crack you up.

PRINCESS: How can you let her stay here? We don't know who she is. You don't listen to me—you only listen to Jakes.

MINGUS: Look—you're just an American's tjerrie, and that means you shaddup and listen or I'll have to cut you up.

PRINCESS: I know about these Jewish girls from Yeoville. They're spoilt. Their fathers give them lots of money—they do what they like. They've all got nannies. Well, I'm not going to be anybody's nanny.

LULU: You're just jealous.

MINGUS: Look, I brought you here. I give you dresses, I take you to bioscope, you're my princess. What else do you want?

PRINCESS: I want that Jewish girl out.

MINGUS: Shaddup or I'll have to cut your spinal off! I didn't bring you from your shack so you can complain.

LULU: I like her. I stared at her face all night. It glowed in the dark. It made me think of the line in this poem, "a host of golden daffodils." I need help with this homework.

PRINCESS: I'll help you.

LULU: What do you know—you're just an American's tjerrie.

PRINCESS: I'll give you a good klap. How can you let her stay here? She doesn't belong here, man. She's a European. Europeans don't live in Sophiatown. It's a native location.

JAKES: It's a freehold suburb—no fences, no superintendent.

MINGUS: Ja, and this house is open. If I say she stays, she stays.

JAKES: Look, she's got guts. I need her. She's a hot story. How many others are there like her?

LULU: There's that white woman living with the police sergeant in Orlando.

JAKES: Regina Brooks.

MINGUS: Ja, she's all right.

LULU: And there's the Afrikaans girl living with the Olifants in Ray Street.

MINGUS: I think she's a relative.

FAHFEE: A relative?

MINGUS: Ja, a relative.

JAKES: And here's Ruth Golden.

PRINCESS: Ja, and what are you going to say when the G-men raid? "Make way for the Jewish—she's a new kind of girl." Just pretend you don't see her?

JAKES: We'll hide her like we hide the booze.

PRINCESS: And who's gonna protect her from the Americans at night?

MINGUS: Me.

PRINCESS: But you are an American, wena.

MINGUS: I'll protect her.

PRINCESS: And the Berliners, and the Gestapo Gang, and the Vultures? Where have you ever seen a white girl in this Sophiatown—where?

FAHFEE: There are always Europeans here—drinking at the Back of the Moon, drinking at the Thirty-Nine Steps. In the nightclubs, in the jazz clubs, at the House of Truth, in the bioscope. What difference if one of them spends the night. Nobody's gonna know. And if they did, nobody'd give a damn.

MINGUS: Except for the Boere.

LULU: And the Princess!

PRINCESS [chasing LULU around the room]: You just watch your mouth.

LULU: Princess of the slum! Princess of the slum!

PRINCESS: Mingus!

MINGUS: Lulu! Tsama hansi! Sit down!

PRINCESS: How can you let her stay here? What does she want here? Is she an angel?

JAKES: I think this young lady's gonna do just fine. She'll help Lulu—and we'll be the talk of the town.

LULU [flopping down]: Ag—I'm finished with school. I hate it. What do they teach us? Nothing! How to be good Christian girls. Rubbish!

MINGUS: You're staying right there. Nobody says Mingus lets his sister on the streets. This house wants a situation—a B.A. Intellectual!

LULU: You've got your situation.

MINGUS: Where?

LULU: This Jewish girl's your situation. I'm going to be a film star—like Dolly Rathebe in African Jim and The Magic Garden.

[She gets up and sings an extract from one of Dolly Rathebe's films.]

"I came to Joburg, to the Golden City,
What did I come here for?"

The household applauds. Enter RUTH.

RUTH: Morning.

JAKES: Hullo Ruth. How did you sleep?

RUTH: Fine.

MINGUS: Are you sure?

RUTH: Yes.

JAKES: Was the bed all right?

RUTH: Yes, fine.

LULU: You were talking in your sleep.

RUTH: Was I?

LULU: Yes. I was watching your face. Did you have nightmares?

RUTH: I don't know.

LULU: I think you were talking about Yeoville.

RUTH: Was I?

LULU: Yes.

RUTH: It must have been the dogs.

MINGUS: The dogs?

RUTH: Yes.

MINGUS: What do you mean, the dogs?

RUTH: Well, the barking kept me awake.

LULU: And Mama's snoring!

MAMARITI: Eh wena! Hai! Wena ungakhulumi umswanila nxa! (Hey you! Hey! You stop talking tripe here!)

MINGUS: Charlie! Get rid of those dogs!

RUTH: No, no. Please it's all right . . .

MINGUS: I'll stone them. I'll shoot them.

RUTH: No, please, it's quite all right really. It'll just take a bit of getting used to. There are dogs in Yeoville too.

JAKES: Of course, yes.

RUTH: You see, I'm just not used to sleeping three in a room.

MINGUS: Jakes, I want you out your room.

JAKES: What?

MINGUS: For the Jewish girl.

RUTH: No, please. Really it's all right.

MINGUS [*turning on her*]: Don't you argue with me.

JAKES: Listen Mingus, give it a few days. I'm sure everything will settle down.

MINGUS: Look here, Jakes, she's a European and a guest and in my house she gets the best.

RUTH: Please, I just want to be like everybody else.

PRINCESS: Well, you never will be!

RUTH: Now that is very unfair! You told me I'd have a room on my own and I'd hardly be in the house at all, and now already there's a whole fuss.

MINGUS: Listen, if you go back to Yeoville and tell everybody you were uncomfortable here, I'll be very much and extremely upset. I want you in Jakes's room.

RUTH: And where will Jakes sleep?

MINGUS: In the front room—on the floor—under his table, I don't know. Charlie! Where the hell is he?

PRINCESS: What are you doing here anyway?

RUTH: Curiosity?

PRINCESS: What?

Enter CHARLIE flustered.

CHARLIE: Outside!

MINGUS: I want you out there tonight with the Baby B and stones. I want those goddamn dogs dead.

CHARLIE: Outside!

MINGUS: What?

CHARLIE: Outside.

CHARLIE and MINGUS exit. Re-enter MINGUS.

MINGUS: Fahfee, Jakes—outside!

The men exit.

PRINCESS: Already you're causing disruptions.

MAMARITI: Hey Princess—leave the Jewish girl alone. I want her here and that's that. Don't you come here with your Princess nonsense.

The men enter carrying a large bath.

MINGUS: Jislaaik—it's heavy!

LULU: A bath! What we going to do with it? Tie it to the water tap outside?

MINGUS: You are going to fill it with hot water from the stove.

PRINCESS: Where are you going to put this stupid thing?

MINGUS: In the kitchen! And you shaddup.

RUTH: For heaven's sake! I didn't realise. The last thing I wanted was a special bath. I've had enough baths at home.

JAKES: We'll all use it.

MINGUS: Ja.

PRINCESS: I'm not going near that thing.

LULU: Me neither.

MINGUS: Ma?

MAMARITI: No.

MINGUS: Ma, shall we try it for size?

MAMARITI: Never! Not me, never!

MINGUS: Lulu.

LULU: No!

MINGUS: Lulu!

MINGUS signals to CHARLIE, who dumps LULU in the bath. FAHFEE attempts to intervene but his back is damaged from the weight of the bath.

RUTH: Charlie, I'm very sorry—I really didn't mean you to go to all that trouble.

MINGUS: Hey! Never, never apologize to Charlie. Understand? He does everything I say. Just keep your damn nose clean.

PRINCESS: Ja Mingus, tell her.

JAKES: Ruth Golden—now the bath's here, somebody's got to use it. And by all accounts it had better be you!

RUTH: I couldn't . . . I really couldn't.

The Cast sing "Tobiansky"

Tobiansky
Tobiansky
Tobiansky
Tobiansky
Why did you do this thing to me?

You gave me freehold suburbs
You gave me title deeds
You gave me everything
A Softown majieta needs
And then you take it away
Tobiansky
Tobiansky
Tobiansky
Why did you do this thing to me?
You gave me Odin bioscope
You gave me Gerty Street
You gave me Softown lifestyle
And everything is sweet
And then you take it away

There is a moment of transition as the bath is moved to one side of the stage.

FAHFEE: This bath is so big, I think the whole of Gerty Street will have to come and bath in here.

JAKES: Fahfee, watter nommer sal die Chinaman trek vanaand? (what number will the Chinaman draw tonight?)

FAHFEE [*indicating the bath*]: 22—American Battleship.

JAKES [*turning to the audience*]: Well, things settled down and within weeks Ruth seemed like part of the family. She wouldn't use the bath and so Mamariti started brewing great quantities of beer in it. I was planning my big break with *Drum*—dreaming of a double page full of pictures.

All those guys thought Ruth was great but I suspected they were just after any white girls. White skin, it's a fatal attraction. Heartbreak and humiliation. I was keeping my distance, as always, just watching.

Ruth wanted to move around with more freedom, so we let her in on some secrets.

Lights change.

SCENE 4

RUTH is having lessons in how to survive in Sophiatown from JAKES, FAHFEE and MINGUS.

FAHFEE: Ek sê, waar's die ouens hier? (I say, where are the guys here?)

RUTH: Hoozit gents! (How's it going, gents.)

FAHFEE: Is Khuvet onder die korset—en met jou? (It's cool—and you?)

RUTH: Die mission is grand. (The mission is grand.)

FAHFEE: En wie is jy? (And who are you?)

RUTH: Ek! Ek is die matara van die dla! (Me! I'm the lady of the house.)

FAHFEE: Wie? (Who?)

RUTH: Die matara van die dla.

FAHFEE: Jy's mooi hey. (Hey, you look nice.)

RUTH: Don't touch. Jy moenie baaiza nie. Sit gents. Sit julle majietas. Die magrizin van die stuk is nie hier nie. (Watch your step. Sit gents. Sit you dudes. The proprietor of the place is not here.)

FAHFEE: Wie?

RUTH: Die magrizin van die stuk?

MINGUS: Not bad, Fahfee, try it again.

FAHFEE: Ek sê, waar's die ouens hier?

RUTH: Hoozit gents!

FAHFEE: Is khuvet onder die korset—en met jou?

RUTH: Die mission is grand.

FAHFEE: En wie is jy?

RUTH: Ek! Ek is die matara van die dla!

FAHFEE: Wie?

RUTH: Die matara van die dla!

FAHFEE: Jy's mooi hey.

RUTH: Don't touch. Jy moenie baaiza nie. Sit gents. Sit julle majietas. Die magrizin van die stuk is nie hier nie.

FAHFEE: Wie?

RUTH: Die magrizin van die stuk?

MINGUS: Right. Grand. And if die majietas kom, and go for you, what do you say?

RUTH: I'm a virtuous well-bred girl, I'm a nylon.

MINGUS: And if they don't leave you alone, they really go for you . . . ?

RUTH: Julle moenie baaiza nie? (Watch your step?)

MINGUS: Ag! Nee man! (Ach! No, man!)

RUTH: I don't know—I'll never learn.

JAKES: Look, it's in the eyes, it's a warning signal which says, "Leave me alone." It's because you're white. White flesh, it's a fatal attraction. They get you into bed—it's a fart in the face for this Prime Minister Strijdom.

MINGUS: Look, if an American comes in here and he wants you, what are you going to do?

RUTH: I'll stop him.

MINGUS: These Americans always get what they want. They see girls and they're mad, mad. They see white girls and they're over the back of the moon. And white girls living in Softown! It's our territory, man. I see something, I go for it. Look at me and Princess. I klapped her till she loved me.

RUTH: Mingus!

MINGUS: The more you love, the more you hit. Now she'll never leave me alone. So, if an American comes in here and goes for you what are you going to do?

RUTH: I don't know. I'll just go back to Yeoville.

FAHFEE: Go back to Yeoville?

RUTH: You want me to learn a whole new language, and you want me to have a special look in my eye, and you want me to klap me until I love you. I think I must be mad to even try.

FAHFEE: You're giving up?

RUTH: Look, I come from an ordinary Jewish family. We've lived in Yeoville for as long as I can remember.

FAHFEE: And now you're going back!

RUTH: I'm trying to change my whole life!

FAHFEE: But you're giving up!

RUTH: I'm tired!

MINGUS: You're tired! What's the matter? Jakes's room not good enough for you? Charlie! Charlie! I told you to get rid of those goddamn dogs!

RUTH: Look—I don't want you to call Charlie. That's one of the reasons I'm tired. Every time a little thing goes wrong—Charlie! Charlie! I'll sort things out for myself.

MINGUS: You're bloody ungrateful. Why don't you bath? I brought it specially for you.

RUTH: You did not! Charlie did!

MINGUS: I told him to go out and get it.

JAKES: Look gents, we want life easy for the lady but not so easy she leaves. If she doesn't want to bath, she doesn't have to. If the dogs keep her awake at night that's tough. If the Americans want her—well, that's how it is. Come on, Miss Golden, cheer up . . . come on . . . smile. The sky can fall on your head anywhere. Come on, we'll take you to Freedom Square, we'll show you the Back of the Moon, we'll take you to Can Themba's House of Truth and we'll teach you hoe om te wietie (how to talk). . . . Does that make you feel better? Hey, Fahfee, why don't we try that little bit of lingo again?

FAHFEE [*clowning for her*]: Torch, torch daai wiebit. Torch daai tjerrie. Ek hak jou. Kom my little matara. Ons wietie, ek en jy. Kom, ons moet Katz en Lourie. As ek jou magrizin request, sal jy my trou? (Look, look at that chick. Look at that cherry. I like you. Come my little lady. We'll talk, me and you. Come, we should get married. If I ask repectfully, will you marry me?)

JAKES: Say, "Yes."

RUTH: Yes.

FAHFEE laughs, RUTH gives him a punch.

FAHFEE: Kom, ons moet Katz en Lourie. Life is—boogie. Dis singalie. (It's grand.) Dis khuvet onder die korset. I'll show you Kofifi, I'll show you Maklera. Ons sal in die main road pedestrie and al die moemishes sal stare, en jy sal die matara van die dla wees. Jy notch? (We will stroll down the main road and all the fools will stare, and you will be the lady of the house. You get it?)

RUTH: Sure I notch. [*To JAKES.*] What's he saying?

MINGUS: In a nutshell he'd like to Katz and Lourie you.

JAKES: Which constitutes a rather unexpectedly early offer of marriage—considering that he's just met you.

RUTH [*playing along*]: Hey, hey don't touch. Jy moenie baaiza nie. I'll give you such a zetz. Sit julle gents, sit julle majietas en die larnie van die stuk will get you a brandy. (Sit fellas, sit young men, and the white person of the house will get you a brandy.)

FAHFEE: Mahok.

RUTH: A larnie's a white girl, right?

FAHFEE: Ja, a smart white person like you.

JAKES: But you're Jewish, right?

RUTH: So Nu? (Yeah, so?) What's Jewish? I don't know what the hell I am. I'm Jewish on Mondays, I'm white on Tuesdays, I'm South African on Wednesdays, I'm a Democrat on Thursdays, and I'm confused on all the other days. Mostly I'm just confused.

JAKES: What the hell am I? The Boere want us in separate locations, but what am I? I speak Zulu, Xhosa, Sotho, English, Afrikaans, and in moments of weakness I even speak Tsotsitaal.

FAHFEE: Hey! Tsotsitaal! Dis die taal van die ouens. (It's the language of the guys.) It's a sophisticated taal.

JAKES: So who the hell am I?

FAHFEE: Vra jou ma, man! (Ask your mother!)

JAKES: I'm a would-be intellectual, living in a wasteland, with no power to change anything except words—and a fat lot of good they do!

MINGUS [*suddenly aggressive, jumps up and moves in on RUTH*]: Come on, we must teach you lang-arm dancing for the Ritz. Arm uit! Daai kant! Ga my skouer. (Arm up! That side! Take my shoulder!) [*RUTH does not understand.*] Ga my skouer, man. [*RUTH hesitates, then takes his shoulder. They take up a position for a waltz.*] And—one, two, three, one, two, three . . .

RUTH [*laughing*]: I can do this! This is just a European waltz.

MINGUS [*offended*]: Nee man. This is for the Ritz, Sophiatown style. And one, two, three. One, two, three. One, two, three. And the lights go low, and the jazz band plays slow, and you are my wiebit . . . my matara . . . Bite my neck . . . Bite my neck!

RUTH: Mingus!

MINGUS: Bite my neck!

RUTH [*pulling away*]: Please!

MINGUS: What's the matter? Don't you like to dance? Or maybe you don't like to dance with Mingus? Kom, fok met my, kom! (Come, fuck with me, come!)

MINGUS chases RUTH around the room.

JAKES: Mingus! Mingus!

MINGUS: Shaddup, Jakes, man. She's got to learn, man. This is not Yeoville here, man. It's rough here. You can't be a larnie and live here. You think your sweet polite words will save you? You think your sweet white words will protect you?

JAKE: Mingus!

MINGUS: Shaddup, Jakes! Here it's bicycle spokes, and jungles, and Baby Brownies, and Lugers. [*To RUTH*] All nice European guns, mind you, from your war. It wasn't our war—it was your war. Look, look at my scars, look at my knife wounds—they're from our own war. You think Sophiatown is just jazz and clubs and the bright lights! It's a war, man—and you want to make this your war! Well, you've got lots to learn. And you can't pretend it's not happening because it will never go away. If you want to live here, white girl, you must learn—or pack up! Voetsak! Go back to Yeoville!

Blackout.

Scene 5

A single tight spot reveals RUTH sitting in a chair. FAHFEE stands behind her. She listens with intense concentration, desperately trying to learn.

FAHFEE [*in a monotone*]: 1 is for King; 2, Monkey; 3, Scawater; 4, Dead Man; 5 is for Tiger; 6 is for Ox; 7 is for skelm; 8 is for Pig; 9 is for Moon; 10, Eggs; 11, Car; 12, Granny; 13, Big Fish; 14, Dead Woman; 15, Slegte Vrou; 16, Pigeons; 17, Diamond Lady; 18, Small Change; 19, Small Girl; 20, Cat; 21, Elephant; 22, Ship; 23, Long Hair; 24, Big Mouth; 25, Big House; 26, Bees.

Blackout.

Scene 6

LULU is working at her homework. MAMARITI is carefully cleaning the type-writer. RUTH is writing in a diary.

LULU: Homework, bloody homework! Every day is homework. Got to wash the dishes for Mama, look after the customers, but these school teachers, they don't understand.

RUTH: What are you doing?

LULU: I'm writing a composition.

RUTH: I'll help you.

LULU: Will you? You're a star, hey!

RUTH: What's it about?

LULU: It's called "My Family." God, my teachers are dumb—what a stupid title: "My Family"!

RUTH: Well, what have you got there?

LULU: First I started writing about my mother.

RUTH: Mmmm?

LULU: She's just a cheeky old woman, breaking the law, working on her beer, and planning for her future which never comes.

MAMARITI: Sis! You stupid little idiot. How can you say all those things about me after all I've done for you?

LULU: Ag Ma, it's just a composition.

RUTH: And?

LULU: I'm also writing about my brother Mingus, who's always stealing goods from the railways.

RUTH: I'm not sure you should say those things.

LULU: But they're true!

RUTH: So?

LULU: Do you know, Mingus and the American gang, they stop the intellectuals, die situations, on the street corner, and to make trouble they make them recite Shakespeare!

RUTH: Shakespeare?

LULU: That's what Jakes told me. He says he's got a special line he learnt just in case, "Oh what a rogue and peasant slave am I."

RUTH: Hamlet!

LULU: Ja. I was going to write it here but Jakes says I shouldn't—he says all my teachers will think it's bad English! So I just write, "Mingus steals goods from the railways."

RUTH: Surely there are nice things you can write?

LULU: My teacher says telling the truth is a virtue.

RUTH: But there are all sorts of truths. It's true to say your brother steals from the railways, but it's also true to say that he gives your mother money to run the house, and money for your school.

LULU: He can keep his money for school.

RUTH: No! He pays for you, why not tell the truth?

LULU: A thief is a thief is a thief!

MAMARITI: Hey shaddup! It's enough now. Mingus brings me money and he's my son. If you tell everybody he's a thief, whatever you've got that's nice, they'll just say it's stolen! Fool!

LULU: Okay Ma!

RUTH: Carry on.

LULU: I wrote here about Princess, who's so lazy.

RUTH: Lulu! There must be something else.

LULU: Well . . . I wrote about her being in jealousy about you.

RUTH: Lulu! There must be something you like about her—she's very pretty.

LULU: She thinks she's pretty—she's always working on her toenails. I think her toenails are bloody ugly!

RUTH: She gives you presents.

LULU: She gave me a present only once—when she first arrived. Now she thinks she's the madam of the house. And now I'm writing about Ruth Golden, who is this strange European lady nobody understands. She's always the centre of the attractions. She thinks if she comes to live here everything will be all right.

RUTH: And I'm writing about Lulu who is the cheekiest sixteen-year-old I know.

LULU: You know, when I first met you, I thought you were Regina Brooks.

RUTH: Ag, I look nothing like her. She's big and fat, and wears a doek!

LULU: How do you know what she looks like?

RUTH: I saw her in Jakes's magazine.

LULU: Everywhere in this house it's just fiction, fiction, fiction. Jakes told me he's writing about you. He must be in love with you.

RUTH: Nonsense, Lulu!

LULU: Yes . . . He told me, he stares at your face and makes up the most fantastic stories. He tells me he's writing all about you, where you come from, what you're doing here . . .

RUTH: He knows none of those things!

LULU: That's what I told him. He told me he makes them up. I told him he's not allowed to, he told me he could. So, what are you doing here anyway?

RUTH: Let's just say I've got my own stories to write.

LULU: Fiction! I want the truth!

RUTH: All right . . . I guess I just wanted to see what the other side of the world looked like.

LULU: And what do your parents think?

RUTH: My parents think I'm in Cape Town!

MAMARITI: Hayikhona!

RUTH: Ja Mama, they think I'm in Cape Town sorting out my life, and here I am in Sophiatown making it more confused.

LULU: You'll get caught in the end.

RUTH: I expect to.

LULU: So why don't you tell the truth?

RUTH: There are different sorts of truths, Lulu. Remember that.

Enter MINGUS and PRINCESS. MINGUS is wearing a trench coat, and chewing an apple. He also carries a Benzedrine sniffer which he sniffs constantly. His hat is low over his eyes. He is acting out the role of Styles in a scene from the film Street With No Name. *PRINCESS follows as his henchman. She has a low-brimmed hat down over her eyes and an imaginary cigar clutched in her fingers. They both speak in ridiculously exaggerated American accents.*

PRINCESS [*offstage*]: All right, Styles, so just tell me what we gotta do.

LULU: Mingus and Princess have been to the movies! [*She and RUTH hide.*]

MINGUS: There's only one guy who's the brain of this outfit, and that's me!

PRINCESS: Right, boss. Just tell me what we gotta do.

MINGUS: First Ginger Girl, just give your daddy a big kiss and then get out a map.

She leans over and gives him an elegant kiss, then spreads an imaginary map on the table. MINGUS studies it.

All right! If we're gonna hit this place, we've gotta hit it hard. So when I give the word [*Sniffs.*] you go that end and I go this end. Scarface covers the rear. [*Sniffs.*] Now remember, when the hit comes out, no shooting till I say. [*Sniffs.*] I'm de brains of this outfit, and that brooks no contradiction. *He takes a hefty bite from the apple.*

PRINCESS: That was a sweet job you pulled in Pittsburgh.

MINGUS: No conviction . . .

PRINCESS: And that was a nice little shooting match in Miami.

MINGUS: No conviction . . .

PRINCESS: And that was a very surprising incident in Chicago.

MINGUS: No conviction . . .

Enter JAKES.

JAKES: Hey, Modimo wa khotso. What's going on?

LULU bursts out of hiding.

LULU: Mingus and Princess have been to the bioscope! Mingus and Princess have been to Balansky's.

PRINCESS: The Odin, wena.

LULU: Mingus and Princess think they're in the movies. Miami—no conviction! [*Mocking MINGUS, she snorts.*] Chicago—no conviction. [*Snorts.*] Softown—no conviction! [*Snorts.*]

MINGUS: I'll give you a blerry klap, man. Shaddup.

JAKES: So what did you see?

MINGUS: *Street With No Name.* Starring Richard Widmark as Styles. God, I'm a new man. From now on, I plan all my robberies with a map. Nothing but the best for Mingus. Nothing can stop me. I rob from the rich and sell to the poor. There's no limit, man . . . White girl, if you live here, you don't say a word.

RUTH: Cross my heart I never will.

Enter FAHFEE.

FAHFEE [*agitated*]: What's the number! What's the number! Number 4—Dead Man, trouble. Number 26—Bees, trouble. It's number 27—Dogs, policemen, trouble.

JAKES: What's the matter, Fahfee?

FAHFEE: I dream of number 8—the Pig, the white man, and I bring news.

JAKES: What news? Is there a story?

FAHFEE: There's a story, but will *Drum* tell this story? It's the end for us.

JAKES: Come, Fahfee, tell your story.

FAHFEE: They're moving us out! Hulle sê die Native Resettlement Act of 1954 sê die hele families wat hier in Kofifi pola, hulle moet klerrie. Hulle sê daar's accommodation in die new location van Meadowlands. (They say the Native Resettlement Act of 1954 says all the families that are staying in Sophiatown must clear out. They say there's new accommodation in the new township of Meadowlands.)

JAKES: Did you get it?

FAHFEE: Yes. Toby Street. They say the first moves are on 12th February.

JAKES: Are you sure about this, Fahfee?

FAHFEE: See for yourself. Notices.

JAKES: How many families?

FAHFEE: One five two.

RUTH: Jakes, what are you going to do?

JAKES: I don't know. Write the story. What else can I do?

FAHFEE: Congress says we mustn't move. We must resist, like in the Defiance Campaign. Congress calls for five thousand volunteers. We've got a plan.

JAKES: The secret M-Plan?

FAHFEE: Ja.

RUTH: How does it work?

JAKES: Nobody knows—it's a secret.

FAHFEE [*suddenly suspicious*]: Why do you want to know?

RUTH: Pardon?

MINGUS: Ja, why do you want to know?

FAHFEE: Why do you want to know?

RUTH: That's great! That's really great. You don't trust me.

FAHFEE: You must earn your trust—you must work.

RUTH: What must I do?

FAHFEE: Stop all this shit.

RUTH: How do you expect me to do that?

FAHFEE: My uncle has been here since 1924. He knows nothing else—and now they want to move him to this Meadowlands. Ons dak nie. Ons pola hier! (We'll never move. We're staying here!)

JAKES: And what do you do when the policemen come?

FAHFEE: Die G-men?

JAKES: Ja.

FAHFEE: We've got a plan.

JAKES: But you hardly know what it is!

FAHFEE: When the time is right, we'll hear.

JAKES: That sounds very unsatisfactory to me.

FAHFEE: I don't care! I'd rather die than move from this place. They can kill us one by one, but we won't move. We'll sit down in the streets and wait for the bullets. There's going to be a war. Petitions, letters, committees—it's rubbish! I'm telling you, it's rubbish. There must be blood. Then things will happen.

MINGUS [*to RUTH in a moment of great anger*]: And it will be your blood.

RUTH: Jakes, please—I can't stand this.

MINGUS: Ja, just run back to Yeoville.

FAHFEE: What am I going to do in this Meadowlands? How am I going to put bread in my mouth? What's going to happen to my business with the Chinaman, the Gong? Where's he gonna be when they move Sophia? And the Indians? And the coloureds? Where's the jazz? Where's the life? Where's the situations? Where's the teachers? Where's the life? Where's the Fahfee? Where's the life? It's just dust and blood and dust!

MINGUS: Go back to Yeoville!

Change of lights. The Cast sing "Meadowlands" in a slow and melancholy waltz time. Then the rhythm changes to an up-tempo jive and they launch into a lively dance.

Meadowlands

Otla utlwa makgowa a re
A re yeng ko Meadowlands
A re yeng ko Meadowlands
Meadowlands Meadowlands
Meadowlands Meadowlands
Meadowlands sithandwa sam'
Meadowlands sithandwa sam'

Otla utlwa botsotsi ba re
Ons dak nie ons pola hier
Ons dak nie ons pola hier
Pola hier pola hier Pola hier sithandwa sam'
Pola hier pola hier Pola hier sithandwa sam'

(You'll hear the whites say
Let's move to Meadowlands
Let's move to Meadowlands
Meadowlands Meadowlands
Meadowlands Meadowlands
Meadowlands, my love
Meadowlands, my love

You'll hear the tsotsis say
We're not moving, we're staying here
We're not moving, we're staying here
Stay here, stay here
Stay here, my love
Stay here, my love)

SCENE 7

The family are gathered around the kitchen table. JAKES flourishes a Drum *magazine with great pride and excitement.*

JAKES: I've got it! [*He lays the magazine on the table.*] I've got it here! Come and see, come right up and see! This is break. No more boxing, no more gangster stories. I'm dealing with socialities. Come on—open it. Who do you see?

LULU [*opening it*]: It's Ruth!

RUTH [*rushing to look*]: Do I really look like that?

LULU: Look here, it's me! Oh, Jakes, in my school uniform! How could you do that to me?

PRINCESS [*pleased with herself*]: Look what I look like!

JAKES: The front page of *Drum* is waiting! Cheesecake, crime, babies, boxing—and more cheesecake. Princess must become a *Drum* girl, a model.

PRINCESS: Do you really think so?

MINGUS: You'll be famous, my sweetie. Let's have a party.

EVERYONE: Ja!

JAKES: Don't you want to hear it? Listen here: "The first of four articles on a Sophiatown phenomenon, 'Ruth Golden' by Jakes Mamabolo."

RUTH: God—if my parents find out they'll die!

LULU: Come on. Who in Yeoville reads *Drum*? It's a native magazine.

FAHFEE: Don't worry—nobody is gonna find out. Jakes, what's the page number?

JAKES: What?

FAHFEE: The page number, what's it man? It's today's winner.

JAKES: Number 23!

FAHFEE: Ah! You see! Number 23! A Dream of Long Hair!

JAKES: Don't you want to hear what it says?

FAHFEE: Com'on, give it here—I'll read it. "Mixing It Up in Softown. Dig that crazy white girl living it up in Gerty Street! Pshoo! Was there a scramble when word went round Sophiatown that a Jewish girl was living at Mamariti's Diamond Shebeen . . ."

MAMARITI: Say that again—that's me!

FAFHEE: "Nobody believed it was possible. Was this just a fantasy? A Jewish girl living in Softown! It's not possible. Is she crazy as a bedbug? Who'd leave the easy white life of Yeoville for the secthing hot-spots of Kofifi? Well, folks, let me introduce you. She is none other than Ruth Golden. Height: five foot three inches . . ."

RUTH: Five foot four!

JAKES: Oops! Sorry.

FAHFEE: Aah . . . Five foot four. "Long black hair pulled back in a swinging switch. A pert but comfortable figure. Curious bright eyes . . ."

RUTH: Come on!

FAHFEE: "She tells me . . ."

JAKES: Uh, uh—that's my bit. "She tells me she worked at Vanguard's, the bookshop, and we all know what happens there! Could she be an eager intellectual? A wide-eyed jazz maniac? A demure but daring do-gooder? Or is it just an advertising stunt?"

RUTH: Jakes!

JAKES: "Hey no man, Ruth Golden's just a gal with a golden heart. With her sweet smile and her helpful ways, she's become a smash-hit attraction at Mamariti's Diamond Shebeen."

MAMARITI: God, me again? I'm famous!

JAKES: "Says Ma: 'She's the best whiskey-glass washer I've had in ten years.'"

MAMARITI: I never said that!

LULU: Ag, Ma. It doesn't have to be true!

JAKES: Listen! "Says Princess, 'She's not so bad.'"

PRINCESS [*magnanimously*]: You're not so bad.

JAKES: "But then I must add, Princess is not so bad herself. She's the other hot girl in the house. A girl with real style and you know these girls don't throw around the compliments. Mingus, that regular church-goer . . ."

MINGUS: What?

JAKES: Okay! Just kidding.

MINGUS: What you got written there?

JAKES: Just listen. "Mingus, reputed to be one of the hot American Gang, says of our Jewish girl, 'For someone of her complexion, she's got spunk. She's all right. She's hot!' And that's a hot compliment from Mingus. So there we are, against all the odds. A Jewish girl living in Sophiatown. Read in the next issue, in her own words, How Ruth Golden Manages."

RUTH: How can you write all that, Jakes? There's just gonna be trouble.

JAKES: Nonsense. We've written about Regina Brooks, we've written about the Americans, we've written about politics. It's what people want to hear. And what's wrong with a Jewish girl living in Softown?

RUTH: There's nothing wrong. But it's illegal.

MINGUS: Look. We're two streets from Westdene. If the G-men come, you're out the door and up the road into the white suburbs in a tick.

RUTH: And all these other articles? I haven't said a word.

JAKES: You will. You will.

MINGUS: Come on, fok the G-men, let's have a big party! Mama, where's this week's booze?

MAMARITI: With the Jewish lady, of course.

MINGUS: Come on, get the booze! We're having a party.

The household breaks into a celebratory song.

A bo tle	(Let it come)
Re bo kga kgathe	(We'll drink it)
Ga bo palla	(If it doesn't taste nice)
Re bo tsholole	(We'll throw it out)
Re bo tsholole	(We'll throw it out)
Serope sa ngwanyana	(Girls' thighs)
Ke Moseletsi	(Are a lot of work)
Se bakela bashimane	(They keep on causing problems)
Dikgathatso	(For the guys)
Dikgathatso	(For the guys)

RUTH fetches bottles of gin, brandy and whiskey, hidden in brown paper packets. LULU hands out glasses. The song gets raucous. RUTH interrupts.

RUTH: I've got a surprise! Along with the usual, a gift from the Yeoville shops. A bottle of special home-made Jewish Friday night wine.

FAHFEE: What?

RUTH: I thought we might all like to try it. It's specially made for Friday night, and today's Friday, so here we are. Who knows, the entire house may be miraculously converted.

FAHFEE: Three drops of this Jewish wine and we're all Softown Majietas.

JAKES: Com'on then, let's hit that bottle. [*He opens the wine and pours.*] Right everybody, take a glass. We'll drink a toast in Jewish wine to the Jewish girl. And here's hoping for an instant rise in circulation.

MAMARITI: Hold it! Hold it! The man at the chemist shop says that we must say a prayer before we drink wine!

RUTH: Right—it's customary in Yeoville.

FAHFEE: A prayer? Ah . . . Please God don't make me too drunk tonight. Amen.

JAKES: I'll do it—just teach me how.

RUTH: It's in Hebrew.

MINGUS: Hebrew! Let's hear it.

RUTH: You really want to hear it?

EVERYONE: Yes!

RUTH: All right. Everyone stand. Put your hat on your head, Mr Fahfee. Baruch Atah Adonai, Elohaynu Melech Ha'Olam. Borai Pri Hagafen. Amen.

FAHFEE: It sounds like Tsotsitaal!

JAKES: What does it mean?

RUTH: Praised be the Lord our God, King of the Universe, who gave us the fruit of the vine.

FAHFEE: Jy sien hier in Kofifi, ons kan nie drink voor die madlozis drink, and so ons maak so. (You see, here in Sophiatown, we can't drink before the ancestors drink, and so we do this.)

He pours some wine on the ground. CHARLIE attempts to catch it in his glass.

Hey man, Charlie, jy's nog nie 'n madlozi nie. Hulle moet eerste drink, ons kan nie alleen drink. Ons moet hulle koek gee. Hulle drink en hulle's all right! (You're not an ancestor. They must drink first, we can't drink alone. We must give them a drink. They drink and they're all right.)

RUTH: You spill some on the ground?

FAHFEE: Ja, vir die ancestors. (Yes, for the ancestors.)

RUTH: We do the same! On Passover we leave the door open, and the ghost of Elijah's supposed to come in and drink the wine. I suppose it's the same thing really.

FAHFEE: Ghost?

RUTH: Ghost, Mr Fahfee.

LULU: What is this Passover?

RUTH: Passover? It's when the Jews were living in Egypt under the tyranny of a wicked Pharaoh and God said he'd send his angel of death to kill all the first-born. But he told the Jews if they'd put a sign on the door they'd be passed over.

MAMARITI: Perhaps we can also put a sign on our door.

MINGUS: No, no, it won't work here. We're all wicked.

JAKES: I suspect this good Lord couldn't give a damn, and even if he does, his voice is very distant. We'll have to fight it out for ourselves.

FAHFEE: You say this prayer is "Blessed be the Lord our God, who made the wine."

RUTH: Blessed be the Lord our God, King of the Universe, who gave us the fruit of the vine.

LULU: How many gods have you got?

RUTH: The Lord is One.

LULU: The Lord is one what?

RUTH: No, no. The Lord is One—unified.

LULU: In our church we say God is Three in One.

RUTH: I admit it is confusing.

MAMARITI: And the ancestors—there are many, many.

FAHFEE: I've got it! You say "Blessed be the Lord because he's King of the Universe"? Blessed is die Lord want hy's die Baas van die Hele Joint. Hy's alles, want hy gee ons die vrugte vir die koek. Hy's all right! Ja, daar's net een religion en daar's net een taal; en daai's Tsotsitaal, Kofifi style. (Blessed is the Lord cuz he's the boss of the whole joint. He's everything cuz he gives us the fruit for the drinks. He's all right! Yeah, there's only one religion and there's only one language; and that's street slang, Sophia style.)

MAMARITI: Ruthiwe, what is a Jewish? The only Jewish I know is the man in the chemist shop and one day he said to me, "Meshugenah-kop chazer." What is this "Meshugenah-kop chazer"?

RUTH: Mama, you don't want to know that.

MAMARITI: Certainly I do.

RUTH: It means, "Madman pig."

MAMARITI: Is that nice? When will these white people learn?

LULU: So what is a Jewish?

RUTH: Well, it's really hard to say. It's not a religion, because you can be an unbeliever and still be Jewish. And it's not a nationality, because you can be South African and be Jewish. It's not even a language, because the only Hebrew I know is this Baruch Atah. Perhaps it's like a tribe. A lost tribe. It's very confusing.

JAKES: God is One, and God is Three, and the ancestors are many, and I speak Zulu and Xhosa and Tswana and English and Afrikaans and Tsotsitaal, and if I'm lucky Ruth will teach me Hebrew, and the Boere and the U.P. and the Congress fight it out, and this Softown is filled with Coloured and Indian and Chinese and Zulus . . . but this Jewish remains a mystery. And Softown is a brand-new generation and we are blessed with a perfect confusion.

MINGUS: Ruth Golden. Come here! I've got a little surprise for you.

RUTH: For me?

MINGUS: Charlie! Go and fetch that little box!

Exit CHARLIE.

RUTH: A surprise for me?
MINGUS: Ja, guess.
RUTH: I can't.
MINGUS: Come on, guess.
RUTH: I don't know. Sweets?
MINGUS: Come on. Better than that.
RUTH: Buttons? I'm really no good at guessing.
MINGUS: Again.
RUTH: Please, Mingus.

MINGUS takes the box from CHARLIE, who has returned.
He conceals it from RUTH.

MINGUS: Come on. Pocket size. Guess!
RUTH: No, please, Mingus.
MINGUS: Pearls!
RUTH: Pearls! For me?
JAKES: Mingus, what you playing at?
MINGUS: Just a present from Mingus, Jakes.
RUTH: Gosh, Mingus, they're beautiful. I'll have to borrow one of Princess's gowns.
PRINCESS: You can't have one of my dresses.
RUTH: Ah . . . what's wrong Princess?
PRINCESS: Absolutely nothing!
RUTH: Come on, Princess—what's wrong?
PRINCESS: There's nothing wrong.
MINGUS: Come, Princess—what's the matter?
PRINCESS: You ask me what's the matter? How can you give her pearls? [*to RUTH*] I'm his girl.
RUTH: Come on, Princess. He's always giving you presents. Dresses, perfumes, jerseys. Oh my God, Mingus—where did you get them? You stole them! God, I'm drunk!
MINGUS: I did not steal them.
RUTH: Of course you did.
MINGUS: Nonsense. Somebody gave them to me.
RUTH: Ah . . . come on!
MINGUS: I'm telling you. I walk into the Ritz—me and my boys. We open the doors—the swing doors. Wam! Wam! And everybody's dancing. I stand for a moment. Very quiet. Just like Styles. I survey the scene from under my hat. And then—Ladies and Gentlemen, Mataras and Majietas, Dames en Here—the music's still playing—"Blue Moon"—but nobody's dancing. They're all looking at me. I say, "Ladies this side, Gents that side." They're all up against the walls. And

I walk to the gents, "Ouens, steek julle linke hande uit." (Guys, stick out your left hands.) And all the left hands shoot out, zip! Al die rappe. (All the watches.) And as I walk I thank each one of them as I go by.

He saunters, hat in hand, reliving the collection of the watches.

And I walk up to the ladies, "Yes ladies, let's see what you got. Show your necks." And they showed! There were the pearls, big ones and little ones. And I say, "Make your gifts," and they make their gifts. And I walk, just like in church collections.

RUTH: I can't take them, Mingus. They're stolen goods.

MINGUS: You've never complained before.

RUTH: You've never given me anything before.

MINGUS: But you know what's going on here.

RUTH: It's none of my business.

PRINCESS: She won't take them, Mingus. She's too clean, too holy, too white. But I'll take them. *She takes them.*

RUTH [*snatching them back*]: I've changed my mind. I'll have them.

JAKES: Before you know it you'll be with him on the jobs.

LULU languidly falls off her chair.

LULU: This red wine is making me sad. I want to be Jewish. I want to be a princess. I want to be the centre of the attractions. I want to be like Dolly Rathebe and sing in all the movies.

LULU launches into a maudlin and drunken version of "Stormy Weather."
Suddenly there is a violent knocking on the door.

FAHFEE: Oh my God! Dis die G-men! Vice en liquor squad!

JAKES: Ruth! You must hide!

RUTH: God! Where?

FAHFEE: Get rid of the bottles!

LULU: You must run to Westdene!

PRINCESS: Hide in the cupboard, with the dresses.

JAKES: You must get out!

RUTH: Jakes, please, you must come with me.

JAKES: I can't. Just move! [*RUTH moves out.*]

MINGUS: Fok julle G-men! Die is onse plek!

JAKES: Shut up, Mingus. Mama, open the door.

MAMARITI: Not me!

JAKES: Lulu!

LULU: No!

JAKES: Listen, Lulu, you're a schoolchild, you're innocent.

LULU: I've had too much of this Jewish wine.

JAKES: Go to the door, play the innocent. Get them to fok off. Tell them you're doing homework.

LULU reluctantly exits. CHARLIE follows. There is more frantic cleaning up.
Re-enter LULU.

LULU: Mama, it's a special notice for you.

MAMARITI: Read it.

LULU: "You are hereby required in terms of the Native Resettlement Act of 1954 to vacate the premises in which you reside. The date given is February 12th. You will be offered accommodation in the new location of Meadowlands."

Enter CHARLIE.

CHARLIE: I'm going to get a house!

Blackout.

ACT TWO

SCENE I

The company storms onto stage, singing "Koloi e." Each character emerges and shouts his or her protest over the music.

Koloi e

Koloi e, ha ena marili
Koloi e, ha ena marili
Ha e tsamaya, ya nyahyatha
Ha e tsamaya, e etsa "Chips"
Ha e tsamaya, e etsa "Chips"
Sutha sutha wena Strijdom
Ha o sa suthe
Sutha sutha wena strijdom
Ha o sa suthe
E ya go gata!

(This car, this car has no wheels
This car, this car has no wheels
When it moves, it moves quietly
When it moves, it dances "Chips"
When it moves, it dances "Chips"
Give way, give way, you Strijdom
If you don't
Give way, give way, you Strijdom
If you don't
It will ride over you)

MINGUS: Strijdom, Strijdom, watch out! Watch out, Strijdom!

FAHFEE: Hey, hey, hey, hey, hey! Die kar van ons (our car)—it's going right over you!

CHARLIE: Ja Strijdom. Ons dak nie, ons pola hier. Gee pad, gee pad, gee pad!

PRINCESS: Hey Boere, watch out! This car it's got no wheels! Gee pad, gee pad!

JAKES: Strijdom, get your ox-wagon out the way! Strijdom—get, get, get!

FAHFEE: Our children, born here, in Gerty Street, in Ray Street, in Good Street, in Gold Street. Don't think you can drive us away Strijdom!

MINGUS: We're here to stay. Dis onse plek. (It's our place.) Voetsak, voetsak, voetsak!

LULU: Title deeds. En nou waar's die law? Fok jou law, Strijdom. Dis 'n rich man's law. (And now where's the law? Fuck your law, Strijdom. It's a rich man's law.)

JAKES: Get your Boere out. The rivers are running. Take your guns, take your Saracens en gaan weg. (and go away.) Give way Strijdom, give way.

MAMARITI: Here we come, Strijdom. Watch out, this car's moving! It's got no wheels. Here we come. We're gonna roll, we're gonna roll right over you.

MINGUS: Kom Boere, gee pad, gee pad, gee pad!

FAHFEE: Strijdom, remember the Defiance Campaign. Ons is in Defiance. (We are in Defiance.) Ten thousand people broke your rubbish laws. Boere gee pad, gee pad, gee pad. Ons pola hier! Gee pad.

The song builds as the Cast prepare for the next scene. RUTH and MAMARITI seat themselves at the kitchen table and cut vegetables. LULU resumes her studies and JAKES sits at his typewriter. The song ends.

FAHFEE: News of the Day! Dikgang tsa gompieno! Congress calls for a fight on all fronts. This year is the year of the Congress of the People. We won't move. What's the number? Yes? Yes? It's 26. 26 June 1955—one nine five five.

JAKES: Hey Fahfee, what's going on?

FAHFEE: You must keep up, Mr Drum. The magic number is 26.

RUTH: Bees.

FAHFEE: That's right. What kind of South Africa do you want? Write it on a piece of paper, any paper—*Drum* magazine, *Star, New Age,* school books. Everybody must have an answer. We are going to make a new South Africa. These Boere be damned!

MAMARITI: That's right.

FAHFEE: This is a big day for news. Congress calls for a total boycott of all schools.

LULU: Agreed! I'm not going back to school any more.

RUTH: No more school?

FAHFEE: That's right.

MAMARITI: Hau, Lulu.

LULU: I don't want this Bantu education, Mama. It's for the gutter.

FAHFEE: Verwoerd's new Bantu Education is for slaves. This is 1955. We want education for freedom. Father Huddleston says, "Close the church schools rather than teach children rubbish."

MAMARITI: Hey wena. I don't care what he says—I want my child back at school.

FAHFEE: Hey Mamawe. They're coming with this new education. They want to move us. Well, I'm telling you, this is just the beginning—the tip on the top of the mountain. And what are we doing about it? What are you doing about it, yes, you Mama? And you, my broer? You just let them stomp all over you . . . Well, no-one's going to stomp on me, they can come with their lorries, their guns and their bulldozers, but they won't find me. Ba tla bona marago a noga! (They'll see the backside of a snake!)

LULU: Ja, they can try to force us back into the classrooms, but we won't move. They can keep their gutter education. These Boere are trying to take over the country.

MAMARITI: Hey Lulu, you don't talk like that.

FAHFEE: Lulu is right, Mama. I'm not going to be anybody's slave.

MAMARITI: Hey wena, Fahfee. What's gone wrong with you?

FAHFEE: I am recruited.

JAKES: Recruited? That sounds like a story.

FAHFEE: I am a freedom volunteer. I am one of thousands. The working people of this country will decide what they want. I am a fahfee runner, that's my job. I work, I decide what kind of South Africa do I want. I write it down on a piece of paper and send it to this Congress where it becomes law. So what kind of South Africa do you want?

MAMARITI: I want to stay right here in my house. It's freehold. My husband bought it. Paid good money for it. It's my right.

FAHFEE: Ag Mama. Freehold is just the beginning. We want decent jobs, decent education, decent food, and decent life for all. [*He takes one of the potatoes MAMARITI has been peeling, throws it into the air and catches it.*] If we grow something, it's ours. If we make something, it's ours. So what's the magic number?

RUTH: 26.

FAHFEE: Hayikhona! Ten thousand in the Defiance Campaign. Do you remember the 1946 strikes, Mama?

MAMARITI: Ja.

FAHFEE: Forty thousand. Forty thousand miners in the rat-holes, saying no. The Chinaman, he's got 36 numbers but I never win. But forty thousand, that's a number I can understand. Imagine a Softown strike! Fifty thousand! Then see if the Boere can move us. So, what else do you want, people?

RUTH: I'd like to find a way for Lulu to be in school.

LULU: I'm not going to school!

MAMARITI: I sell mbamba day and night to send you to school. Look at my hands. They're working for your future.

LULU: There is no future, Mama. Unless we make it. This education is rubbish.

MAMARITI: You must go to school—anything is better than nothing.

LULU: No, Mama. This is less than nothing. What do they teach us? Nothing!

Which natives live in which native reserve; education for certain forms of labour; whites originate in Africa; civilisation comes from Europe; English only from Standard Six.

JAKES: English only from Standard Six? Now that's a terrible thing to do. If there was one thing we got from our church schools, it was a love of English.

LULU: Ja, they want us illiterate.

RUTH: Well you're not going to be illiterate if you can speak Zulu and Xhosa and Sotho.

JAKES: English is the language that unifies us.

RUTH: Okay. But you don't want to lose your own language.

JAKES: Look—you're Jewish, right?

RUTH: So?

JAKES: Well, can you speak Hebrew? Besides this Baruch Atah.

RUTH: No.

JAKES: But you're still Jewish, right?

RUTH: Look, I'm a South African first.

JAKES: And what does that mean?

RUTH: I'm a white, English-speaking South African.

JAKES: But you're still Jewish and you can't speak Hebrew, right? And that proves my point.

RUTH: Well, frankly I wish I could speak Hebrew. Jakes, I just think it's a terrible thing to lose a language. Imagine if I was the last person who could speak Hebrew? When I died, those words would be gone forever.

JAKES: You don't look so worried.

RUTH: I am worried.

JAKES: What's gone is gone. You can't hold on to the past. These native reserves that Verwoerd wants, what have they got to do with Sophiatown? Here we listen to Bach and Beethoven. We listen to great American jazz. We read great Russian novels. We are a brand-new generation.

RUTH: Well, Lulu's not going to read anything if she doesn't go to school.

LULU: Even if I wanted to go to school, I can't. The school is going to be closed in April. Anyway, we'll be in Meadowlands.

FAHFEE: You must never say that, you hear! You give up before the fight!

RUTH: If you don't go back to school, what are you gonna do?

LULU: We're going make our own schools—under trees, in dance halls, in special clubs, in shebeens . . .

RUTH: In the shebeens?

JAKES: Yes—Mamariti's Special Shebeen School for Young Girls!

FAHFEE: Don't make jokes, Mr Drum.

LULU: It's not a joke. There are going to be schools in shebeens.

RUTH: And who is going to teach in these new schools?

LULU: I don't know. The teachers.

RUTH: Yes, that's the problem—new schools, Verwoerd's teachers.

FAHFEE: I'll teach her. Mathematics—dis my forté! I'm an expert on numbers. What's 49 times 49? Yes! Yes! Yes! Two thousand four hundred and one!

JAKES: How did you do that??

FAHFEE: I worked it out yesterday!

JAKES: I'll teach English literature . . . Africa's use of the short story.

RUTH: I'll teach English composition and biology. I was great in biology at school.

Enter MINGUS.

MINGUS: Charlie! Where the hell is he? What's going on here? Restaurant? Princess! Waar's daai tjerrie? I'll moer her! She's a rubberneck. (Where's that chick? I'll fuck her up! She's got her eye on all the men.) Head this way! Head that way! This morning she's dressed up to kill—she won't even tell me where she's going.

Enter CHARLIE.

MINGUS: Charlie! Gaan vat daai Delilah and bring haar hierso. (Go get that Delilah and bring her here.) She's 'n rubberneck. Gaan! Speed!

Exit CHARLIE.

MINGUS: So? Sny my nou die mello. (Tell me what's happening.) Cut me into the story. What's going on here?

FAHFEE: Listen, Mingus, we need the Americans' help. We're not going to move. Ons pola hier.

MINGUS: Niks. Politicians is one thing Americans is another.

FAHFEE: Luister, Mingus, if we move from Sophia, these Americans, these Berliners, these Vultures are finished.

MINGUS: Never—we're not going!

FAHFEE: It's easy to talk—talk is cheap. We must organise. Remember the 1949 tram boycotts? The Berliners were there, man, fighting the police.

MINGUS: The Berliners were there, all right, but were they smart? No! One side only. In the tram boycott the Americans were smart, man. The Congress wants us to hit the tram users. So, early in the morning we move out. "Hey—where you going? Don't you know it's boycott? The city wants to rob you man." Kah! Kah! We hit them, man. And we get paid. Then at night the tram companies pay us to use the trams as if we're coming home from work—twice paid! That's what I call American style.

FAHFEE: You can't do that. It's one side or the other.

MINGUS: Money is money, Fahfee!

FAHFEE: Luister, Mingus. The G-men are always after you, right?

MINGUS: Right.

FAHFEE: Why?

MINGUS: Because we are the enemy man. They can't get us—we're too smart.

FAHFEE: Yes, but they're always after you.

MINGUS: Aah! Fokken spies! We'll get them. Just one day we'll get them.

FAHFEE: Mingus, have you ever been to Freedom Square? Seen the thousands of people there? Why are the G-men always coming with Sten guns to break up the meeting?

MINGUS: Why?

FAHFEE: Because the politicians are the enemy, man, just like the Americans, just like the Berliners.

MINGUS: Don't talk to me about the Berliners!

FAHFEE: Listen, you stupid Mingus. You and the Berliners, you fight each other—you should fight the real enemy.

MINGUS: The Berliners are the real enemy.

FAHFEE: We need you Mingus. We need the Americans to fight. We need the numbers, man. We need fighters. We need planners. We need the Berliners and the Americans and the Vultures and the school children, and the journalists to fight. Can't you see what's going on?

JAKES: What's going on? Hundreds of people living in shacks, paying rents so home-owners can get rich—that's what's going on. Nobody's going to stop them moving. They're going to get houses.

FAHFEE: Where? Twenty miles from town. So Verwoerd has a clean white city.

MINGUS: The trains, hey, easy pickings. An American's paradise.

FAHFEE: Sis, Mingus. The Boere are making a little thief out of you, robbing people on trains. This is history—we're in history and we're fighting for freedom.

MINGUS: Hey teacher, what is this history? They teach Lulu history in school. What does it help? I stole this, I stole that. Is that history?

JAKES: It's only history if you steal something really large—like a country. Then it's history.

FAHFEE: Ja, well, we're going to steal it back. And we start with Sophiatown. We must organise. What are the numbers? Seven to a street—with a leader. Seven leaders to a ward. Seven times seven. Forty-nine. Forty-nine times forty-nine. The magic is in the numbers. We'll steal back our country with numbers.

Enter CHARLIE carrying PRINCESS. She is protesting wildly.

PRINCESS: Put me down! Put me down! You're a bloody stupid! Charlie, what are you doing? Put me down!

She is released and stands in the middle of the room. She is wearing a stunning but dishevelled outfit.

MINGUS: Ja—where have you been?

PRINCESS: What's it got to do with you?

MINGUS casually walks up to PRINCESS and then suddenly cracks her across the face.

MINGUS: Kom, jong, shoot die six, Princess. Sny my nou die mello. (Come on, kid, fill me in, Princess. What's going on?) Cut me into the story.

PRINCESS: I've got a job.

MINGUS: What job?

PRINCESS: I've got a job as a model for a photographer.

MINGUS: Ja. And who's this photographer?

PRINCESS: He's from Holland.

MINGUS: Aah! A larnie Hollandse photographer! Come show me what you do.

PRINCESS: What you mean?

MINGUS: Show me!

PRINCESS: What?

MINGUS: How you do this modelling.

PRINCESS: Come on, Mingus.

MINGUS: Show!

[*She makes a half-hearted attempt to strike some poses.*]

You . . . you do that for this photographer?

PRINCESS: Yes.

MINGUS: Come on, take off this dress—it's mine!

PRINCESS: No, Mingus.

MINGUS: Com'on—I want to see how you look without my dresses.

[*He attempts to pull off her dress. She resists, then runs off screaming. He runs after her, shouting, followed by the others. Only JAKES and RUTH remain.*]

MINGUS [*running after PRINCESS*]: I want them all back. My dresses, the jewellery, die bloody lot. Come, let's see if you look like a princess then.

RUTH: I don't know why she doesn't leave.

JAKES: If I were you I'd stay right out of it. This is one thing you'll never understand.

RUTH: It's just plain bullying.

JAKES: She belongs to him, and that's that!

RUTH: Now that I don't understand.

JAKES: Look, to be frank—there is plenty that you'll never understand because you'll always be looking from the outside.

RUTH: In that case, I'm a lot like you. You're always looking from the outside, watching.

JAKES: Rubbish!

RUTH: Well, why don't you join Fahfee? He needs you. You can't watch for ever, you know.

JAKES: When I decide the time is right, I'll be a different person.

RUTH: I think you're just scared.

JAKES: Well, what about you?

RUTH: I'm here.

JAKES: You think that is enough? If you were a princess in Princess's position, what would you do?

RUTH: I'd fight. There's no question. Nobody treats me like that. I wouldn't tolerate it.

JAKES: Mingus would just fuck you up.

RUTH: Well, if I was treated like that, I would just leave.

JAKES: Where would you go? She's a princess from the slums—no name, no home, no family. She'll sleep wherever she can find a place. Now she's got a place—she'll stay. The truth is, no matter wherever you go, if something really happens to you, you'll just go home to Daddy or Uncle or just the whites—rich and warm and loving. It's just another kind of laager.

RUTH: Well, you're in your own kind of laager, aren't you Jakes? Buried in this new journalism, and the African short story. Why don't you get out for a while? Look at me. You write about me, but you never look at me properly. Try to see beyond your own fictions. It's me, Ruth Golden, the girl with the golden heart, pert, comfortable, curious. Why don't you look at me properly, Jakes. Just once?

Blackout.

Scene 2

Spotlight on RUTH. She is concentrating intensely.

RUTH: 17, Diamond Lady; 18, Small Change; 19, Little Girl; 20, Cat; 21, Elephant; 22, Ship; 23, Long Hair; 24, Big Mouth; 25, Big House; 26, Bees.

Blackout.

Scene 3

Enter the four men dressed in immaculate evening dress, white jackets, bowties, walking sticks, and hats pulled over the eyes. As they sing, they execute dance steps reminiscent of the Manhattan Brothers.

Bantu Bahlala

Bantu bahlala ngenhliziy' ezibuhlungu
Sophia ngeyami
Sophia ngeyami
Bantwana baydlala
Bazali bayakhala
Bakhalel' ilizwe labo
Sophia ngeyam'
Sophia ngeyam'

Sithi yebo yebo yebo yebo
Sophia ngeyami

Sophia ngeyami
Nanka amabhunu
Afikile ngebulldoza
Adiliz' imizi yethu
Sophia ngeyam'
Sophia ngeyam'

(People stay with sad hearts
Sophiatown is mine
Sophiatown is mine
Children are playing
Parents are weeping
Weeping for their land
Sophiatown is mine
Sophiatown is mine

We say yes, yes, yes, yes
Sophiatown is mine
Sophiatown is mine
Here come the Boers
Coming with the bulldozers
They destroy our homes
Sophiatown is mine
Sophiatown is mine)

Blackout.

SCENE 4

It is midnight. Enter RUTH in a nightdress, carrying a paraffin lamp. She sneaks up to the typewriter and begins to read one of JAKES's stories. Suddenly there is a noise behind her. Enter MINGUS. He is dressed to kill, hat brim pulled low, trench coat. He has returned from a job. He stands in the doorway.

MINGUS: What are you doing?

RUTH: Oh God, Mingus—you gave me a fright.

MINGUS: Come on Ruth Golden, what are you doing?

RUTH: I couldn't sleep.

MINGUS: Ja, and so you scratch in Jakes's things. What do you want?

RUTH: I'm just looking.

MINGUS: Why? What do you think you'll find there that you don't know already? Haven't you seen enough?

RUTH: Look, I couldn't sleep.

MINGUS: Why? Does Princess keep you awake, that you have to wander around at night?

RUTH: We manage.

MINGUS: Ja, and how does Sophiatown look now? Two in a bed—or does Princess sleep underneath?

RUTH: You kicked her out, and your mother wants the rent, so we manage.

MINGUS: Ja, and when the majietas come? One underneath and one on top! Sophiatown style.

RUTH: What do you want, Mingus?

MINGUS: From you, Miss Golden—nothing.

RUTH: Good, I'll just go right back to bed.

MINGUS: Hold it!

RUTH: What do you want, Mingus?

MINGUS: Come here! Come on. Give me your hand. I've just been on a job. Here—feel.

He puts her hand under his jacket.

RUTH [*pulling away*]: Ah.

MINGUS: Tonight there is no sleep for either of us. What I need now is a drive, a ride in the moonlight. I need to look at the moon.

RUTH: Why don't you go, Mingus?

MINGUS: Hold it. I want you to come with. It's lonely out there on your own. I want to look at your hair, your face, the rest of you.

RUTH: I'm tired. I'm going to bed.

MINGUS [*blocking her exit*]: If you want to see Sophiatown you gotta see all sides. This is Sophiatown by night.

RUTH: Look Mingus, it's late. I don't feel like going for a drive.

MINGUS: Don't make no fuss. Mingus will begin to think that you don't care for him and he'll wonder why. What's the problem with the white girl that she won't get in a car and come for a midnight ride? Or is there something about Mingus's face she doesn't like?

RUTH: Look Mingus, that's not true and you know it. I'm not dressed. Look at me!

MINGUS: That's what I'm doing.

RUTH: I can't go out like this.

MINGUS: Luister! Al die tjerries van Softown will come out with Mingus any time. But because you're too much of a larnie, you make yourself a can't-get, a nylon.

RUTH: Mingus, why are you making it so difficult for me? I'm living in Sophiatown, having a good time, and you're making it impossible.

MINGUS: You call this a good time? Julle larnies, julle is fokken mal. (You whites, you're fuckin' crazy.) You come all the way from the white suburbs where it's all bloody fancy, and what is happening there? Niks. So you come here and Mingus is offering you a nice ride in the moonlight underneath the madness of the moon, and you say no.

RUTH: I just don't feel like it, okay?

MINGUS: Hey, what's the matter with you? What are you doing here anyway?
RUTH: Not what you think.
MINGUS: Luister, nobody says no to Mingus.
RUTH: Well, this person does!

Exit RUTH. MINGUS begins to follow her, then changes his mind. He makes for the exit, then turns back suddenly and shouts after her.

MINGUS: Hey! Nobody says no to Mingus, you skorrie morrie. You make promises with your eyes, and your bloody tits, shaking your bloody backside! And when the money's down you give nothing. How long do you think you can stay clean? Jou hoendervleis! You think I must lick your arse to get a ride with you? Jy's net 'n gemors. A weggooi! Kom hierso! Ek is moer se cock (You're just a piece of trash. A piece of rubbish! Come here! I've got the hots for you) and you're hiding right underneath your bloody corset. You bloody nylons, you're all the same, man. You try and you try but once a nylon, always a nylon! Bloody bitch!

Blackout.

SCENE 5

Enter JAKES, dishevelled. He sits himself at his typewriter. He looks as if he's been up all night.

JAKES [*pounding away*]: The bastards, the tricky bastards! What kind of a brain do you have to think like this? God give me the right words!
MAMARITI [*offstage*]: Hey, Jakes, it's five o'clock in the morning. Hey, tula wena! (Hey, be quiet!) I want to sleep. Tik-tik! Are you mad, man? Hey, you must find somewhere else to live if you want to work at five o'clock in the morning!

Enter LULU wearing a nightdress.

LULU: What's going on?
MAMARITI: Hey Lulu, tell that madman from *Drum* to stop die geraas. (the noise.)
LULU: Jakes, it's five o'clock in the morning.
JAKES: You tell your mother I pay good rent. This is my bedroom. You see the chalkline on the floor?
LULU: So?
JAKES: Well, I work in my bedroom, so leave me alone!
MAMARITI [*offstage*]: Luister! You bloody keep quiet—or out!
JAKES: Jesus, Ma, you're like the Boere. You want me on the streets. I'm working, I pay rent, this is my space, pitiful as it is, and history is being made right now—and you want silence!

There is a knocking at the door.

Jesus Christ! What now? Surely not today?

Enter FAHFEE, carrying a suitcase.

FAHFEE: They got me. They knocked down my shack before my eyes.
MINGUS [*offstage*]: Come on, come on—move these boxes! Charlie, you useless! You must move, man.

Enter MINGUS and CHARLIE. They are in a panic. They're carrying piles of boxes. There is an immediate uproar.

MINGUS: Make space! Make space! We got work to do.

Enter RUTH in a nightdress.

RUTH: What's going on?
LULU: What's all these boxes?
JAKES: What's the story, Mingus?
MINGUS: Come help! Don't just stand there—move your arse! Get these boxes in—com'on. Hey, hoendervleis, kom help. (Hey, white girl, come help.)

Exit MINGUS, LULU, RUTH and CHARLIE to carry more boxes.
Enter MAMARITI.

MAMARITI: What's happening? It's five o'clock in the morning.
JAKES: Toby Street removals, Ma. Three days early.
MAMARITI: Jesus!

Exit MAMARITI, enter MINGUS.

MINGUS: Don't just stand there, Jakes, come and help.
JAKES: What's the story Mingus?
MINGUS: There's no story. Work for your living for a change! Have you ever done a stroke of honest work? No! Just sit down and tik-tik-tik all day. Kom, help.
JAKES: Com'on Mingus, what's the story?
MINGUS: Those bastard G-men knocked down my store-room in Toby Street. I've been like a rat all night—dodge here, dodge there! I'm everywhere!

Exit MINGUS for more boxes. Enter MAMARITI, dressed.

FAHFEE: Where you going, Ma?
MAMARITI: I'm going to see.
FAHFEE: No, Ma. There's trouble out there.
MAMARITI: Hey, wena, I'm going to see.
FAHFEE: You just stay right here.
MAMARITI: I'm going!

Exit MAMARITI. Enter MINGUS and CHARLIE, who move some boxes into JAKES's space.

JAKES: Hey Mingus, how long are these boxes going to be here? Where do I sleep?
MINGUS: You're lucky you've got a room at all. In fact, you're on one minute's

notice. I'm sick and tired of you. Uit! You bloody situations, you're full of words. And what have they done? Have they saved my store-room in Toby Street?

FAHFEE: Ja, Mingus is right. Congress is always sending letters to City Council. It's rubbish. They just laugh and send an official apology. Words on paper—useless. It must be guns against guns. Then things will happen.

RUTH [*coming in carrying a box*]: What did happen, Mingus?

MINGUS: Ja, white girl. What do you do? You never work. You just want, want.

RUTH: What's going on Jakes.

MINGUS: You're a bloody good-for-nothing! You whites, you're breaking down all our houses.

RUTH: I'm doing no such thing!

MINGUS: Well, who's doing it?

FAHFEE: They came three days early, like tricksters, con men. They're loading people onto trucks and nobody's doing a thing. It's pitiful—families everywhere. They went for the leaders.

MINGUS: Ja, white girl—it's your fault!

RUTH: My fault? How can you say a bloody stupid thing like that?

MINGUS: What are you doing to stop them?

RUTH: What are you doing? Jakes, tell him to lay off.

RUTH finds protection behind JAKES. MINGUS moves in on her.

MINGUS: Don't cry to Jakes, it's your fathers and uncles and brothers who are doing this to us.

RUTH: My father has never hurt anybody in his life.

MINGUS: Don't talk to me like that. I'll cut you up. I'll kill you! I'll kill you!

FAHFEE: Luister, Mingus. This is only Ruth Golden. Choose your targets carefully. Daar's wit mense in Congress—baklei die Boere. (There are whites in Congress—fight the Afrikaners.)

JAKES: Ja Mingus—what have you done to stop them?

MINGUS: I was working.

FAHFEE: Stealing.

MINGUS: That's my business. They steal from us—we steal from them.

FAHFEE: Ja, and how does it help?

JAKES: How does it help, Fahfee? Where's the M-plan? Where's the strike? Where are the gangs? How can I make a story out of this? The largest move in the history of the 1950s and nothing has happened.

FAHFEE: Some people have moved into the church to avoid the lorries.

JAKES: And you?

FAHFEE: I'm hiding—I need a place to sleep.

MINGUS: Sleep in the bath under the boxes!

Enter PRINCESS, immaculately dressed, carrying a suitcase.

PRINCESS: You can sleep in my place—I'm leaving.

MINGUS: Charlie! Let's get the hell out of this hole.

Exit CHARLIE and MINGUS.

PRINCESS: Ja, you can all stay here—in the rubble. I'm going to Hillbrow. Nobody's going to catch me like a fool in Meadowlands. Princess is Number One. I've got a flat. I've got a man with manners. I got perfume—and chocolate. I'm going. This Softown, it's finished.

Silence. They all look at her. She exits.

Fade to black.

SCENE 6

MINGUS is tying up his stolen goods and possessions. On centre stage, ropes and boxes abound. CHARLIE and MINGUS attempt to make some order.

MINGUS: Come on, Charlie, we gotta load all these things on the G.G.'s truck. Looks like junk doesn't it, Charlie, but we know it's not. Come on, what's in that box? Jewellery! from Katz en Lourie. And that box? No, no, no—you gotta handle it with utmost care. Gently. Put it down. Turn it over now. And do you know what's in that box? Stetson hats. When I get down to Meadowlands, I'll be selling them there. I hear say these trains from Meadowlands are going to be easy pickings, and if the fences keep us in, they'll keep the G-men out—you'll see. Do you know what's in that box? I thought as much. You don't know a damn thing—all your life you're depending on this brain, living on this man, and what have you learnt? Nothing. Just dumb hands for carrying and dumb legs for running behind my tail.

[*Exit CHARLIE.*]

Well, four rooms in Meadowlands doesn't seem such a bad prospect.

[*Enter CHARLIE with a small tattered suitcase.*]

Hey hey hey! What do you think you're doing? Where you putting that suitcase of yours?
CHARLIE: I'm going to get a house.
MINGUS [*laughing*]: One thing is very clear—that suitcase does not belong to me, Charlie, so the best thing for you to do is move it right away.
CHARLIE: I'll get a house!
MINGUS: Come on Charlie, you'll get a labour camp! I think I'm right in presuming that it is only my assets and properties that are going with me to Meadowlands. So I think the best thing for you to do is to get your suitcase well away!
CHARLIE: No!
MINGUS: What you mean, Charlie? The time has come for you to go your way and I get going my way.
CHARLIE: No!
MINGUS: Look, Charlie, for your own good—just move your stuff away.

CHARLIE: No! I'm going with you.

MINGUS: Just move it away!

CHARLIE: No! I can't stay here. What will I do? Everything I've done for you.

MINGUS: I'm not going anywhere with you. Now get that into your head. I can't keep watching for you all your life. It's the end! So just move your things away. I'm going to live in Meadowlands. There's no place for you there. So just leave me be.

CHARLIE: Ons dak nie. Ons pola hier.

MINGUS: Are you kidding? We've already lost. We'll stay wherever they want us to.

CHARLIE: So you want to leave me here to die! You're just going to dump me. I'm not staying here. I'm coming with you.

MINGUS: Now, Charlie—be a man!

CHARLIE: I am a man! Where must I sleep? In the rubble? Where will I live? Where are the old cars? Where are the tin shacks? Where are all the houses?

MINGUS: Charlie! I didn't know you had so many words in you! I'm amazed!

CHARLIE [*immediately at a loss*]: I'm Charlie . . .

MINGUS: Now Charlie, relax. Look, I've got a plan. Now listen. When I get to the house, I'll send a driver back to come and pick you up—with your suitcase—in style.

CHARLIE: No, man!

MINGUS: Look, we're gonna have a full truck but I'll get someone to fetch you. Now sit, Charlie, take your suitcase and sit. I'll be back in a minute.

CHARLIE: You're lying to me! You'll never come back.

MINGUS: I will.

CHARLIE: No you won't. Don't try and stop me.

MINGUS: All right! Now just do yourself a worldly favour . . .

CHARLIE: No no no. Don't try and talk to me. You just want to dump me.

MINGUS: Will you listen! If you listen I'll explain.

CHARLIE: No!

MINGUS [*with uncharacteristic compassion*]: Charlie, do you know who you are? Have you ever looked at yourself, stared at that face of yours, and asked yourself who you are? Looked in the car mirror and asked, "Who am I?" You just can't come with me.

CHARLIE: I will!

MINGUS: No! Listen. You can't come with me because you're a coloured. Me—I'm a black, black as the ace of spades. But you're coloured. Me, I'm going to Meadowlands because we lost, but you can't. Just understand one thing, Charlie. We lost Sophiatown and you're on your own. So just take your suitcase and say goodbye. Please, Charlie, goodbye.

CHARLIE and MINGUS freeze in their positions of parting on opposite sides of the stage. RUTH enters from one side, JAKES from the other. RUTH is carrying both her suitcases.

RUTH: So this is it.

JAKES: This is it.

RUTH: I can't stay here, I know that. And I can't come with. So this is the end. I've come to say goodbye.

JAKES [*curtly*]: Goodbye.

RUTH: What is the matter with you, Jakes? I've been waiting for weeks for you to show me a sign, one sign of real interest.

JAKES: Ja.

RUTH: You won't let me reach you. You're like a brick wall. What do you want me to do?

JAKES: There is nothing you can do.

RUTH: If you had opened up for a moment, anything would have been possible.

JAKES: It isn't possible, because I've decided that it isn't possible. I'm not letting some white girl put her hands around my heart when she feels like it. You want to ride me over like a bulldozer and leave me here for dust. But I'm not going to allow it. We lost what little chance we had.

RUTH: We never took it.

JAKES: Well, let's just say we failed. We let the Boere drive a wedge between us. Who gives a damn whether a black journalist and a white storyteller can or can't meet? When the war comes, as it will, it will be fought in the barren ground between us, and it will be so large as to make us invisible.

RUTH: I'm not talking about a war. I'm talking about us.

JAKES: We can't begin to talk about us—not until this war has been fought and won.

RUTH: There are other countries.

JAKES: There's nowhere to go, except Yeoville and Meadowlands. No matter where we run, these places will always haunt us. Ruth in Yeoville, Jakes in Meadowlands. Truth is, all the time you've been with us, we've both known you have a back door to Yeoville.

RUTH: That door is closed, Jakes.

JAKES: No, it's not.

RUTH: Yes, it is.

JAKES: Nonsense.

RUTH: Jakes. Right now I don't know where I'm going, but the door to Yeoville is shut.

JAKES: No . . .

RUTH: I'm the one who's closing it.

Lights change.

SCENE 7

The cast sing "Boph' umthwalo" as they enter.

Boph' umthwalo sigoduke	(We pack up and leave)
Boph' umthwalo sigoduke	(We pack up and leave)
Boph' umthwalo sigoduke	(We pack up and leave)
Boph' umthwalo sigoduke	(We pack up and leave)
Siya' shiya iKofifi	(We're leaving Sophiatown)
Siya' shiya iKofifi	(We're leaving Sophiatown)
Siya' shiya iKofifi	(We're leaving Sophiatown)
Siya' shiya iKofifi	(We're leaving Sophiatown)

As the Cast sing, they slowly place a lifetime of furniture and possessions in a pile around JAKES's desk. The old bath is carefully laid on its side. MAMARITI climbs onto her chair which has been placed on top of an old tin trunk. The other members of the Cast each take up a special position and recite their monologues over the singing. The stage becomes very quiet, only the hum of the song remaining. The lighting is moody. Faces are picked out by spotlights.

MAMARITI: The day they moved us out, it was the day the big rains fell. That was the day of the tears and the day of the Saracens.

LULU: We watched them move the first street, Toby Street, where Dr Xuma was. The rain was falling and we were only a few. The bulldozers were knocking down the pillars of the first house. I don't remember the name of the people. That was Toby Street where Dr Xuma was—right next to Westdene. Father Huddleston, Dr Xuma, Bo Resha and Oliver Tambo were there.

MINGUS: The bulldozers bulldozed five houses: one, two, three, four, five at the same time. As they were bulldozing the houses, the lorries that were supplied by the G.G. were taking the loads out to Meadowlands.

MAMARITI: The day my house was removed, it was half past five in the morning. I think it was on a Thursday. They knocked at my door. Three loud knocks. Five tall Dutchmen. They said the day had come. I wished for a special sign on my door, but there was none.

LULU: The lorries were waiting. Even as we packed, the labourers with the Boere were hitting the pillars of the verandah with big hammers.

MAMARITI: I said to them, I wished they would give us enough time to pack, as I was going to have my cups and plates broken.

LULU: And they said, "Jy praat te veel. Moenie praat nie." (You talk too much. You must not talk.) And Ma said, "I have the right to talk for my things." By eight o'clock we were already moved to Meadowlands. The walls and the floors of the house were rough cement. Everything was awful and we were very much unhappy.

MAMARITI: I was sitting on my chair on the lorry and I started shouting, "I'm not getting down! I'm not going to stay in that Meadowlands house. I'm afraid. Take off the load from the lorry but I'm not getting down. I'd rather die. Dump me anywhere, I'd rather die!"

The Cast complete the song.

FAHFEE: These Boere, they are very tricky. Three days early they came, and we weren't prepared. There were two thousand G-men lining the streets. Everywhere, there were slogans on the walls: "We won't move." "This is home." "Hands off Sophiatown." But what could we do against eighty lorries and two thousand police? We tried to organise a general stayaway. At three o'clock the following Monday morning we ran through the streets hitting the telegraph poles with iron bars. Wake up!

[*CHARLIE strikes one of the telegraph poles with an iron bar. Sharp lighting change.*]

Vukani! [*CHARLIE hits the pole.*] Strike! [*Hits.*] General stayaway! [*Hits.*] I remember the last time they hit the telegraph poles it was before the 1950 riots. The Youth League. They wanted real violence and the Berliners were ready, but Congress said no. Stone the street lamps! [*Hits.*] Let the Gatas move in the dark. [*Hits.*] Watch out! [*Hits.*] Watch out! [*Hits.*] Watch out! The Gatas are coming! These Berliners! These Americans! They could fight. [*Hits.*] Pole against street lamp. [*Hits.*] Bar against telegraph pole. But the time was not right. The Gatas did their job, and the buses left for work as usual. I signal Bees. If this number comes up—26—we signal Bees. Bees mean trouble, large crowds, army. Well, I signal Bees. Ja, I signal Bees. They can't stop us forever.

The Cast resume the song as they regroup on the stage to resemble a family portrait. JAKES rises to speak.

JAKES: This bitterness inside me wells up and chokes. We lost, and Sophiatown is rubble. The visions of the mad Boere smashed this hope, turned it to rubble. And out of this dust, like a carefully planned joke, Triomf rises. What triumph is this? Triumph over music? Triumph over meeting? Triumph over the future? Sophiatown was a cancer on a pure white city, moved out at gunpoint by madmen. With its going, the last common ground is gone. The war has been declared, the battle sides are drawn. Yeoville and Meadowlands, and a wasteland in between.

I don't want to die like Can Themba, of alcohol poisoning, in a country that is not my own. I don't want the streets of New York to take me, as they did Nat Nakasa. The streets of New York broke his bones, but South Africa broke his spirit. Exile—an interminable death. It eats out the very centre of your heart. Arthur Maimane, Todd Matshikiza, Bloke Modisane, Lewis Nkosi, Hugh Masekela, Dollar Brand, Miriam Makeba, Jonas Gwangwa—all our best and brightest driven out by this Triomf.

And 65 Gerty Street? Princess and her Dutch lover escaped the Immorality Act by going to Europe. Lulu is without education. The G-men, they caught up with Mingus, and he served time in Number Four. Coming out, he was a qualified plumber. Mama died of a broken heart. Fahfee disappeared. Some say he was recruited—joined Umkhonto We Sizwe.

Ruth we never see. We tried for a while, but meeting seemed impossible.

Oh yes—Charlie . . . Charlie we found stabbed to death in the bricks and rubble at the old house. He was living in a pipe and got into a fight. Some say he crawled five blocks to get to Gerty Street. His body was found lying in the brick and the rubble over the upturned bath.

This destruction is called Triomf. I hope the dust of that triumph settles deep in the lungs like a disease and covers these purified suburbs with ash. Memory is a weapon. Only a long rain will clean away these tears.

The cast sing "Izinyembezi zabantu."

Izinyembezi Zabantu

Izinyembezi zabantu
Izinyembezi zabantu
Izinyembezi zabantu
Sophiatown, Sophiatown, Sophiatown
Izinyembezi zabantu

Kwadum' izulu, lana
Kwanyakaz' umhlaba
Siyakushiya Sophiatown
Siyakushiya Sophiatown
Izinyembezi zabantu

Sibon, kughamuk' amaphoyisa
Kudum' ibulldoza
Kwaghamuk' umntwana
Kwaphuma bonk' omakhelwana
Siyakushiya Sophiatown
Siyakushiya Sophiatown
Izinyembezi zabantu
Izinyembezi zabantu
Izinyembezi zabantu

(Tears of the people
Tears of the people
Tears of the people
Sophiatown, Sophiatown, Sophiatown
Tears of the people

It thunders, it rains
The earth trembles
We are leaving you, Sophiatown
We are leaving you, Sophiatown
Tears of the people

We see the police appearing
The bulldozer thunders
A child jumps out
All the neighbours appear
We are leaving you, Sophiatown
We are leaving you, Sophiatown
Tears of the people
Tears of the people
Tears of the people)

Fade to black.

Horn of Sorrow

(1988)

Nicholas Ellenbogen

Nicholas Ellenbogen was born in Bulawayo, Rhodesia in 1948. He attended the University of Cape Town, the Royal Academy of Dramatic Arts, Arts Educational Trust, and the London School of Economics before embarking on a career in acting and directing that began with considerable training and practical experience during two sojourns in London and Paris. In South Africa, he has worked for the three major government-supported performing arts councils in Johannesburg, Cape Town, and Durban, as well as appearing on television, in films, and at the Market Theatre. He has produced new South African plays by Zakes Mda and Paul Slabolepszy, among others. He established the Amstel Playwright of the Year Award to nurture new South African writers and served as Artistic Director of Drama for the Natal Performing Arts Council for six years. In 1990 he founded Theatre for Africa, the only environmentally oriented theatre company in South Africa. He has created more than fifty-six works, alone or in collaboration, for this company, which has toured throughout Africa as well as to Europe, the United States, Canada, and East Asia. Ellenbogen has garnered numerous awards and honors in South Africa and abroad, including two playwright awards for A Nativity *(1990), a best costume design award for* Kwamanzi *and* Elephant of Africa *(1993), best musical score for a film version of* Nativity, *called* The Angel, the Bicycle, and the Chinaman's Finger *(1992), four Scotsman* Pick of the Fringe *Awards and the Herald Angel Award for best drama (*Guardians of Eden, *1996) at the Edinburgh Festival, and a command performance of* Kawamanzi *for the British Royal Family at Balmoral Castle (1992).*

Theatre for Africa uses its international tours to raise money for environmental preservation projects. In South Africa, it has used theatre for environmental and AIDS-prevention education in impoverished townships and rural areas. The company, under Ellenbogen's leadership, aims at bringing various environmental issues to public attention, developing the distinctive qualities of South African theatre, and creating entertaining spectacles from the diversity of life experiences in South Africa. Horn of Sorrow *won the AA Life Vita Award for Best Script in 1989; in 1990 it won a Pick of the Fringe Award at the Grahamstown Festival in South Africa and a* Scotsman *Fringe First Award at the Edinburgh Festival in Scotland.*

Ellenbogen's Theatre for Africa is one of the most prolific and popular theatre companies in South Africa. Its blend of vigorous physicality, engaging music, ingenious mime, striking visual tableaux, plentiful humor, and environmental themes has made it popular with a broad, loyal, middle-class audience in South Africa. It has also pleased others, ranging from villagers in Tanzania to heads of state in Europe. Theatre for Africa's works rely heavily on a stunning array of inventive stage business and lose a great deal when transferred to the page, but Horn of Sorrow *retains a number of appealing features even in print. First, it is an object lesson in the essentially corporeal and performative nature of theatre. Whereas many dramatic texts allow the reader to cling to the literary pleasures of plot, character, and verbal repartee, this one reminds one constantly of the presence of bodies on stage and of the rhythm and pacing with which the action unfolds in time. If some of what the actors are doing on stage is difficult to imagine, the sense of pacing and shifts in tone that enliven the performance can be easily sensed in reading the text. Second, much of the play's humor and its pedagogical thrust are well-preserved on the page. The play is noteworthy for its attempt to modulate the environmental concerns of the world's affluent population with the economic concerns of impoverished rural people. Sympathy is shown for poachers as well as animals, and condemnation is shifted from individuals driven by poverty to networks of trade and uneven economic development that stretch around the globe.*

Horn of Sorrow *toured Natal and the Cape while apartheid was crumbling. Rather than drawing upon the sharp contemporaneous social drama of civil unrest and governmental repression, the play looked to underlying social inequities and neglect that South Africa's unequal development fostered but that were likely to outlive apartheid. The play anticipates the concerns of the new South Africa in looking at abiding difficulties for the country's wildlife and its rural poor and begins to develop the promises of the new cultural dispensation in its combination of Anglo and township performance styles.*

Horn of Sorrow *premiered under a fig tree in the Umfolozi Game Reserve in August 1986 and then at the Loft Theatre in Durban, 6 September 1986, with the following cast:*

    Lindelani Buthelezi
    Roger Charteris
    Bheki Mkhwane
    Madoda Ncayiyana
    James Ngcobo

Colleen Nicholas

Ellis Pearson

Robyn Uren

The revised version printed here was performed at the Baxter Theatre in Cape Town in 1988. It uses six actors who were originally:

ACTOR 1/VULTURE	Ellis Pearson
ACTOR 2/SKUWIT	Madoda Ncayiyana
ACTOR 3/PORTUGUESE	Brendan Grealy
ACTOR 4	Bheki Mkhwane
ACTOR 5	Nandi Nyembe
ACTOR 6	Anthony Reade

Directed by Nicholas Ellenbogen

HORN OF SORROW

Enter ACTOR 3, hitting two pieces of wood together with a rhythmic beat. Enter ACTORS 2,4, 5 & 6 carrying carved wooden rhino horns. They put them down in a row on the ground, down stage center. They all then join ACTOR 3 in making sounds of nature. Enter ACTOR 1 with large cardboard box filled with horns. He trips, picks box up and repacks the horns, anxiously looking around him. Repeats fall, more anxious, apologetically placing the baby horns from the box with the others on the stage. He sits embarrassed on the box which collapses. He nods to ACTOR 2 who picks up two horns, snorts, takes up the stance, and becomes a rhino. ACTORS 5,6 and then 4 follow suit.

A chant follows.

ACTOR 2: Ubejane. He smells the wind!
All: Ubejane!
ACTOR 5: He sees as if in the mist!
ALL: Ubejane!
ACTOR 6: He hears the air! [*They sniff the air*]
ALL: Ubejane!
ACTOR 4: Isilwane Esinamandla Sase Africa. (The animal who has power in Africa.)
ALL: Ubejane!
ACTOR 3: His anger flares, he thinks on blood, he stamps the ground!

They stamp the ground.

ACTOR 1: Can he hide from the killing?

ACTOR 3: Death comes from across the river! He knows the sound of a gun.

All sniff the air. Gun shot.

ACTOR 3: His safe place is now his trap. He must charge the danger. [*Does so, charges downstage*] For he is . . . Ubejane!!
    ALL: Ubejane!!

All sit.

ACTOR 2: [*Stands up, puts his horns down center stage, in a pile*] Ubejane! filled with holes, horn of sorrow, hacked away. Your courage bleeding, black, into the dry earth, rotting in the sun to please a far away need in Man.
    ACTOR 5: [*Putting her horns down*] A need to possess your health, your courage, to possess your power.
    ACTOR 4: [*Putting horns down*] Ubejane—they will come until your stamp, your snort, are but memories on this earth.
    ACTOR 6: [*Putting horns down*] But, Ubejane, oh, Ubejane, they will never possess you. For if you live it is to be free.

All crouch down.

ACTOR 2: Man is the one who sees so little, so late. [*Indicates horns*] Ubejane, oh, Ubejane, your loss will live forever to mock Man.

He goes back and ACTOR 4 comes forward, shaking a match box. Music and harmony begin—1. Jew's harp, 2. Two nails (tapped together), 3. Plastic packet (shaken rhythmically together between hands), 4. Big pair of scissors, 5. Small branch-cutting saw with jagged teeth and a long nail to play it with. Shaking things, wind and animal sounds etc. Song and mime of activity of animals on the earth.

ACTOR 1 [*Crash landing badly as a vulture and laughing*] Oh, nearly made it that time, eh! Trouble with the landing gear again! You know, we vultures, are not known for our landing capabilities. We are in the cleaning up business. I'm here on a very cheap day return. I'm staying at a local hotel—Hage Hall (whichever hotel is local to the area). Oh, what a smart place! The rooms!! I pressed a button, a towel came out. I pressed another button, the maid came out. I pressed the maid, my teeth came out. Dsssh!! But, you know, that's not a problem because where I come from, it's such a tough neighborhood, if you've got teeth they think you are a bloody sissy! Well, I know you're here to hear about the black rhino. Now, white or black, they're both in the same predicament, but it's that black rhino that I really go for. Now, that chappie, he's got guts—miles and miles of delicious guts! But, to give you an overview of the whole tragic story, I'd like to introduce you to a very special little individual—Thembalethu. [*Marimba starts playing*] Now, her story began not far from here, oh, about 12 years ago. I remember well because I was just finishing off a rare and delicious nibble of giraffe tongue, rounded off by warthog bladder, still full. [*ACTOR 1 is really getting into the description of his meal, savouring the details. ACTOR 4 whistles, irritated, wanting to get on with the story*] Oh, the story has begun.

ACTOR 5 on ACTOR 4's back. ACTOR 3 covers her with a plastic bag. All three then form a rhino. Music. Rhino walks around and baby —ACTOR 5—is born. Mother stands by as she tries to walk, staggers and falls. Chooses the small horn, bumps mother, climbs underneath, looks around, butts mother, and then drinks.

Song—THULA, THULA:

Thula sana lwami	(Hush my little child)
Umama Uyeza	(Your mother is coming)

Only baby, still as rhino, does not sing. ACTORS 3 and 4 reform rhino. Noises of hyenas whooping. Rhino butts air, stabs around. Others, as hyenas, grab baby. Mother fights them off. ACTOR 1 dies very noisily, again hogging the limelight, until his vulture mask is dropped in front of him.

ACTOR 1: Oh, sorry. I was getting a bit carried away there. Man, what a battle, hey! Blood all over the place—I love it! D'you see that hyena that broke its back here? I was following that chap [*he flies*] and thinking, "Ummmm, I'm going to share a bit of baby rhino with that hyena." I landed up eating him instead. Life has a very funny twist in its tail. But now, that Thembalethu, what a plucky thing! Did you see what they did to her? They ripped her ear to shreds. They tore a bloody hole this size in her ear. [*Indicates huge hole*].

ACTOR 3: Ah, ah!

ACTOR 1: Oh, maybe it was a bit smaller, [*bringing in hands to indicate a smaller hole*] but it was still a big hole, and that's how I recognized her, wherever she went.

ACTOR 4: Pum, parara, parara, parara, parara, Pum parara . . . etc.

ACTOR 1: Oh, time for the ethnic number.

All dance, clap and sing Pantsula Jive. *ACTOR 2 arrives with bicycle handlebars covered in colored tape, with a bell and a horn attached. Waves, greetings, etc.*

ACTOR 2: My name is Skuwit. I'm the talk of the village. Outside the shop I park my bike and I parp it a bit and it goes . . . [*sound of parp parp*] and all the girls come and surround me. I climb off Washesha and speak fanakalo. Hey, wena funa mina thanda wena! (Hey, you, me love you much!) [*Laughs*] Ja, all the boys envy me because I'm from Jo'burg. I speak English—hey, bugger off, man! I also speak Afrikaans--hey voetsak, man! [*All laugh*] Me, I'm a playboy! Excuse me please, baby, if you don't mind. [*Taking ACTOR 5 by the hand*] Thank you. I wonder if you'd be generous enough to be my [*He smells*] armpit? [*All react, girls whoop with excitement and act coyly*] Ja, all the girls like to call me their under armpit—to keep me secret from their man. From Jo'burg I bring them Zulumoto sweets on which are written "I love you, my armpit. You are my Kentucky Southern Fried playboy." [*ACTOR 5 is carried by ACTOR 2 as they ride the bike. He then hands bike to a member of the audience*] Could you please look after Washesha for a second? If he gives you trouble, shout, I'll be around. Don't be shy. [*Dances and sings* Pantsula Jive *with all, others echoing his moves, but lastly especially with ACTOR 5 who he dances over his shoulder and through his legs*] Thank you for looking after Washesha. Did he give you any trouble? Nothing? Ja, he's well mannered. Say thank you, Washesha. [*Rings bell*] He says thank you, and with a smile. Now we are going to share our armpits with you.

Music and dance. Instruments mimed: one playing the drums, one the trumpet, etc. Gradually dies down and changes to bush sounds.

ACTOR 4: Why have you come?

ACTOR 2: I've come to show you my bicycle.

ACTOR 4: Boasting again. You know what they do? They leave us behind for a city that is full of Umcebo [*indicates money*] and when they come back they take everything that we have—our girlfriends, our hope. We don't have money. They're the ones with money.

ACTOR 2: There's money here for you, too.

ACTOR 4: How?

ACTOR 2: Ubejane.

Both talk secretly in Zulu together.

ACTOR 4: Hey wena musa ukuzenza isilima. (Don't be stupid.)

ACTOR 2: I've contacts in Jo'burg. Everyone is looking for the horn. Now you must bring me a horn.

ACTOR 4: But how, Skuwit?

ACTOR 2: Oh, you've trapped ntebane. You've eaten impala. Now you must go for the big ones.

ACTOR 4: Skuwit, you catch them with the wire?

Music stops.

ACTOR 2: You will need a gun.

ACTOR 4: A gun!

ACTOR 1: [*Moves on stage quickly to cut across the tension*] Did you hear that? Now I was on the outskirts of that village, cleaning out the cranium cavity of an old dead dog. When I overheard that conversation I thought, "Mmmmmmm, Man!" And you know, that's where Thembalethu's trouble all began. But now, Thembalethu. I didn't see her for the next, ummm, four years. When I did see her again it was down by the riverside. Oh, yes, down by the riverside, down by the riverside. [*Mimes guitar, song:* Down by the Riverside] For those of you who like geometry, this next scene has got a lot of hypotenuses in it.

All are hippos in a dam, all heaped together. Noise, come up above water, open mouths wide. Loud fart. ACTOR 1 makes bubbles rise up and indicates foul smell. All cough and splutter. ACTOR 2 becomes a jacana bird (like a lily trotter) walking on backs of hippos and on lily pads. All make bubbles, mud plopping noises. Bird lands on ACTOR 1's head and using finger as beak, digs in his ear. Flies away and settles again. Thinks of putting his beak in ACTOR 5's bum. Very tempted, but changes mind and flies away. All become flamingoes and fly away. ACTORS 2 and 6 as rhino, using dropped arm as penis indicating male. Lots of bird and animal sounds.

Rhino, walks backwards and forwards, defecates, paws ground, walks marking terri-
tory. ACTORS 3 and 4 form another rhino which behaves in the same way as the
first one. Actor 5 as baby. Big rhinos charge. Baby tries to interfere. Tries
to come close to mother, pushed aside by interested male.

ACTOR 1: I felt sorry for her. Thembalethu was going through a very difficult
time. Adolescence. Oh, I know a couple of jokes about adders. These two snakes
were leaving the ark and Noah said to them, "Go out and multiply." They said, "We
can't. We're adders!" Little joke I threw in. Wish I'd thrown it out. Anyway, I got
another for you. What d'you call a gay snake? A poefadder!! After that Thembalethu became a bit of a wanderer, off by herself you know. I got busy up North,
there in the Zambesi valley. There're shooting these things indiscriminately.
They take off the tusk, they tear off a horn, they don't even touch the meat. Man!!
Why does he have to be so greedy? Why can't he learn a lesson from the lion, and
only take what he needs? You know, the way things are going there'll be no horn
left at all. Anyway, I was getting homesick. On the way back I flew over that same
village I was talking about. Now I'd just peeled an old squashed frog off the road—
padkos . . . paddakos . . . padkos! (food for the road . . . frog food . . . road food!)
Some maniac in a big red, fast car had been past. [*Noise and demonstration of car
running over frog*] But I tell you what. I'll let these chappies tell you all about that.
There you are, fellows, take it away!!!

ACTOR 4 starts township song as he herds cattle:

Mabo
Zinyana Lesilo (Child of a lion)
Zinyana Lenyamazane. (Child of a buck)

All others are cattle except ACTOR 1, who is a dog. ACTOR 4 kicks him away. He
howls and urinates on a member of the audience. ACTORS 3 and 6 become scratch-
ing hens. ACTOR 2 arrives in his car, i.e. carrying a steering wheel. All greet him
and then form tableau for red car song.

ALL: Bum, Bum, Bum Bum
Bebarp, red car,
going up the hill
Bebarp, red car, bum, etc.
going up the hill,
Bebarp, red car, bum, etc.
going so fast . . .
ACTOR 4: going so fast,
ACTOR 1: The cows walk past!
ALL: Bum, bum, bum, bum
Bebarp, red car
going up the hill
Bebarp, red car, bum, etc.

going up the hill
Bebarp, red car, bum, etc.
going so fast . . .
ACTOR 4: going so fast,
ACTOR 1: The abafazi walk past!

All laugh.

ACTOR 2: Hey, shut up, shut up.
It's going up the hill . . .
ACTOR 5: Oh shame!
ALL: Shame, shame, shame, shame!
Bebarp, red car,
going up the hill, shame, shame, shame
Bebarp, red car,
it's going up the hill, shame, shame, shame
Bebarp, red car,
It's nearly at the top . . .
ACTOR 3: It's stopping at the top!
ACTOR 6: It's stopping at the top? It's boiling hot!

ACTORS 1 and 4 make sound of car boiling over. ACTOR 2 leaps out of car, open-ing and closing his door. He opens the bonnet—arms of ACTORS 1 and 4. Hot water spurts out. Lots of hissing and engine noises. Closes bonnet and noise stops.

ACTOR 5: What's going on, Skuwit?
ACTOR 2: Never fear, baby, when Skuwit is near. [*He turns on wipers—arms of ACTORS 3 and 6*]
ACTOR 5: Aaah, Skuwit!! [*ACTOR 2 stops wipers and an aerial comes up*] Aaah, Skuwit!!
ACTOR 2: Automatic, baby, automatic. Cassette, tape deck cassette!

He puts it in ACTOR 1's mouth. He garbles on fast forward. ACTOR 2 turns him off and turns ACTOR 3 on.

ALL: [*Gathering speed*] Bum, bum, bum, bum
Bebarp, red car,
It's going down the hill
Bebarp, red car,
It's going down the hill
Bebarp, red car,
It's going so fast . . .
ACTOR 5: It's going too fast. . . !

Tableau falls apart. Cries of "Skuwit." ACTOR 2 turns round and round with wheel, ACTOR 1 swivels in center, indicates a large tree with his arms, car crashes into it, tree falls. They fall into the farmyard scene and run away like chickens.

ACTOR 2: O.K. It's enough. The car will be fixed up. My grandmother is a panelbeater! Ja, this is my old car, Sputnik. Sputnik is his name because, like a shooting star, he flies, leaving a trail of dust behind him. The cows, grazing miles away, they give way for Sputnik. And the girls are behind the wheel with me all the time [*Protests*] Ja, Skuwit and his armpits, of course.

ACTOR 4: [*Holding wooden model rhino*] Ja, more, Skuwit. (Good morning, Skuwit.)

ACTOR 2: I'm Skuva Kuva—Somkatakata.

Jozi Manyaledi Indawo Zokuba mbezela.

Yeyi farmboy . . . Kom hier, jou farm boy. Wat verkoop jy? (I'm Skuva Kuva from Johannesburg, a suburb called Manyaledi, where everyone holds me. Hey, farmboy . . . come here, you farm boy. What are you selling?)

ACTOR 4: Uthini Manje. (What do you want?)

ACTOR 2: I see, you're still wearing the same short trousers.

ACTOR 4: Hey, Skuwit, this is a new one, man.

ACTOR 2: You still cannot afford a longer one?

ACTOR 4: Skuwit, I now sell my carvings in order to afford my own armpits.

ACTOR 2: Small cash, no armpits.

ACTOR 4: You're right, Skuwit. It's time I made money. I need more.

ACTOR 2: You need quick cash.

ACTOR 4: What?? [*He is confused*] Ahawu! (exclamation of amazement)

ACTOR 2: Now there's big bucks in the horn.

Actors move off.

ACTOR 1: What is all this madness about rhino horn? Oh, yes, they say it's supposed to fix up your tummy when it gets a bit wobbly like mine often does. Now, I've tried it, and it doesn't work. You may as well chew your finger nails--it's made of the same stuff, you know. And as for this aphrodisiac, potency [*indicates with arm*], make you a man business--ROT. You may as well go and sniff a bottled hippo fart for all the good it does. Anyway, the ones I feel sorry for are the poachers. Those chaps get next to nothing for the horn. It's the business men overseas who are making all the money. The poachers get nothing, and they get shot into the bargain. Oh yes, I've seen poachers there in the Zambezi valley, poachers lying there dead, shot! Well, this whole poaching nonsense was getting a little close to home. I thought, "Mmmmmmm, maybe I'd better keep an eye on Thembalethu." Well, with an ear like hers, it wasn't hard to track her down. [*He flies around and finds her*]. So I came in and landed in the top of an old acacia tree, but it was full of those weaver birds. What a bloody noise, man!

ACTORS 4 and 6 as weavers (with whistles in their mouths), 3 and 5 as a giraffe, 1 and 2 as another giraffe. ACTOR 6 then forms back of second giraffe. Bird noises. Giraffe walks around, down to drink, nervous, restless. ACTORS 3 and 5, as Thembalethu, charge giraffe.

ACTOR 4: Pasop, Ubejane! (Be careful, rhino!)

All laugh. Thembalethu walks around, rolls in mud, and backs onto ACTOR 1, who is a tree, rubs against him, charges him and urinates against him. He is at first scared, then offended, then he laughs at the joke.

ACTOR 1: What a sense of humour! Oh, Thembalethu had grown into a delightful little thing—all nine hundred kilograms of her! Well, the years rolled on. I was just recovering from an oversupply of offal of aardvark, when I was called in to clear up this dead donkey. Now, this donkey had been killed in a head-on collision with a Zola Budd, a taxi, outside a store on the Mozambique border. When you get to be an old chappie like me, you like to have your meals well prepared. This donkey had been beautifully pureed by about 50 bakkies. [*Indicates, with sound effects, cars flattening donkey*] While I was enjoying all the good things of life, the situation inside that store was quite different.

ACTOR 4 starts song and all form into queue-like group. ACTOR 3 stands apart, reading magazine. [Humming interspersed with the following lines]

ACTOR 2: . . . . itea baba . . . . i5 roses (tea sir . . . 5 roses)
baba . . . . itea bags . . . . i5 roses
tea bags, baba.
ACTOR 4: . . . . imilk . . .
ACTOR 2: . . . . i5 roses, baba . . . .
ACTOR 4: . . . . imilk, baba . . . [etc.]
ACTOR 1: . . . . . isunlight soap . . . .enkhulu baba (the big one sir) . . . isunlight . . .
ACTOR 5: . . . . i5 roses [etc.]
ACTOR 4: . . . . imilk . . .

They all ask all together.

ACTOR 3: Shut up!!!
ACTOR 5: . . .ebaba . . .i2 cents chappies, baba . . . (sir . . . two-cent bubblegum, sir)

All ask again.

ACTOR 3: Thula umsindo. (Keep quiet.) [*All watch the Portuguese store keeper as he threatens them*]. These people are all the same. I've got a cousin in Jo'burg. He's got a big house in Sandton, a BMW 750i, time sharing in Umhlanga Rocks. He thinks I'm mad. He says, "Why d'you want to live in this gat?" But, I remembers what happened to my father in L.M. When the ANC come, me pack one suitcase, whtt!! gone. He sit with M-Net decoder, eletrix fence around the house. How I make my money? I'm selling dagga to Taiwanese sailors. One day they comes to me and say, "We want horn rhino horn." I say to them, "No problem. I can get you plentsh, plentsh, plentsh rhino horn!" Now, I sit with a big account in Switzerland, but one problem. If I leave—pooff!! Japanese Mafia very strong. You think that's funny? I'll tell what's funny. Me, I've never seen a rhino. Voetsak, voetsak! [*He shoos them out of his store.*]

The singing increases and they move from tableau. Township night noises.

ACTOR 4: Hey, Skuwit, why are you still here?

ACTOR 2: This time I come back for leave. I bought a dozen live chickens for my wife, but when I came back, she was not there. She had fallen pregnant by that farmboy uNgcebo so she fled. Washesha, my bicycle, and Sputnik, my car, have all gone too, and so it is the end of my armpits. Now I need to stay here with my five kids. At this shop the Portuguese man wanted to shoot me, but he changed his mind. He said he'd give me some money, only if I bring him a horn.

ACTOR 4: But . . .

ACTOR 2: I know it is tough in the bush, but it's worse in the mines. You cannot run away when the earth falls on you, but in the bush there are many trees to climb. This Portuguese man will help me, if only I can bring him a horn.

ACTOR 4: Skuwit, how are you going to find a horn?

They talk quietly together in Zulu.

ACTOR 2: Sibali lalela kahle. (Come brother, listen here.) We must go through the wire late one night, kill quickly, take off the horn and get out before the vultures come to tell their stories, before the dogs come sniffing.

ACTOR 4: Skuwit, why do you have to risk your life so much?

ACTOR 2: They've killed our cattle, they've taken away our pride, they taught us about money which never filled our milkpots. What are we going to do for lobola? What are you going to offer to your ancestors? Our customs are endangered. We need cash to replace what has been taken away from us. Who owns these ones? [*Indicates the model rhino*] We, the people of Africa!!

ACTOR 4: Skuwit, how much do you get for a horn now?

Silence.

ACTOR 2: 1,000 Rand!! Imali engaka! (Big money!)

ACTOR 4: Eh, he!!! 1,000 Rand! Uyayithatha sibali? (Are you in friend?)

They slap hands, talk quietly in Zulu and then leave. Music. Rhinos, ACTORS 2 and 6, and 3 and 5, rub each other, snort and follow around. Mating routine.

ACTOR 1: Now, I didn't know all this hankie-pankie had been going on. I'd been away down south, visiting a couple of cousins and when I got back I was sitting at the top of an old tree, looking at a fat, juicy dung beetle. This fellow'd just got a new job at the local rhino midden and his work was piling up. I was trying to decide whether to pop down there for such a small morsel when suddenly Thembalethu appeared and, oooh, she had a surprise for me. But first let's show you that dung beetle, hey. Oh, what's brown and sounds like a bell? Dung!! That's my favorite joke—brown, and sounds like a bell. Dung!!! I can do it with my glasses up—dung!—or down—dung!!

ACTOR 2: That's enough. Dung beetle.

ACTOR 1: They've got no sense of humour, these people.

ACTORS 3 and 6 form dung. ACTOR 1 is the beetle. Kicks the dung which rolls and then ACTOR 6 becomes Thembalethu's baby. Same baby routine with ACTORS 3 and 5 as mother. Song of baby rhino:

Thula sana lwani   (Hush my little child)
Umama Uyeza   (Your mother is coming)

Hunting song of ACTORS 2 and 4: [*Make drumming sounds on collapsed cardboard box*]

Dedela Bhejane   (Let go rhinoceros)
Dedel Uphondo Lwakhe.   (Let go of your horn)

ACTOR 1 gives gun to ACTOR 2, Zulu war dance, drums, shot fired. Thembalethu staggers injured and falls.

ACTOR 2: Right, cut out the horn quickly.
ACTOR 4: O.K.

They talk in Zulu.

Iyephila lento. (This thing is alive.)

Thembalethu up and charges. Baby follows, afraid and uncertain. Thembalethu falls and kicks, baby nudges her. ACTORS 2 and 1 form a helicopter with chain on a stick. ACTOR 1 talks as if a game warden, through a walkie-talkie. He darts Thembalethu, who lies still. Helicopter lands.

ACTOR 1: So they darted Thembalethu and took her and her calf to the boma. Now on the first night it was touch and go. On the second night, Thembalethu died. [*ACTOR 5 with great pathos puts her horns down*] Now, I'm not one to mourn the dead, in fact I like to eat them, but there was one thing that worried me. This little one here [*indicates baby*]. Here he was, condemned to depend on Man. What is the future of this little one here?

Slow rhythmic clapping. All pick up horns. ACTOR 1 has large wooden box marked "Taiwan." As each actor speaks he puts his horns into the box.

ACTOR 2: Ubejane! Filled with holes, horn of sorrow, hacked away, your courage bleeding, black, into the dry earth, rotting in the sun to please a far away need in Man.
ACTOR 5: A need to possess your health, your courage, to possess your power.
ACTOR 4: Ubejane! They will come until your stamp, your snort are but memories on this earth.
ACTOR 6: But, Ubejane, oh Ubejane! They will never possess you. For if you live, it is to be free.
ACTOR 2: Man is the one who sees so little, so late. Ubejane, oh, Ubejane, your loss will live forever to mock Man.

They pack the horns into the box and nail it down. As they exit, ACTOR 6, as the baby rhino, snorts and tries to escape.

ACTOR 3: Bamba!! (Catch him!!)

ACTORS 1 and 4 catch him and drag him, kicking and squealing, upstage to where the box is. All stand with their backs to the audience. ACTOR 1 walks forward with the model rhino, looks at it long, hard, and lovingly. Puts it down in the center of the bare stage and goes to join the group of actors with backs to the audience. Pool of light diminishes slowly on rhino model.

Blackout.

The End.

And the Girls in Their Sunday Dresses

(1988)

Zakes Mda

Zanemvula (Zakes) Kizito Gatyeni Mda was born 6 October 1948 in Sterks-
pruit, Herschel District, an impoverished rural area in the eastern Cape Province.
The family moved to Soweto soon after his birth but maintained ties to the area,
where Mda received some of his education. In 1964, the family moved to Lesotho
soon after Zakes's father, a lawyer and prominent member of the Pan Africanist
Congress, received political asylum there. Zakes Mda attended high school in
Lesotho and then studied fine arts through a correspondence school in Switzerland.
He began writing plays in junior high school, but his work did not receive professional productions until 1979 when, after winning the South African Amstel
Playwright's Merit Award for We Shall Sing for the Fatherland, that play and
two others were presented in Soweto, at the Market Theatre in Johannesburg, and
at the People's Space Theatre in Cape Town. While continuing to write plays, he
earned an M.F.A. in the United States. He has traveled extensively as a UNICEF
consultant on social mobilization, taught at the National University of Lesotho
(while working with the Marotholi Traveling Theatre there), held a Research
Fellowship at Yale University, and earned a Ph.D. from the University of Cape
Town for his work on theatre for development. He is now a professor of theatre at
Witwatersrand University.

    And the Girls . . . , although written when protest against and resistance to
apartheid in South Africa was at its height, looks beyond the immediate struggle
in South Africa to the post-colonial conditions of poverty, dependency, uneven
development, and corruption that plague large sections of Africa and could become
an issue in South Africa in the future. The play is distinctive for its treatment of
a political theme without any of the grand narrative visions and stark contrasts
between good and evil so often deployed in political drama. The Woman makes a
theatrical denunciation of corruption and upper-class disdain for the plight of the

downtrodden at one point, but, rather than turn on this gesture, the play suggests it is inadequate for understanding or changing the situation. The play uses absurdist elements to break down the significance usually attached to social stereotypes and narrative unity in pedagogical plays and to infuse the unapologetically didactic ambitions of the play with a healthy dose of humor.

The turn to the concerns of women distinguishes this play from most earlier political drama, which usually focused exclusively on men. The passive, domestic roles assigned to women by the patriarchal society are vividly highlighted by setting the scene in a line waiting for discounted government rice, but this setting also politicizes and makes public the women's private domestic worlds. The public qualities of private life are also borne out in the women's professions. Whereas sex and housekeeping are generally considered home-bound occupations, these women engage in them in a public market, although not with satisfactory results. The office women in their "Sunday" dresses represent an ideal of social legitimacy and financial independence that the two characters look on with envy and do homage to by waiting in line. The play's Kafkaesque and absurd turns are designed to undercut the authority and promise that keeps the women waiting upon the whims of the powerful.

And the Girls in Their Sunday Dresses *premiered at the Edinburgh Fringe Festival, Springwell House, Edinburgh, Scotland, 14 August 1988 with the following cast:*

THE LADY: Gertrude Mothibe

THE WOMAN: Tokoloho Khutsoane

Directed by Teresa Devant

Produced by Meso Theatre Group from Maseru, Lesotho

AND THE GIRLS IN THEIR SUNDAY DRESSES

Scene One

THE LADY is about forty and a bit overdressed, albeit in the latest fashion. One can see that there was a conscious effort on her part to make herself appear very chic and sexy. Her mannerisms are of a sophisticated woman of the world, but of course at the end of it all she appears pretentious—even ridiculous. When the lights go up she is sitting on a chair, making herself up. She is looking at herself in a compact mirror and dabs a little powder on her cheeks. On her lap is all the paraphernalia used in make-up; lipstick, eyebrow pencils and mascara. She uses some more lipstick on her lips and tries to shape them in what she thinks is a sensuous way. Her old lizard bag lies opened on the ground. THE WOMAN enters holding a small parcel of food. She is much more simply and soberly dressed. Indeed she looks like someone's mother. She is roughly the same age as THE LADY.

WOMAN: The queue hasn't moved an inch since I left.

LADY [*busy with her nails*]: Did you come with our lunch?
WOMAN [*throws packet to THE LADY*]: Here. Can't afford much more than that. Moreso we don't know for how long we'll be here.

Catches the packet, then puts her make-up paraphernalia into her handbag.
She opens the packet and wolfs the food. Almost half-way through
she remembers THE WOMAN.

LADY: Did you eat?
WOMAN: You know very well I did not eat.
LADY: I'll leave you some.
WOMAN: I'll eat it when I am on the chair.

THE LADY has finished eating her share, and she gives what remains
to THE WOMAN. Pause.

LADY: It is the third day now.
WOMAN: Fourth.
LADY: Third.
WOMAN: For me it is the fourth.
LADY: And you managed without the chair. The first day, I mean. Before I came.
WOMAN: It had not rained then. I sat on the ground.
LADY: Yeah. It's wet all over now, so you need my chair. We need each other because I also need the food that you buy for both of us. You see, I didn't bring any money with me, and . . .
WOMAN: You told me already.
LADY: I just want you to understand that hands clean each other. You need my chair, I need your food. I don't want you to think I am stranded or something.
WOMAN: Maybe we should go.
LADY: Go? We wait here for days, then just when things are about to get right we go. Very clever.
WOMAN: How do you know things are about to get right? See, they are about to close and go for lunch.
LADY: They'll come back.
WOMAN: They always do. But we continue to wait.
LADY: Yeah.
WOMAN: So how do you know things are about to get right?
LADY: Dammit man, is it my fault that we have to wait here?
WOMAN: Nobody said it is.
LADY: Then stop bugging me, okay?
WOMAN [*coolly*]: We can all lose our temper if we want to, you know. We've all got it somewhere, and we can just as easily lose it. [*There is the sound of a gong*]. Ah, they are closing for lunch now.
LADY: I am sure when they come back things will be all right.

WOMAN: They are filing out of the storeroom.

LADY: And out of the offices.

WOMAN: Don't the office girls look beautiful in their summer dresses?

LADY [*contemptuously*]: Well, to you I am sure they do.

THE LADY stands up, and they both wave at the throngs of people who are passing by.

WOMAN: Goodbye, *marena-a-rona*!

LADY: Have a beautiful lunch.

WOMAN: As you chew think of us who are sitting here in the hot sun, and in the rain!

LADY [*to THE WOMAN*]: Why did you say that? Are you protesting or what? Do you want them to keep us here much longer than we have been? [*To the throngs*] She didn't mean it *bo-ntate le bo-'me'*. What she was trying to say is . . .

WOMAN: Who told you to speak on my behalf? I know exactly what I am trying to say. [*To the throngs*] What I am trying to say is, for how long do you think we'll wait here?

LADY: You see they are laughing at us. You want to make us a laughing stock of the storemen and office girls.

WOMAN: Listen! That other man answers. He says they are still sewing the bags. There is nothing they can do until all the bags have been sewn.

LADY: Of course they did tell us that right from scratch didn't they? People have been buying a lot of this rice they said. So it got finished in these storerooms, they said. They had to send trucks to fetch more rice from other hoarding places throughout the country. Now they are putting it into bags and sewing the bags. Some bags are tattered so they've got to be sewn before grain can be put into them.

WOMAN: It seems there is a lot of sewing happening in there.

Suddenly they both run for the chair. THE LADY gets there first and sits.

WOMAN: It is my turn.

LADY: What?

WOMAN: To sit. It is my turn.

LADY: How do you know it is your turn?

WOMAN: I have been counting the hours you have been sitting there. I've got to sit too now.

LADY: Let me finish my make-up, okay? Then I'll let you sit.

She begins to make herself up again

WOMAN: You lay it on a bit thick, don't you?

LADY: What?

WOMAN: The make-up.

LADY: What would you know about it?

WOMAN: I am not stupid. I've got eyes, and I can see layers and layers of thick gooey stuff all over your face. [*THE LADY laughs mockingly*] It makes you look like a whore.

LADY: I *am* a whore.

WOMAN: You mean you are . . .

LADY: Of course. At least that's what people like you call us. But that's not why I use this stuff. People use it generally, you know, to improve their looks. I am sure even where you come from people use it.

WOMAN: But not as thick as that. You look like a ghost.

LADY: Not like a whore this time, eh?

WOMAN: Well, I am sorry. Maybe it was not the right thing to say.

LADY: Don't be sorry. I ply my trade openly. Everyone knows me in town. But, you see, to put you at ease—for you seem concerned with the thickness of my make-up—contrary to what many of you civilians may believe. I wear it thick because my skin is a mess. Messed up by the follies of my youth.

WOMAN: I can see that. Not the follies of youth, I mean. The skin.

LADY: Yeah it's in a mess. Got messed up when I was a little girl. You remember the skin lightening creams we used, eh?

WOMAN: Very well. *Ambi Extra, Artra . . .*

LADY: *Super Rose* and all the rest. When we were girls we used them, 'cause we wanted to be white. We bloody hated ourselves, so we used them. They've got something called hydroquinone in them, but we didn't know it then. All we wanted was to have white skins. Hydroquinone, sister woman, it destroys your skin.

WOMAN: Sister woman?

LADY: That's what I call all my girl friends. They call me that as well. Anyway it eats your skin. I was lucky. It didn't eat much of mine.

WOMAN: Yeah, I have seen people whose skins are completely destroyed. The whole face!

LADY: So that's why I use this stuff. To hide all the ugly blemishes. [*She has finished her make-up*] There! You see! As good as new. You should try some of this stuff too.

WOMAN: No thanks.

LADY: How old are you?

WOMAN: About forty.

LADY: See what I mean? We are about the same age, but look at you. Frumpy!

WOMAN: I think I am all right the way I am.

LADY: You think so. But do other people think so? We are not so selfish as to look beautiful for our own selves, you know. We do it for other people, so that they should have something to admire.

WOMAN: I think you have finished your make-up now.

LADY: Of course.

WOMAN: So let me sit on the chair.

[*THE LADY reluctantly stands up, and THE WOMAN sits*]

Phew! I thought I'd never sit.

LADY: I don't like standing up for long periods. It's not good for my figure. I don't think this is a good arrangement.

WOMAN: It was a good arrangement when you ate my food. A single hand cannot wash itself, you said. Two hands clean each other.

LADY: I am not complaining.

THE WOMAN takes the little packet left by THE LADY and begins to eat.

WOMAN: So you knew we're going to be here for days.

LADY: Not really.

WOMAN: Then how come you brought a chair with you?

LADY: Because I know that the wheels of government move slowly.

WOMAN: Maybe you'll explain that.

LADY: I can see you are new to this country.

WOMAN: I was born here.

LADY: But don't live here, I am sure.

WOMAN: Well, I work in Cape Town. In Mowbray. I am a flat cleaner there.

LADY: That's why you are not used to the waiting game. I have lived here all my life. I know about the waiting game. You are a novice. An absolute amateur.

WOMAN: I think I am beginning to know about the waiting game.

LADY: You don't know half the story. Let me tell you. When I go to the post office to buy a stamp, I take my chair with me. When I go to the bank to draw money—I used to have a respectable balance in my account, by the way—I take my chair with me. Why, because I know there is going to be a lot of waiting there. When I go to government offices for any service whatsoever I know I have to wait while bureaucrats have endless conversations about their lovers, and the great parties they have been attending lately. You go to these offices, sister woman, and the particular person who has been assigned to deal with your particular case has gone out. No one knows where. So you wait. Or they can't locate the file. Or perhaps the person who has to sign something has gone to a meeting somewhere. They always go to meetings. So you wait. I tell you, sister woman, all of us spend ninety-five percent of our waking hours waiting. Sooner or later this nation will learn from me. [*Shouting*] Bring your own chairs with you, and let's relax while waiting for something to happen! So you see why I am not very much amused when I have to share my chair with you?

WOMAN [*apologetically*]: It's just that it rained.

LADY: Another lesson in this waiting game. Get drip-dry clothes. You know, wash-and-wear. You never know when it's going to rain while you wait in some line. Look at the mess you are in, just because it rained like shit on us, and your clothes are all shriveled up. Look at me. As fine as ever.

WOMAN: When it gets dry I won't need your chair. I'll sit flat on the ground, and keep my place on the queue. See who's going to feed you.

LADY: Ha! It won't get dry. Rain never behaves that way. As long as we are waiting here, it's going to rain every time and the ground won't dry up.

The sound of the gong.

WOMAN: The workers are coming back. The storekeepers and the office girls in their beautiful dresses.

LADY [*shouting*]: We hope you've had a lovely lunch, and God bless you. [*They both stand up and raise their arms as if in supplication*] We greet you, our lords and masters!

LADY: *Marena!*

WOMAN: *Nkosi yamakhosi!*

LADY: *Melimo ea lefats'e!*

Lights gradually fade to black.

Scene Two

THE LADY and THE WOMAN. Still on the queue. THE WOMAN is sitting on the chair, and THE LADY is impatiently pacing the floor.

LADY: It is the inertia that kills me.

WOMAN: What's that?

LADY: Inactivity.

WOMAN: We could kill time by playing some game.

LADY: Like what?

WOMAN: *Liketo.* We could get some small stones and play liketo.

LADY: On this wet ground?

WOMAN: I forgot about that. The wet ground. We could devise a game. Something we can play while one of us is sitting on the chair and the other is standing up.

LADY: Maybe we could lay every guy on this queue.

WOMAN [*standing up and horrified*]: What!

LADY: Lay them, you know. The poor guys have been standing here for days, and I am sure quite a few of them are horny. We could have a ball.

WOMAN: I think that's disgusting.

LADY [*with relish*]: Yeah, let's all be disgusting.

WOMAN: But then, it's something you are used to. It's your profession, you said.

LADY: Just for kicks this time. We wouldn't dream of charging these wretched souls a cent.

WOMAN: Why did you become a prostitute?

LADY: Eh?

WOMAN: You heard me.

LADY: You expect a sob story, I am sure. A broken home. Abused as a child by a step-father. Family so poor we had to scrounge for food any way and anywhere we could. I am sorry to disappoint you. I was from a very happy family. We were not millionaires, but we had enough to eat. You can even say we lived almost on the wealthy side of the street. I went to a private school. Even up to university. Attempted a BA. Didn't finish though.

WOMAN: Then why did you become a prostitute?

LADY: Choice! Goddammit, can't a woman choose what she wants to do with her life?

WOMAN: You are such a beautiful woman. You could have made some lucky man a good wife.

LADY: I did make somebody a good wife. I was so damn good that he left me. Ran away with the maid.

THE WOMAN has seen something that excites her.

WOMAN: Look, they are loading it into the trucks!

LADY: What?

WOMAN: The fucken rice we are waiting for. They are loading it into those trucks.

LADY: Don't worry. They'll surely leave something for us.

WOMAN: It's not fair! We have been waiting here for days, and those trucks just drive in and get loaded with rice. It's not fair!

LADY: They'll leave some bags for us, I tell you. I am sure they have counted the number of people in the queue and they'll leave some bags for us.

WOMAN: That's not what concerns me, er . . . sister woman, as you say you're called.

LADY: Yeah, sister woman!

WOMAN: That's not what concerns me. You see all those trucks? They have the names of different companies written on them. Wholesalers, general dealers and jobbers. They're buying all this rice here because it's cheap. They're going to sell it in their shops. At a very high price.

LADY: So what? They're in business.

WOMAN [*shouting at the trucks*]: Fuck you all, big-bellied businessmen. That is our rice!

LADY [*trying to stop her*]: Shut up, for God's sake. You are going to make things worse for us. They are going to keep us waiting here for the next ten days just for that.

WOMAN: Listen, we have rights as well as any person here. We have been waiting for days. And these big men with big trucks just push in and load the rice.

LADY: Nobody forced you to come here, you know that. Nobody said, "Sister woman, you are forced to go and buy rice from the government food aid depots. Go or face the firing squad!"

WOMAN: If it's food aid it must be given to the poor for free. And in many cases it helps to keep them where they are—poor.

LADY: The poor, yes, and you and I don't qualify. Let's face it, you came because you heard it's a bargain. You knew before you came that the countries that donated it meant for it to be distributed among the poor for free. But you came to buy it still. You shout at those big guys, but you are not different from them.

WOMAN: Do you have to bundle me with them?

LADY: All we need is patience, and our turn will come.

WOMAN: Where does this rice come from anyway?

LADY: Italy. You see the writing on all those bags? It's in Italian. I can read it because I was once married to an Italian chef. I learned a little bit of the language.

WOMAN: You have been doing a lot of marrying it seems.

LADY: Only once. Never got married again.

WOMAN: What about the man who ran away with the maid?

LADY: That's the same Italian chef. When I met him I was a student at the university. He had a restaurant just outside the gate of the main campus. My friends and I used to eat and drink there while at the same time competing about who was going to catch him first. I won. We lived together and for a while I was a queen. He took me to places and spent good money on me. We went to Mauritius. We went to all the gambling dens you can think of. We went to Sun City.

WOMAN: And now you have nothing to show for it

LADY: A daughter. A good-for-nothing teenage daughter. She gets laid all over town and doesn't bring a cent home. Spends it all on herself. Flashy clothes and jewelry.

WOMAN: You are in the same trade then?

LADY: Same trade? Sister woman, I taught that girl everything she knows. Every little trick. Every little movement. The ungrateful brat!

The gong.

LADY: It is time up! They are going home for the day.

WOMAN: They can't do that without serving us.

LADY: It's four-thirty, sister woman. They're knocking off.

WOMAN: All this sister woman rubbish! It irritates me, you know that?

LADY: I don't see why it should. I think it's nice. We got it from some black American customers who once came here years back.

WOMAN: Well, I hope you'll stop calling me that.

LADY: I don't see why you should be irritable. It's not my fault that these people are going home without serving us. Ah, there they are coming. Let's greet them nicely. It humours them.

THE WOMAN sits down on the chair.

WOMAN: I am not going to do that. I am sick and tired of kowtowing to these bastards who don't have any regard for us.

THE LADY waves feebly.

LADY [*wanly*]: Good night, my lords and masters. Do have sweet dreams.

WOMAN: I say let them all go and fry in hell.

LADY: Sh . . . They'll hear you.

WOMAN: Of course I want them to hear me.

LADY: Shit, why did I sit with you here?

WOMAN: We both didn't have any choice. We are in a queue.

LADY: Listen, I know the system, okay? You just come from Cape Town and you want to mess up everything for everybody. Those people are civil servants, do you hear that? You don't just talk to them as though they are the woman who sells fat cakes at the street corner.

WOMAN: Listen, I think I am going home now.

LADY: Why? You don't want the rice anymore?

WOMAN: I need the rice, but I am not prepared to wallow in degradation for it.

LADY: Well, if you think you are a better buttock than all these people who have been waiting here who am I to stop you?

WOMAN: Indeed who are you to stop me. Okay, it was nice meeting you. I must go now.

She makes to go.

LADY: Sister woman, wait! What will your children eat?

WOMAN: I'll just have to buy for them in the shop. It's more expensive there of course, but what choice do I have?

LADY: You have been waiting here for many days. Surely you can wait for another night. I am sure in the morning they'll serve us.

WOMAN: You have been saying that from the very first day we met. I am sure when they come back from lunch, they'll serve us. I am sure . . . I am sure . . . I am sick and tired of all that. I must go now.

LADY [*appealingly*]: Please, sister woman. Don't go. Listen, I'll even let you use my chair for ever. Bequeath it to you. Only please don't go now.

THE LADY holds THE WOMAN tight in an attempt to stop her from going.
THE WOMAN tries to break loose.

WOMAN: Let go of me, bloody whore! What do you want from me, eh? What is it that you want from me?

LADY [*pleading*]: Please don't go. How am I going to live without you? [*she kneels*] Look, I am kneeling down on the wet ground in my beautiful dress pleading and begging.

WOMAN: I thought as much. It is my money you are so much interested in. If I go you'll have to find another victim who'll buy you meals while you wait in your perpetual queue.

LADY [*standing up and mustering as much dignity as she can*]: I am broke. I don't have a cent to my name. The only money I have is the ten bucks with which I'll pay for the rice. That's all.

WOMAN [*coming back*]: But you led me to believe you were a prosperous street walker.

LADY [*greatly offended*]: I am not a street walker. I have never stood at street corners waiting for clients to come and pick me up in their cars. No one can claim to have ever seen me in front of the Victoria Hotel soliciting for the clientele. I am not an orphan of the night. I am a courtesan. A courtesan, do you hear that?

WOMAN: Okay, I am sorry. You are a courtesan, whatever that means.

LADY: It means that my clients are from the upper crust of the society. I entertain Ministers and Ambassadors. I am a high-class hooker. I service rich capitalists when they come to town on business.

WOMAN: Then what are you doing on this queue with low-lives like us?

LADY: I am broke, I told you.

WOMAN: Courtesans don't make enough to make ends meet these days?

LADY [*breaking down and weeping uncontrollably*]: Oh, sister woman. I am old. I don't know what to do.

WOMAN [*trying to comfort her*]: You are not old. You're only forty. You are still a beautiful woman.

LADY: They don't come anymore. The johns don't come anymore.

WOMAN: Johns?

LADY: The clients. The customers. The johns. The young girls have taken over. Teenage whores line the streets by the dozen, and no one wants to screw us old whores anymore. The competition is hard, sister woman, very hard. And now we are dying of hunger.

WOMAN: And you've read books, and you've a lot of learning. You could have easily become like one of the office girls who have been coming in and out of this yard in their beautiful Sunday dresses.

LADY [*pride taking over again*]: What's the difference? Many of them have to sleep with someone to get their jobs. They have to lay some dirty old man to get a promotion. We are in the same profession, sister woman. Only I do it openly and on my own terms, as a free agent. They get laid and still have to sit behind office desks and typewriters before they get their porridge. [*She looks at herself in the compact mirror*] Oh damn, the tears have messed up my make-up.

WOMAN: Don't worry. Nobody will notice. It's getting to be night anyway. You'll do it again in the morning.

LADY: Honestly, do you think I am old, sister woman?

WOMAN: Forty is never old.

LADY: Then why don't they come, sister woman? Why don't the customers come any more? I am not ugly. I am still beautiful. Look at my body. *U ntse u lutlisa mathe.* Why the hell don't these bastards come, sister woman?

WOMAN: As you say, there is all this young blood now. Like your daughter.

LADY [*desperately*]: Am I old, sister woman? Am I ugly?

WOMAN [*reassuringly*]: Not at all. It's just that men are fickle. That's the whole problem.

LADY: Yes, the bastards are unreliable. They find you when you are nice and fresh and young. They use you in many different ways, and then throw you away like the marrow of a horse when they have drained you of all flesh and blood. I hate the bastards. I was young once, sister woman. I was young and beautiful. I was the campus queen. That's when the father of my daughter met me. He lavished all his love and money on me. I always had booze and cigarettes for myself and my friends. I even left varsity for him. I gave birth to his daughter. Then the bastard left me. I heard he got a job as chief chef on some luxury liner.

WOMAN: Maybe that's because he was a foreigner. You should have got yourself a local man and settled down.

LADY: Local men? They are bastards as well. Maybe even worse. They take you for granted. They don't treat you like a lady. They treat you like scum and you got to be at their beck and call. Do everything for them. Even have to wipe their arses. No, sister woman. Men are all the same. That is why I got into this profession. I have been used. So I use them. The men I sleep with, in them I see the Italian chef. All of them are representative of him. That is why I am going to lay them to death, and take their money to boot. I hate the bastards, sister woman.

WOMAN: Yet you make love to them.

LADY: Those are johns. They are not human beings. Even as they undress I look at them and I feel like spitting all over their shriveled bodies. I find them pathetic. Pathetic and disgusting creatures. I wish I had AIDS, then I'd spread it like wild fire. Kill all the bastards.

WOMAN: We are all victims of a social order that allows this to happen. But I don't think yours is the solution.

LADY: What would you know about it? You went to Cape Town to work for the Boers. Clean after their filth.

WOMAN: Look at you now. All scared and worried because the johns don't come anymore. That's the problem with your kind of job. Old age comes quite early. And there is no insurance against that.

LADY: There is insurance. It's just that I was unfortunate things didn't work out for me. I thought that my daughter would be my insurance in my old age. You should see her, she is a beautiful little thing. An expert in the job, for she was trained by the best. But a good-for-nothing brat who doesn't care for her mama who brought her into the world and taught her all she knows. One of the major insurance policies, of course, is marriage. All of us, as we do our rounds we are looking for a John who will fall head over heels, and marry. There are many of us who are married all over Europe, married by former clients who wanted to keep this thing for themselves for ever. Married by European businessmen, contractors, engineers, aid workers and so on, who initially came as experts sent by their governments, or as tourists. These women now lead respectable lives as housewives. Or have forged careers for themselves. Only a few days ago, I met one of my old colleagues. She is visiting home, you know, from Switzerland where she has a successful marriage and a successful career as a singer. She sings gospel music all over the place. Sometimes she gets invited to sing in anti-apartheid rallies all over Europe. You can't get more respectable than that. No one would ever know about her past. Except for the fact that she is saved. Not only does she sing gospel all over the show, she preaches it as well, and tells everyone she was once a hooker.

WOMAN: I am sure she is the same person I saw the other day. They told me she used to be a call girl, then she got married in Europe and got saved.

LADY: She must be the one, sister woman. She goes to Victoria and preaches to the ladies of the night.

WOMAN [*preaching*]: My sisters, my sisters in the Lord. Isn't it a wonderful feeling to know that someone's blood can flow?

THE LADY is now the preacher's audience. She sits down on the ground. Sometimes she will stand up as the spirit moves her. Lights dim, for it is now night.

LADY: Yes. It is our blood. Very inconveniencing when one is on duty.

WOMAN: I am talking about the blood of Jesus Christ our Lord. The blood that flowed to save us from our sins. The blood that shows to one and all how much the Lord loves us. It is love that I am talking about, my sisters of the night. Not the love of the flesh. But the love that is everlasting.

LADY: Amen! Hallelujah!

WOMAN: I am talking now about repentance. Repentance from our sins. Once upon a time, I was like you. I moved from hotel to hotel trying to get men. I jumped from bed to bed. I used to be a harlot of Sodom and Gomorrah. Then one day I saw the light. [*She sings a hymn. THE LADY joins, and they both dance and clap their hands. It is obvious that the spirit has moved them.*] I saw the light, sisters of the night.

LADY: Amen.

WOMAN: Jesus spoke to me. He said: "My daughter, I gave you your body, and it is the temple of the Lord. *Hobaneng joale ha u ntse u fana ka eona hohle moo?*" I used to lead the same kind of life. But I got saved. Now I live in my villa in Geneva, and I praise the Lord all the time. I urge you to repent. I urge you to be saved! Do I see repentance, my sisters of the night?

LADY: Amen!

WOMAN: Do I see signs of repentance?

LADY [*greatly moved by the spirit*]: I will repent. I feel the spirit. I will repent. But first let me find myself a john who will marry me and take me to Europe with him, or who will build me a house in Maseru West, and furnish it. Then I'll repent! And be saved! And work for the Lord . . .

Overcome by the spirit, THE LADY collapses. Lights fall to black.

SCENE THREE

The queue. THE LADY is now sitting on the ground and is smoking a cigarette. She is dishevelled and is no longer fussing about her looks. THE WOMAN looks as she did in the previous scenes: simple and neat. She is whistling or humming the hymn of the previous scene.

LADY: I wish you'd stop that. It irritates me.

WOMAN: You can have your chair. You don't have to sit on the wet ground.

LADY: You don't have to patronise me.

WOMAN: It is your chair after all.

LADY: I don't care any more. I can sit anywhere I want. I can even lie flat on my belly in that mud puddle. It is not your business at all.

WOMAN: Well, if it suits you.

LADY: You are gloating.

WOMAN: About what?

LADY [*bitterly*]: Now that you know so much about me you think you can sit in judgement.

WOMAN: I didn't say anything.

LADY: I can see you. You think I am going to allow you to pity me, and to patronise me. You are Miss Perfect and I am a fallen whore.

WOMAN: If it will make you happy, let me tell you that I am not perfect.

LADY: How's that?

WOMAN: When I went to Cape Town for the first time it was with a man.

LADY: So what's wrong with that?

WOMAN: He was my boss.

LADY: Yeah?

WOMAN: I ran away with my boss to Cape Town. He was a young man *oa Letaliana* (an Italian). I was his maid. I looked after his house while he ran his restaurant business.

LADY: See how strange life is?

WOMAN: He was a philanderer, *Letaliana leo*. Brought different women home every day. Mostly ladies of the night. But oh, he was charming, with an impish sense of humour. It was the easiest thing to fall in love with him.

LADY: Same with mine. These *Mataliana* (Italians) are all like that it seems.

WOMAN: Yeah. Then he made one of his many women pregnant, and decided to live with her. I couldn't bear another woman living permanently in that house, and I told him I was quitting. He wouldn't hear of it. [*Mimicking Italian accent*] I cannot live without you, *ausi*. Let us run away to Cape Town. I have many brothers there. They will get me a job in a nice big hotel. His business was not doing well. In fact he had gone bankrupt. So we ran away to Cape Town.

THE LADY is engrossed in the story. She sits still, one hand on her cheek, looking fixedly at THE WOMAN.

WOMAN: My first trip to South Africa, and I was with a white man. It was before they had scrapped the Immorality Act, so I passed as his maid. Which in any case I was, besides the fact that we were lovers also. We drove to Cape Town and got ourselves a flat in Mowbray—one of those self-contained flats where they supply you with everything, including kitchen utensils. For a while we were very happy, although at every knock at the door we would jump: "Police!" Then one day he says: "Dammit, we can't live like this, like animals in a cage." I tell him: "But you knew when we came here that there are strange laws in this country."

"Yeah, I knew, but I didn't think it would be so bad."

"So let's go back home."

"Where is back home."

"Where you took me from."

"My home is in Italy."

We forgot about the whole thing, and were happy again for a while. Then one day he didn't come back. Just disappeared like a fart in the wind. He had left in the morning to meet his "brothers" to talk about a job. He didn't come back. [*Screaming*] What am I going to do? Please, what am I going to do? I stayed for a few days and the groceries ran out. The complex manager kept on phoning me about the due rent. [*Screaming again*] I don't know where he is! I don't have any money so I can't pay rent! Please try to understand! Meanwhile I was desperately trying to phone the numbers he used to phone. [*Shouting on the imaginary phone*] Where the hell is this man? Tell me, didn't he tell you where he was going? Didn't he leave a message for me? A tiny little message, anything? But no one knew, or maybe they didn't want to tell. Until at last one of his "brothers" told me. He'd got a job as a cook on a ship. The ship had sailed to Hong Kong days ago. Meanwhile the manager of the flats wanted his rent. So I had to work there for months cleaning the flats, in order to pay him back. Well, even after I had paid him back, I decided to stay and continue working.

LADY [*sadly*]: See what I told you, sister woman. Men always do these things to us. The scum!

WOMAN: I just wanted you to know that I don't live in the past. What happened happened and I remember it only in so far as it is a lesson learned never to be repeated.

LADY: You are not bitter then?

WOMAN: I have no time for bitterness. I rebuilt from the ashes. Got myself a small room in one of the locations. I have a regular job as a flat cleaner. Mind you, I am not saying things are easy. We are struggling on. Like everyone else.

LADY: So they pay you well as a flat cleaner?

WOMAN: That's one of the things we struggle about. I am a member of the Domestic Workers Union. We struggle for better wages and better working conditions. Things are still bad, but we are going to win.

LADY: I know about these unions. It's politics, that's what it is.

WOMAN: Is it not through politics that the laws that have created these terrible conditions for us are made?

LADY: They are not our politics. They are the politics of another country.

WOMAN: I work there so everything that happens there affects me. It affects you too, although you've, like most others, decided to wear blinders and pretend that you live in a never-never land that will smoothly map out its destiny irrespective of all the turbulence surrounding it. One day it's going to dawn on you, and on the rest of all the others who think like you, that this struggle is not just South African. It is Southern African.

LADY [*taken aback*]: My God, you stand with a person in a queue for the whole four days and you think you know them! You are an agitator, and you won't survive here if I must tell you.

WOMAN [*laughs mockingly*]: That's what they call us over there too. Agitators!

It is as if when you are forced to sit on a hot coal stove someone else must come and teach you that your buttocks are burning. I tell you, my working there has put me through a baptism of fire. I won't sit back and take abuse from anyone. That is what I have been trying to tell you. You don't have to take abuse from anyone.

LADY: Hey, who says I take abuse? Just because I have patience and I take my chair with me doesn't mean I take abuse.

WOMAN: It is now time for us to change things. To liberate not only ourselves, but the men themselves, for we are all in bondage! Yes, the men in this free and independent country are in bondage, mostly in their attitudes. That is why you see them sitting back and swimming in the glories of the past. Oh, our ancestors were great! They defended this country against all sorts of invaders! Oh, we are descendants of the great warriors who through their wisdom created this nation. That is all they ever do. We do not see much of what they are doing for the future. It is as if the past will take care of the future without any effort from the present.

LADY: Look, I think all these things you say are making me uncomfortable. People here don't just say things like these in public places—particularly when we are waiting here to be served. But what I don't understand is you say you don't take abuse, but you have been waiting here with the rest of us.

WOMAN [*laughs*]: Through your persuasion. But frankly though, I suffer from the same disease from which we all seem to suffer. We say: Well, this is home, we are prepared to accept shoddiness. We are still a young nation so these things are expected to happen. In other words what we are saying is that we don't think we are capable of producing the best results, so we are prepared to tolerate inefficiency and corruption.

LADY: Sister woman, I think you have gone through a lot of pain in that place where you work. And I have been sitting here thinking it was the end of the world for me just because the johns don't come anymore. I feel such a fool.

WOMAN: You are not a fool at all. And yes there has been a lot of pain. But there has been hope as well. Sometimes hope in death. There is a coloured woman I work with. I was visiting her one day in her location when we saw her son being gunned down by the police. In cold blood. She ran to her son and knelt down by his side. When mothers whose sons have been ripped to pieces by bullets are able to say "My son's death is a victory for the people. He wasn't just mine. He belonged to the people." Then you know that victory is indeed certain, and liberation day is just around the corner. [*Laughing*] Now, I know you will tell me that these are their politics and not ours. Perhaps you think that when bullets fly they choose!

LADY: I am sorry, sister woman.

WOMAN: About what?

LADY: I don't know. I just feel that I have got to be sorry about something.

The gong.

WOMAN: Ah, they are coming back to work.

LADY: Should I greet them, sister woman?

WOMAN: It is up to you.

LADY: Are you going to greet them yourself?
WOMAN: No, they do not deserve it.
LADY: Then I won't greet them too.

They watch the throngs as they pass. THE WOMAN has a contemptuous look.

WOMAN: Jealous down, the office girls do look lovely in their summer dresses.
LADY: I don't want to seem disagreeable, sister woman, but you don't know much about summer dresses. To you those are beautiful because you don't have much expertise on clothing. You can tell me about your politics, but leave fashion to me. Now, if you are talking about cloth, you are talking of me. Even now that I don't earn anything you can see that I haven't lost my taste for a good cloth. I could have been a model. Don't you think I could have been a model, sister woman?
WOMAN: You are all mud now, so it's hard to tell.
LADY: Jealous down, sister woman.
WOMAN: Well, I might not know much about fashion, but I notice that people in your profession tend to be more on the fancy side.
LADY: It's only when we go out to work. We have to be recognisable to prospective clients. At the same time we have to be sexually attractive—physically I mean. It's all part of the job. Like a uniform or something. When we are not at work we change. [*With nostalgia*] I remember in the past—I doubt if the current generation still does that—we used to choose a day each week when we would all don our Sunday dresses and we would take our regular lovers and husbands for a night out in town. On this day, even if the wealthiest johns came to town and wanted to do business, we turned them down, for this was the day for our lovers and husbands.

[*There is a pause. Each of the two women is lost in thought. Then there is a sudden outburst of rebelliousness from THE LADY. She goes to THE WOMAN in a very challenging manner. She is in a fighting mood.*]

You are a flat cleaner in Cape Town. All sorts of men go there with their mistresses and with the likes of us. You clean their filth! You are not better off!

Lights fade to black

SCENE FOUR

It is dawn. The two women are still in the queue. THE WOMAN is sleeping on the chair. THE LADY stands hovering over her.

LADY: Sister woman.
WOMAN: What is it?
LADY: Are you awake?
WOMAN: No, I am asleep.
LADY It's a new day today.
WOMAN: Every day is a new day.
LADY: I feel something very important is going to happen today.

WOMAN: Congratulations.

LADY: For what?

WOMAN: For feeling something important is going to happen today. Now let me sleep, okay?

THE LADY walks around for a few paces, then goes back to THE WOMAN.

LADY: Sister woman.

WOMAN: What now?

LADY: I am sorry I attacked you yesterday.

WOMAN: I understand.

LADY: What do you understand?

WOMAN: Well, I think you were under some kind of pressure.

LADY: You know, one other thing I hate about you, sister woman, is that you always pretend to be some kind of saint. You are a hypocrite. I hate hypocrites, sister woman.

WOMAN: Thank you.

THE LADY wakes THE WOMAN up violently.

LADY: Don't thank me dammit. Listen, I attacked you. I attacked you for no apparent reason. And all you can say is: "I understand" and "thank you."

WOMAN: What do you want me to do then?

LADY: Slap me! Kick me! Whatever!

WOMAN: Listen, I am tired, and I am not at all prepared to argue with you. Especially at this ungodly hour.

LADY: You are a hypocrite, that's what you are. You are a wishy-washy liberal. And I hate liberals. Come here! [*The two women stand facing each other.*] Slap me.

WOMAN: What for?

LADY: To defend yourself.

WOMAN: Against what?

LADY: Against me. I attacked you last night, remember?

WOMAN: That was last night.

LADY: And what did you do about it?

WOMAN: I could have beaten sense into you if I wanted to. In fact the way you have been carrying on, I should have done that a long time ago. But what would be the point?

LADY: There you start patronizing me again.

WOMAN: You talk about defending oneself. You don't know a thing about that. Otherwise you'd not be carrying your chair with you everywhere you go.

LADY: What's my chair got to do with it?

WOMAN: Everything. When they violate you, you wait. You patiently wait until such time that they come around to doing something about it. You have the patience of a saint. When they violate you, you avenge yourself by laying men all over the place. Then you hope things will be all right.

LADY: For me certainly. I get the satisfaction of making them pay—draining their blood and money.

WOMAN: And presto! The world has changed. Injustice has been eradicated! The unequal distribution of the country's wealth has been remedied! Bureaucratic red tape has been eliminated and nobody has to stand on the queue for days on end anymore!

LADY: What do you want me to do then, Miss Politician? What have you done yourself?

WOMAN: Not much. But we should demand a change and be willing to suffer for it, rather than suffer in silence as we have been doing here. Tell me, why are we still here? Why are we still waiting? We are even fighting over the use of the chair. Because we are waiting. Life passes by and we are onlookers. We are like the sedated who sleep through a revolution.

LADY [determined]: I was never an onlooker. I am all action. When the revolution comes I want to carry a gun. I don't sit on the sidelines and darn socks for the fighters.

WOMAN: It is here already.

LADY: Well, I haven't seen much of it. I am still waiting for it, and when it comes . . .

WOMAN: You don't wait for a revolution. You make it happen.

LADY [carried away]: No, I don't sit on the sidelines and sing songs and ululate with meliletsane to make the blood of men boil so that they may bravely march into battle. I carry the gun. I march into battle.

WOMAN: There is hope for all of us yet.

The gong.

LADY: They come again in their Sunday dresses.

WOMAN: Sunday dresses, and summer dresses. That's the same thing then?

LADY: There are winter Sunday dresses and there are summer Sunday dresses.

WOMAN: I never had summer dresses and winter dresses. I just had dresses. I don't have special dresses that I wear on Sundays.

LADY: Sunday dresses are not only worn on Sundays. They are worn on any day when one wants to look beautiful. That is why you see the office girls in their Sunday dresses.

The gong again, repeatedly.

WOMAN: What's that now? Don't tell me they are going back to lunch just after coming in.

LADY: Look, there is a man with a megaphone. He is going to address us.

They listen.

WOMAN: What is he saying?

LADY: He says we must keep order in our queue. Aha, he says rice is now ready. No pushing. We must move in an orderly manner to the window over there.

WOMAN: At last! Let us move with the queue.

LADY: Should we really?

WOMAN: That's what we have been waiting for, is it not?

LADY: Yeah. For all these days.

WOMAN: So let's get moving.

LADY: To that window.

WOMAN: And what happens there?

LADY: We fill in the forms. Come, *'mè*, come! We don't have all day to deal with you.

THE WOMAN is now a rice buying customer and THE LADY an office girl.

Are you going to talk or not? Why do you just stand there staring at me as if you have just swallowed a rat?

WOMAN: I have come to buy rice, *'mè*.

LADY: Of course that's what we sell here. You have come to buy all the rice in this depot?

WOMAN: No, just one bag.

LADY: So, why don't you say so? You people like wasting time. Do I have to prompt you all the time?

WOMAN: One bag of rice, please *'mè*. And here is the money.

LADY: You don't pay at this window. Here we only fill in the forms, in triplicate, then you go and join the other queue where you pay. Is that clear?

WOMAN: It is clear.

LADY: Good. You will fill in your name here. But there is more information that we need from you before we can sell you a bag of rice. You see, here I need to fill in your age, and on this line your place of birth. Place and date of birth actually. Then here of course I fill in your sex. Male or female?

WOMAN: Female, *'mè*.

LADY: Good, now here you fill in . . . You can write, can you?

WOMAN: Yes.

LADY: Then you can fill in the information yourself while I finish eating my fat cake. But first of all let me show you the other information that we need. Here you fill in the colour of your eyes.

WOMAN: For buying rice?

LADY: The government needs all this information. Colour of your eyes here. On this line colour of your hair. And here your height and weight. On this line you fill in, as you can see, the number of teeth in your mouth.

WOMAN: I don't know. I haven't counted them.

LADY: You'll have to count them. You can pay our messenger fifty cents and he'll count them for you. On this line here you fill in whether you have had any communicable diseases or not, and of course here we need your address and telephone number. Name and address of your next of kin here.

WOMAN: Is that all?

LADY: That will be all for now. Next!

WOMAN: Wait. But where do I go from here?

LADY: 'Mè, I don't have the whole day to waste on you. I told you to join the other queue at that window. That is where you pay.

WOMAN: Then I get the rice?

LADY: Not yet. You have to go to the third window where they will stamp your papers with a rubber stamp.

WOMAN: Then finally . . .

LADY: After that you have to join the other queue where you will present your papers to the Right Honourable the Keeper of the Stores. He will assign you a person with whom you'll go to choose your bag of rice. Then of course you've got to sign for it.

They discard their roles as office girl and customer.

That, sister woman, is what we'll go through.

WOMAN: At least now everything will be over and done away with.

LADY: I am not going through with it.

WOMAN: You are not?

LADY: No. I am not. I am going home now, and I am not taking the chair.

WOMAN: What about the rice?

LADY: To hell with the rice! I am going home, and I know that never again will I need the food-aid rice, and my chair of patience. Are you coming or not?

WOMAN [*excitedly*]: You know what? I love you. I think you are a great human being. Of course I am coming. I am coming.

LADY: Let's go then.

They make to go. There is a great warmth between them. They hold each other's hands and there is a pause for a while.

LADY: Sister woman, do you ever think about him?

WOMAN: Who?

LADY: The man.

WOMAN: The man I ran away with? Yeah, sometimes.

LADY: The man who left me. Sometimes.

WOMAN: Well, mine left me too.

LADY: Men . . . They are the same. They are like children of one person.

Lights fade to black as the two women go out.

Mooi Street Moves
(1992)

Paul Slabolepszy

Paul Slabolepszy was born in Bolton, England to an English mother and Polish refugee father. When he was three, the family emigrated to South Africa, and Paul grew up in Pietersburg in the Northern Transvaal. He majored in English and Drama at the University of Cape Town. In 1972 he became a founding member (along with Athol Fugard and Yvonne Bryceland) of the Space Theatre, the first major, integrated, independent theatre to emerge after the repression of the 1960s. He began his theatrical career as an actor but has established his reputation primarily as a playwright. His plays explore the insularity and unease of lower-middle-class White male culture in South Africa. His Saturday Night at the Palace *(1982) is considered the first major play to capture the nihilistic despair, ignorance, and misdirected anger of this social group. When his plays deal with the bonding rituals and sports fanaticism of White men, they can be very humorous, but when they deal with interracial relations and the future, they are often very somber. His darkest assessment of the South African situation and his most scathing condemnation of petty bourgeois aspirations among marginalized Whites is rendered in* Small Holding *(1989). In more recent years, in plays such as* Mooi Street Moves *and* Victoria Almost Falls *(1994), Slabolepszy has been exploring the possibilities of rapprochement between lower-middle-class Whites and Blacks. His writing and performance in* The Return of Elvis du Pisanie *(1993), a wistful and humorous one-man monologue on the grandiose dreams and sordid reality of lower-middle-class life, won more awards than any other production in the history of South African theatre.* Mooi Street Moves *won the Amstel Playwright of the Year Award in 1992.*

In 1992, the ANC's negotiations with the National Party over the future of South Africa were threatened by a rising tide of violence throughout the country. In the same year, Slabolepszy's play portrays the (at first uneasy and tentative) rapprochement of an individual White and Black against the threatening back-ground of urban violence. The play reflects the political tensions of the day in that the rural Afrikaner, whose interests had traditionally been protected by the National Party, now finds himself adrift in a rapidly changing, unfamiliar world and must rely on the good graces of an urban Black, whose group is now a dominant political force. The play speaks to the country's anxieties about wide cultural differences and a disintegrating social structure with hope and humor tempered by abiding fears.

Dramaturgically, Mooi Street Moves offers an unusual blend of realistic elements. It is essentially a domestic drama: the scene is Stix's home and the action opens with him offering Henry food and a place to sleep. But the setting is also Stix's place of business—living quarters, warehouse, and office—and the absence of women or family turns the drama away from the concerns of private life to the more semi-public concerns of male-bonding rituals—the apartment more club-house than home. This world in which home, work, and leisure fold in upon one another resembles the constrained, narrow world of the struggling African petite bourgeoisie, of which Henry comes to realize he is a member. The lack of family ties lightens the sense of constraint initially by minimizing the young men's responsibilities but ultimately leaves the men more isolated, their camaraderie their only protection from the hostile world outside the apartment, where business and political relationships all reduce to crime and violence.

Mooi Street Moves was first performed at the Great Hall, Grahamstown Festival Fringe, June 1992. The final, full-length version premiered at the Market Theatre, Johannesburg, 27 January 1993 with the following cast:

STIX LETSEBE: Seputla Dan Sebogodi

HENRY STONE: Martin le Maitre

Directed by Paul Slabolepszy (assisted by Lara Foot)

MOOI STREET MOVES

CHARACTERS

STIX LETSEBE, a city slick black dude in his mid-to-late twenties. Street-wise, charming-when-he-wants-to-be, but as dangerous as a sharpened bicycle spoke when the chips are down.

HENRY STONE, a white country bumpkin, also in his twenties. Slow and somewhat nerdish, he is out of his depth in Jozi and flat-broke.

THE SET

The action takes place in a bachelor flat in a run-down Hillbrow (Johannesburg) tower block. The time is now.

A large, sparse room. An old mattress lies on the floor. Around the room are pristine cardboard boxes, all shapes and sizes—marked Telefunken, Sanyo, Panasonic, and so on. Milk crates serve as chairs, there are pictures of Orlando Pirates on the walls. If the place resembles a squatter shack, so much the better.

On lights up, we find a white man in his late twenties standing room centre. He is wearing an open shirt, slacks, and well-worn shoes and clutching a large brown paper bag with New York (or some such logo) on it to his breast. Facing him, holding a tin plate of steaming pap, is a black man of the same age, flashily dressed. The black man silently offers the white man the food. There is no response.

STIX: Thatha. [*Pause*] Take it.
HENRY: It's okay.
STIX: Take it.
HENRY: It's okay.
STIX: For sure, it's okay.

> *STIX holds out the plate. HENRY clutches his paper-bag-suitcase.*
> *There is a pause—a frozen tableau.*

STIX: Thatha.
HENRY: I don't like pap.
STIX: You don't like pap?
HENRY: No.
STIX: I make food. You don't want food?
HENRY: I've never liked pap.

STIX slowly turns and goes to his portable cooker—downstage—scooping the pap from the plate back into the pot on the flame.

They study each other furtively during a long, awkward pause—STIX slowly stirring the pap with a metal coat hanger. The central light bulb flickers. They both look to the light. The white man is startled by the black man's angry cry.

STIX [*shouting to the heavens*]: Ningazi ngama simba ...! Si badala irent lana ...! (Don't come with shit ...! We paying rent here ...!)

Eventually STIX turns off the flame and, rising, moves to his mattress—still exchanging the odd wary glance with the white man. He sits down on his bed and begins to eat from the pot with his fingers, blowing at the food.

HENRY mooches about, still clutching his paper bag. Every now and then, he looks toward STIX, who goes on eating. HENRY stares out of the window and sighs, perplexed.

STIX: Sorry—?
HENRY: Sorry—?
STIX: You say something?
HENRY: No. I was just ...
STIX: Aha. [*Pause*]

HENRY: I don't understand it.
STIX: Nami. (Me neither) [*Pause*]
HENRY: I don't . . . I dunno. I'm . . . I dunno.
STIX: Sekunjalo. (this is how it is)
HENRY: No, but, I mean—he didn't . . . there was no . . . why would he just . . . ?
[*Pause*] Doesn't make sense.

> HENRY *paces about, confused—unsure of his next move.*

STIX [*to himself, in the vernacular*]: Stupid mugu. I make him pap and he doesn't
want to eat it. How can a person not eat pap? Stupid mugu.

> HENRY *stops pacing.*

HENRY: Unless . . . unless he just . . .
STIX [*in the vernacular*]: Be hungry. I don't care.
HENRY: Unless one day he just decided to—you know? [*Pause*] But then why
didn't he tell me?
STIX: Tell you?
HENRY: Yes. Why didn't he . . . ? He could of written.
STIX: A letter?
HENRY: Yes. He could of said, listen—I'm—you know—I'm sort of . . . I'm sort
of . . .
STIX: He didn't do that?
HENRY: No.
STIX: No letter?
HENRY: No. Unless . . . unless he wrote me a letter and I didn't get it.
STIX: You didn't get it?
HENRY: Yes. No. That's if he wrote it, that is.
STIX: Yes. If he didn't write it, you wouldn't get it.
HENRY: No.
STIX: You have to write a letter and send it, for somebody to get it.
HENRY: Yes.
STIX: Write it. And then—ka-plak—in the post.
HENRY: I can't understand why he didn't do that. [*Slight pause*]
STIX: So this is what I'm saying, you see.
HENRY: What?
STIX: This is the story.
HENRY: What?
STIX: This.
HENRY: This?
STIX: Ja. [*Pause*]
HENRY: You think so?
STIX: This is what I'm thinking. Me, myself.
HENRY: That he just . . . he just . . . ?
STIX: Ja. [*Pause*]

STIX: Unless you got the wrong place.

HENRY: Oh, no—he lived here. This was his porsie—no doubt about that. I remember exactly what it looked like . . . I mean, here was the . . . whatjoo-callit? Right over here . . . one a' those—um—I even slept on it . . .

STIX: What . . . ?

HENRY: One of those arm-chair-couch kinda' things that you—sort of—er—you do things to it and it . . . and it . . . sort of it . . . and it becomes a sort of a . . . it becomes a sort of a bed.

STIX: A bed?

HENRY: Yes. You sort of—[*demonstrating*]—up and out . . . and it turns into a . . . turns into a kind of a bed.

STIX: Aikona! Chair that says—hey, mfo!—I'm also a bed?

HENRY: You never seen them?

STIX [*in the vernacular*]: I must get me one of those.

HENRY: And then . . . and then over there . . . on that wall there—no, wait a minute—that wall over there—he had a TV unit.

STIX: TV unit?

HENRY: Yes. Except he had no TV. He was going to get a TV, but at the time he still didn't have one. Well, he had one, but it was a small one—little one—black and white. He got the unit first so that when he eventually got the new one, he'd have a place to put it, you see. He wouldn't have to worry about —you know . . .

STIX: Where to put it . . .

HENRY: That's right. And over here, he had a coffee table and a . . . a gram-tape-deck sorta'—radio. Carpet on the floor—pictures on the wall—smart-fancy lamp-stand . . . all sorts of things.

STIX: All the mod cons.

HENRY: Sorry?

STIX: Modern appliances. You know—zabba-zabba—[*whistles*] Phee-phoo . . . ?

HENRY: Ja, for sure. He had lots of those.

STIX: But no TV?

HENRY: He was planning to get one. New one. He had an old one, but he was gonna get another one. Nice one.

STIX: Too bad he's not still around, I could organise a very good colour TV. Easy terms. Codesa-desa, the price—no VAT! (bargain the price—no tax!) [*Takes his pot—collects plate*]. You not looking maybe for a good colour TV, huh? Philips? Telefunken? Remote Control? Zabba-zabba . . . ! [*Looking him up and down*] No? Too bad.

He rinses off the plates in a plastic bowl filled with water. HENRY is staring at the bowl.

Water is off, my bra. To get it, we must go to the river. [*He laughs at Henry's wide-eyed reaction*]

STIX crosses to his bed, patting his wet hands on HENRY'S back. He grabs his *newspaper (*The Sowetan*) and begins to read it. The lights flicker again and then snap off. In the darkness, STIX yells at the top of his voice.*

STIX: Bulala bathakathi . . . !! (Kill the Whites/wizards . . . !)
HENRY [*petrified*]: Juss-laaik . . . !!

*STIX guffaws and flicks a cigarette lighter, holding it close to his face.
He shouts to the heavens yet again.*

STIX: Hey! Madala . . . ! Woza . . . ! I-switch! (Old one . . . ! Come . . . ! The switch!)

He begins singing a tribal song ["Impi . . ."]—an eerie feel in the light of the flickering lighter. Presently the lights come on again and STIX blows out the flame.

STIX: Aha! And Madala said—Let There Be Light!

*HENRY could be forgiven for thinking he is slap-bang in the middle
of a third world lunatic asylum.*

HENRY: How long you say you been staying here?
STIX: Me? Longtime.
HENRY: How long?
STIX: Long-long.

[Pause]

HENRY: How long is that?
STIX: Too long.

HENRY stares at him—lost. He paces about.

HENRY: Wait a minute. I gotta do some thinking here, boy . . . I got to do some quick bladdy thinking now.
STIX: Ja. Thinking is free, my bra. Coevert!

*STIX watches HENRY as he mooches about. He takes a flashy tie from
beside his mattress—inspects it.*

HENRY: I'm sorry—I'm just trying to sort out sorta' . . . what I'm gonna do now. I'm a bit—I'm a bit . . .
STIX: Deurmekaar.

[Pause]

HENRY: Okay. Look. Where can I find the caretaker?
STIX: Hah. Take care of what?
HENRY: How about a landlord?
STIX: You mean the owner?
HENRY: Man sort of—um . . . Man in Charge.

STIX laughs—thinly. Crosses to a clothing rail.

STIX: Last time I see guy like that is 1988. [*He holds up five fingers*] Five years.

HENRY: That's bullshit . . .

STIX: Aikona. Is Hillbrow.

HENRY: Where do you go to pay the rent?

STIX [*hanging the tie on the clothing rail*]: Hah!

HENRY [*a beat*]: You saying to me—what you saying is, you don't pay rent . . . !?

STIX laughs. HENRY stares at him.

STIX: Hey! Where you from, my bra? Nothing is for mahala, jong. (Nothing is for free, kid.) [*In the vernacular, tapping his head*] Use your upstairs, white idiot—vuka wena! (wake up!) [*Back to English*] He comes to collect once a month. N'kosi malanga. (Lord hero.) The Godfather.

HENRY: Godfather . . . ?

STIX: That's right, my broe . . . three rings—priiing-priinggg-prrriiinnggg . . . ! Look-out—big shit! Some people call him Comrade Kommissar—Chairman Mao. But, hey—this political shit, is safer just to call him—you know—like the top dog. He's the . . . he's the . . .

HENRY: The supervisor?

STIX: Aikona. He's the Godfather. But he's not like Al Pacino-Marlon Brando, uh-uh. He's like—er—George Foreman. George Foreman with a sore head. Mike Tyson. Mr T. You know Mr T . . . ? It's always—come, come—what you got, bra?—whatever you got—doesn't matter! Some bucks . . . Jack Daniels . . . Dulux Weatherguard.

HENRY is speechless. STIX crosses to his bed.

STIX: Whatever you got, bra. [*Clicks fingers*] Come, come—Give Me Your Slice. Golden Banana.

HENRY [*a beat*]: He a painter, or what?

STIX: Who?

HENRY: What's he want with Dulux Weatherguard?

STIX guffaws and taps his head, mumbling to himself.

STIX: Why you not eat pap, my bra?

HENRY cannot make head nor tail of this guy.

STIX: Pap makes you big. Makes you strong.

*HENRY stares at him long and hard, before turning on his heel
and heading for the door.*

STIX: Hey! Where you go now?

HENRY: Hey?

STIX: Where you go?

HENRY [*a beat*]: I gotta go find my brother . . .

STIX: How you gonna do this? You know what the time it is now? Come. Sit down. Put down your bag. Have some food.

STIX leads him back in—sits him down.

HENRY [*quietly protesting*]: No, it's . . .

STIX moves to the "kitchen corner," picks up a fresh half-loaf of bread, a bottle of atjar—slaps them onto a plate—and offers it to HENRY.

STIX: Thatha.

HENRY stares at him.

STIX: Bread. Fresh bread. White. [*Checking the jar*]: This . . . ? This is atjar. [*HENRY stares at him, nonplussed*] You don't know atjar? You don't know many things, wena? Don worry. You come a long way and you don't know what's going on here. Is okay. [*He goes back to his paper*]
HENRY: Where can I find the bloke who's in charge?

STIX stares at him, unable to believe this bloke.

STIX: There is no Bloke Who's in Charge, my bra!
HENRY: I gotta find someone who can . . .
STIX: Listen to me! You not listening . . . ! [*Patiently, spelling it out*] Kyk. (Look.) The building—okay?—this building—okay?—is run by the Action Committee representing the dwellers—that's all the peoples who's living here. But the Action Committee is in delicate negotiations with a representative of the owner who cannot be found right now because he is missing.
HENRY: The owner?
STIX: That's right. In Sandringham or Kensington or somewhere like that— nobody knows. Some guys are even talking Toronto.
HENRY [*a beat*]: Who's this now—the Godfather?
STIX: Aikona. Aikona. The Godfather is someone else. He is on the other side. There is another disagreement at present because the Action Committee is claiming that this Godfather is not representing THEM, but ANOTHER Action Group who is trying to sequestrate the building from the owner on behalf of ALL the peoples living in this area on the grounds of lack of adequate infrastructure— lights, running-water, sewerage—things like that. Is a—whatjoo-call?—is what they call a two-prong breakdown on two fronts. Is a double dispute.

HENRY stares at him.

STIX: In other words—it's a foggop. You understand a foggop . . . ?
HENRY: Yes.
STIX: Good. You understand something.

STIX takes out a knife, moves to cut the bread.

STIX: This explains, you see, why when you come in this building—you see some people are making fires in the electric stove. 'n Boer maak 'n plan (an Afrikaner makes a plan), but a Black Man—he goes all the way, Lion Lager.

He prepares a thick slice of bread with atjar.

STIX: I know some guys who living here from longtime before. I ask them tomorrow, maybe they know where he's gone—your brother. They know every-thing—these guys. Everything. [*Plonking atjar-filled bread onto a plate*] Okay. You eat this, my bra. You don't eat it, I give it to the street childrens—I'm not throwing it away.

HENRY does not budge.

HENRY: Can't we go find these guys now?

STIX: Is two o'clock in the morning, my bra. You knock on somebody's door this time, they kak on your head—throw you down the stairs. The only reason I'm not throw you down the stairs is that I'm a happy-go-lucky. I'm what they call a night bird. [*He makes for the door, plate in hand*] Goodnight, bra.

HENRY: Where you going?

STIX: I'm going to find some hungry kids.

HENRY: Wait a minute—

STIX: Ah. You want it? Good—

He thrusts the plate into HENRY's hand. He is left standing holding his bag and the plate—still rooted to the spot. STIX stretches out on the mattress and picks up his copy of the Sowetan, *perusing the back page.*

STIX: Ai—ai—ai . . . ! Aikona—! Fani Madida—ai! [*He "scores" a goal*] La-duuuuuuu-ma . . . ! [*Paraphrasing an article*] Zane Moosa is unhappy with Sun-downs . . . ! We waiting for him. Free Transfer. Ace Khuse—Ace Khuse scores again . . . haai! What d'you think of Ace Khuse?

HENRY [*distracted*]: 'Scuse me?

STIX: Khuse? Ace Khuse? Kaiser Chiefs? [*He looks up from his paper for the first time*] What's wrong, bra?

HENRY: Hey?

STIX: Hey? Hey? Your brain is gone on holiday, my bra. Is gone to Durban? PE? What is wrong, my friend?

HENRY: No, I'm just . . . if I don't find my brother tonight, I'll have no place to crash.

STIX: Crash? Where is this crash?

HENRY: Huh?

HENRY is at the window again, looking out over the Hillbrow flatland—lost—stranded.

STIX [*Looking at him long and hard*]: What kind of malaka is this, huh? How can you come to a place after ten years and think everything, she will be the same?

HENRY: Six years . . .

STIX: Mandela is free, my bra. Soweto has come to town. Things are different, jong.

HENRY: Ja, I know that.

STIX: You know that?

HENRY: I can see that.

STIX: What can you see?

HENRY: I've noticed.

STIX: You notice?

HENRY: Ja.

STIX: What you notice?

HENRY: Hey?

STIX: What you notice?

HENRY: No, that . . . you know . . . things are different.

STIX: Different?

HENRY: Things are different.

STIX: How are they different?

HENRY: Hey?

STIX: How are they different? In what way? You say things are different. What is this different?

HENRY [*a beat*]: What you trying to do here?

STIX: Where . . . ?

HENRY: You trying to make me say something I don't wanna say . . . !

STIX: Or is it who . . . !?

HENRY: You trying to . . . you tryna' put words into my mouth . . . !

STIX: How can I put the words into your mouth, my bra? Words are not something you can eat—like bread!

STIX takes the plate from him, moves away. HENRY is about to leave. Not looking at him, STIX calls out.

STIX: I know where's your brother.

HENRY stops. Turns.

HENRY [*a beat*]: You know where my brother is?

STIX: I know someone who knows. [*Pause*]

HENRY: Since when?

STIX: Since long time.

HENRY [*a beat*]: You lie.

STIX [*shrugs*]: Okay. [*Pause*]

HENRY: Where is he?

STIX: I don't know—but this guy—I know where to find him. We go find him tomorrow.

HENRY: Tomorrow?

STIX starts clearing away the pap pot and so on.

STIX: Don't worry about tonight. Tonight you stay here, tonight.

HENRY: Here . . . ?

STIX: I've got blanket here. We can make place here. Is okay. [*Getting a place prepared*]

HENRY: No, no—it's okay.

STIX: For sure, is okay.

HENRY: No, I'm saying—it's okay. I'm fixed up.

STIX: Where you fixed up?

HENRY: Hey?

STIX: Where's this place you fixed up?

HENRY: No, it's sort of . . . [*points off vaguely*] It's okay. [*He hovers about*] I'll come back tomorrow.

STIX: You come back?

HENRY: Ja. I gotta find my . . . sheesh! [*He smiles, sheepishly—backing out.*] Thanks for the—um—[*pulling up, abruptly*] Oh, ja—er—what time?

STIX: Time?

HENRY: What time tomorrow?

STIX: Tomorrow.

HENRY: Ja, but what time? Eight o' clock? Nine o' clock? [*STIX stares at him*] Okay, look I'll come . . . I'll come sort of . . . first thing. Um—okay. See you then.

HENRY goes. STIX mutters under his breath in the vernacular. He flicks at an orange with his foot—plays soccer with it, skillfully. Goes back to his Sowetan. *Presently, HENRY reappears. He looks shocked, frightened.*

STIX: Ja? What you want? If the lift, she's broken, you must use the stairs.

HENRY: There's a guy out there, he's got a knife . . . !

STIX [*mock horror*]: A knife!?

HENRY: Outside there . . . it's a big bladdy . . . !

STIX grabs him, melodramatically.

STIX: Hey, wait—he's got one eye . . . ?

HENRY: Ja, ja—it was all sort of white . . .

STIX [*laughing*]: Ah, don't worry about him, my bra. That's Mashubane. He's in the business.

HENRY: Business . . . ?

STIX: Ja. Thought he was gonna steek you? Come and have a dop. [*Turning away*] Hey—they call him One Eye Jack. He's selling the girls from the building . . .

HENRY: Girls . . . !?

STIX: Hey, you wanna girl? Nice one? [*Indicates an ample figure*] Electric blanket . . . ?

HENRY: You mad, man . . .

STIX [*laughing*]: Just checking. Come. Siddown.

He moves to the "kitchen area," hauls out a bottle of whisky, pours a shot in a tin mug and offers it to HENRY.

HENRY: No, it's—er—

STIX: You want a glass?

HENRY: No, no—I don't . . . I don't drink.

STIX: Hey-yoh! You don't eat. You don't drink. Wena, you must say your prayers. He is coming to get you—that Big Makulu Boss in the Sky. The one with the white beard . . . the white shirt . . . sitting on the white cloud . . . all the white little angels . . . [*Afterthought*] White maid . . . [*Offers again*] Thatha.

HENRY: No thanks.

> *HENRY, nervous about going off down the passage, hovers about.*
> *STIX chuckles, watching the white man.*

STIX: Hey, witgat. My broe. Tell me something. Do you think God is white?

HENRY: Hey?

STIX [*sipping at the whisky*]: God is not white. Uh-uh. The white people, they think God is white. But God is not white. God is the Bushman. On the other side of the moon. He comes in the night . . . while you are sleeping. He shoots you in the gat. [*Indicating his backside*] Ktoeeei . . . ! If the arrow is the good one, things are good. If the arrow is the bad one . . .

HENRY [*chortling*]: Huh.

STIX: You don't believe?

HENRY: Shoots you in the gat?

STIX: Right here. [*Indicating his rump*] Tzak!

HENRY [*considering this*]: Nah . . .

> *STIX laughs, shaking his head. HENRY laughs and then squirms, embarrassed at having dropped his guard in the black man's company. He moves to the door. Stops.*

HENRY: Um. Sorry. Listen. Can you help me out with a couple of . . . ? Just till tomorrow . . . [*Toying with an automatic teller Help-U card*] I'm sort of . . . um . . .

STIX: You got no money?

HENRY: This is—um—this thing doesn't work.

STIX: What is that?

HENRY: No, this a Help-U card, but it's . . .

STIX: Help-U card? [*Taking it from him*] What good is Help-U card if it doesn't help you?

HENRY: No, I said to them in Richards Bay—before I left—I hate these things. I never wanted it in the first place. I said to them, I rather . . . ag . . . ! Gotta find my boet—my boet'll sort it out.

STIX: Ja, jong. Any man who puts his money in a video machine in the street is asking for trouble.

HENRY: Ten-twenty rand . . .

STIX: Williams?

HENRY: Hey?

STIX: Your name is Peter?

HENRY: Henry. Henry Stone.

STIX [*staring at the card*]: Who is P Williams?

HENRY [*a beat*]: No, man—ag, it's a long story.

STIX: Ja, these things, jong. That's why God gave you socks. You put your bucks in your shoes. Or by your ballas. They see you with a big cock—[*Indicating running away*]—psheeeow . . . ! Zola Budd . . . !

HENRY: Ja. Look. I pay you back when we find Steve. My boet. I promise.

STIX laughs at him, waving the card.

STIX: Ha—haaa . . . ! What's the story?

HENRY [*embarrassed*]: Ag . . . please . . .

STIX: Tell me the story. I like stories.

HENRY [*a beat, wearily*]: Ag, man. It was at the station. This bloke comes along and . . .

STIX: Who is this?

HENRY stares at him, gloomily.

HENRY: Tonight. When I got off the train.

STIX: You rob this guy's card . . . !?

HENRY: Are you mad? He took mine! Just talk, boy. All it is. Talk-talk-talk. [*STIX stares at him. HENRY cringes*] I thought he was trying to help me . . .

STIX stares at him.

STIX: Help-U . . . ?

HENRY [*this is not easy*]: I get off the train, and I haven't got any money, so . . . so I'm trying to get some money outa' this machine . . .

STIX: Ja . . . ?

HENRY: So there's this man. He's dressed up all nice and smart and he kind of . . . comes up to me . . .

STIX: He says—let me help you . . . ?

HENRY: No, he says—um—he says, are you saved?

STIX: Are you saved?

HENRY: Ja. But now I'm tired from all this time on the train and so I'm thinking—ja, well, he's talking about my savings and are they all sort of okay, you see—so I say, yes, yes—I'm saved, I'm fixed up. So then he says—Hallelujah, he says—Praise the Lord!

STIX: A—a—a—a . . .

HENRY: So now he can see I'm having problems with my card, you see, so he says—are you having problems with your card? So I say, ja, well, I dunno—I'm not getting any bladdy joy here. He says—ah-ah-ah-ah—don't swear! Hey? I say—hell, I'm sorry, I mean . . . jirre . . . I'm not having any luck getting money outa' the machine. He says, ah-ha! He says he knows all about this because this is exactly what happened to him before he decided to invest with the Lord.

STIX: Invest with the Lord?

HENRY: Ja.

STIX: This is what he says?

HENRY: So he says let me show you. Then he takes out my card and then he sticks in his card and he starts punching all these numbers . . . it comes out . . . and then he says, look—look what the Lord has seen fit to give me since I turned my back on Evil.

STIX: A—a—a—a . . .

HENRY: And it's written there, more than ten-thousand rand.

STIX: Hau . . . !

HENRY: No, so he says to me—how much do you want? So I say, no, it's okay—thank you very much—I only want my forty rand to see me through tonight. He, says—no, no—[*Mock preacher*] Do You Believe? I say—ja, no, well . . . we all mos believe, man.

STIX: Ja . . . !

HENRY: So he says—Hallelujah—Praise the Lord, what's your number?

STIX: What's your number?

HENRY: What's my number . . .

STIX: He wants your card number . . . !?

HENRY: I didn't know what he was doing, so I . . .

STIX: You give him your card number . . . !?

HENRY: What else could I do . . . ?

STIX: Hallelujah!

HENRY: Okay. Anyway. He takes out his card . . . he puts back in my card. He punches away . . . it comes out . . . it's got 8 500. He says—Hallelujah! The Lord loves you. I say, ja—fine, fixed up—can I please have my . . . ? So he takes out the card, gives me the card—says, ja—I must go home and pray and then tomorrow if I want, I can go draw out as much money as I want.

STIX: And then he—pssshhhheeow!—Zola Budd?

HENRY: No, like an idiot . . . ! [*Hitting his head*] I waited for him to leave because I didn't want him coming back to worry me again.

STIX: He's got your card?

HENRY: I didn't know it until I sorta'—you know—had this thing spitting out all the time and I looked and saw the name.

STIX spits the card out of his mouth—highly amused.

HENRY: It's not actually very funny. I had all my money in that account—four-hundred and eighty-five rand.

STIX: Not anymore, my bra. [*He crosses to Henry—laughing like a drain*] I see this guy, he comes in here—he's holding this bag. I say, why is he holding this bag like somebody is going to take it away from him all the time? Now I know. You been Saved once—you don't want to be Saved again. [*He slaps HENRY on the back, falling about now*] "Invest with the Lord . . . Are you Saved . . ." [*Sitting down, an afterthought*] The Lord Giveth and the Lord Taketh Away! [*Packs up again*]

HENRY manages a brave smile, seeing the humour of it all. A brief pause.
HENRY looks about.

HENRY: Listen—um. You said . . . it was okay . . . if I kind of . . . kip over.

STIX [*a beat*]: You mean . . . crash?

HENRY: Dos down . . .
STIX: Tiep?
HENRY: Stay the night.
STIX: Ja. You can sleep here, ja. [*Smiling, enjoying this play on language*] La-la-panzi. (Lie down and sleep.)
HENRY [*getting with it*]: Hit the sack.
STIX: S'coevert. [*Pause*]
HENRY: Hey, um . . . [*Heartfelt*] Thanks.
STIX: No problem. No problem. Is not the Carlton.
HENRY: Sorry?
STIX: Is not the Carlton.
HENRY: [*Looking around*]: Roller-towel?
STIX: Hotel. Carlton Hotel.
HENRY: Oh. Ja.

*Lights fade to blackout. Cross sound–light cue: "Jericho"—from the Johnny Clegg/
Savuka album "Cruel, Crazy, Beautiful World."*

*On full lights up, it is the next morning. HENRY sits at an upturned box eating
bread and cheese, a blanket around his shoulders. Presently STIX enters—wearing a
flashy pair of sunglasses in addition to his fancy threads. He carries a number of new
shoe boxes—an expensive haul. He stashes them on the pile of goods.*

HENRY: So? What happened . . . ?
STIX: Shhh . . . !

*He tosses HENRY a carton of cigarettes and shouts off—to some
unseen person in the hallway.*

STIX: Manalapo . . . !!
HENRY [*staring at the carton*]: I only wanted one . . .

*STIX sticks his hand into his crotch area and hauls out his wad of
notes. He counts them.*

STIX [*shouting off, in the vernacular*]: If you run away, I'll cut your balls off . . . !

*He tucks the money back into his underpants and darts off—chatting animatedly
to someone in the hallway. He reappears and immediately begins
counting the shoe boxes.*

HENRY: So. What's the story?
STIX: Huh?
HENRY: 'Ol Steve?

STIX spins around—pissed off.

STIX: Hey! What day is it today?
HENRY: Hey?
STIX: What day is it today?

HENRY: Um. Tuesday.
STIX: Tuesday. Tuesday is a working day.

STIX does a recount of the shoe boxes, examining them one by one.
HENRY watches him, intrigued.

HENRY: What you doing?

STIX glances at him—back at the stuff.

STIX [*a beat*]: Operation Hunger.
HENRY: You?
STIX: We are all hungry, my bra. Some people are more hungry than others.
[*Placing the atjar jar before him*] Try this. You like it. Coevert.

HENRY absently obeys him. STIX gets a small old suitcase. He opens it up and
begins going through several piles of tickets, wrapped in elastic bands. He holds them
up to the light, examining them. Throughout, he sings and hums.

HENRY: Oh, ja. While you were out, I think he came. Three long rings—
triing-triing-triing! [*STIX stares at him*] S'true's God, I nearly shat my pants . . . !
I just shaddap and pretended no-one was here and he must've . . . split. [*STIX
resumes his "work"*] I'm not so sure about the Godfather, man—he sounded more
like . . . Shaka Zulu!

STIX ignores him, comparing the tickets. HENRY looks on. STIX
clearly does not like to be spied on.

STIX: What you looking?
HENRY [*Looking away*]: Sorry.

STIX selects several tickets and approaches HENRY. He slaps them onto the floor as
if he is about to do some card trick—swapping and switching them
around like a would-be magician.

STIX: Okay, my bra—look sharp. Eat carrots. Which one is the right one?
HENRY: The right one?
STIX: The real one. Genuine article.
HENRY: Hey . . . ?
STIX [*holding them up*]: Which one?

He swaps and switches like mad, con-trick time.

HENRY [*taking a stab at it*]: That one.
STIX: This one?
HENRY [*confused*]: That one . . .
STIX: That one . . . ?
HENRY: This one.
STIX: You sure . . . ?
HENRY: Wait . . .

STIX: This one . . . ?

HENRY: Wait, man—I can't see the numbers . . .

STIX: Don't look at the numbers. Watch the birdie. Is like the Help-U Card trick, heh? Tsak-tsak . . . !

HENRY: What are they?

STIX thrusts one into his hand, pocketing the other.

STIX: For you. Don't thank me, thank the zabba-zabba . . . ka-tshakka-ka-tshakka . . . ! When you the friend of the machine—you go where no man has never gone before.

HENRY [*reading*]: "Ivory Coast . . . ?"

STIX: Saturday. FNB Stadium. They lose one more time—pssht . . . ! I never go again. Twenty-five bucks a seat. Daylight Robbery. I want goals. I want six goals— six goals before half-time . . . or they can all fok-off!

HENRY: Soccer-match?

STIX: Nigeria . . . ! Phhht . . . ! Zambia . . . ! Phhht . . . ! Zimbabwe! Phhht! Ons is kak, man. (We are shit.) Orlando Pirates—we the only team that's beating Crystal Palace when they come to South Africa—but there's not one Buccaneer in the national squad! Not one! Instead, we got Philemon Masinga. [*Raving off, angrily*] When Philemon Masinga is playing for South Africa, he doesn't know where is the goal. There is the goal—[*Imaginary goal*]—Philemon Masinga is kicking all the way to Jabulani . . . ! Kings Park Stadium! He thinks the crossbar, she's on top of the Brixton Tower! Boem!—La-duuuuuuuuuuuuu-ma . . . ! Ja. La-duma in Hartleyvale, Cape Town! [*He swears in the vernacular about useless arseholes who play for Sundowns*] Bring back Screamer. We want Screamer. At least Scream-er he's a Tshabalala and not a bladdy Portuguese from . . . from Spain or wherever he comes from!

STIX whips up his tickets—back to his suitcase. Begins restacking them.
HENRY watches him.

HENRY: So, did you manage to find him? This bloke?

STIX: What bloke?

HENRY: The bloke who knows where my boet is?

Irritated, STIX clumps the stacks of tickets in the suitcase, mumbling
to himself—packing it away.

STIX [*in the vernacular*]: What must I do with this idiot? He comes here now and lands me in the shit just when I was getting organised. [*Back to English*] Do this! Do that! Do this! Split focus!

HENRY changes tack—toys with his soccer ticket.

HENRY: Ja. Soccer. I'm not so mad for soccer myself, actually. Me, I like rugby.

STIX: What is this?

HENRY: Rugby.

STIX: What is this?

HENRY: Rugby, man. Rugby. You don't know rugby?

STIX: Is this the game they play, the ball she's like the banana?

HENRY: Banana . . . ?

STIX: What is a ball, my bra? You know what is a ball . . . ? [*Grabbing his orange*] The ball, she's round. This is why they are calling it the ball. A ball is not like a banana—you run that side, the ball she's this side . . . ga-dooiiinngg . . . ! You run this side, the ball she's—ga-dooiiinngg . . . ! [*He runs around playing the dof whitey chasing a haphazardly bouncing rugby ball*] Where's the ball . . . ? Oh, there is the ball . . . ! Where is the ball . . . ? Oh, there is the ball . . . ! Oh, no—the ball, she's— where is . . . ?—ga-dooiiinngg . . . !

HENRY: It's not like that, man . . .

STIX: This running around is not something you can call a game. This is not something men with brains they are doing. This is a whole lot of boere-Afrikaner- monkeys—chasing the banana. [*Imitating a baboon*] Hoh-hoh-hoh . . . ! Hey, Fanie—ho-hoh—vat hom, Fanie . . . hoh!

He is enjoying himself immensely, doing a fair impression of a baboon chasing a bouncing banana. He unscrews the cap of his Sparletta cool-drink and takes a long drink, chortling to himself. He points at the large picture of the Orlando Pirates soccer side on the wall.

STIX: Me. Football, my bra . . . soccer. Once a Pirate . . . always a Pirate! Up the Bucs! [*He makes the crossbone sign. A pause*] So you a fan of the Blue Bulls, hey? Naas Botha?

HENRY: No, uh-uh . . . I like Faffa . . . Faffa Knoetze. Western Province.

STIX [*disdainfully*]: Faffa . . . !? [*Miming a man whistling, calling for his dog*] Faffa . . . phwee-phwoo . . . Faffa, Faffa . . . !

HENRY [*sheepishly*]: No, man . . .

STIX: What kind of a name is Faffa . . . !?

HENRY: It's a nickname, man. His mother called . . .

STIX: No, bra. Now, soccer players . . . soccer players, they have names. Guys like . . . [*With great pride, these guys are gods*] Doctor Khumalo . . . Ace Ntsoeleng . . . John "Shoes" Moshueu . . . [*His voice soaring*] Augustine "The Horse" Maka- lakalani . . . ! Teenage Dladla . . . ! Those . . . are names, my bra.

HENRY: Ja. Um. Maak-a-kakkie who? (Take-a-crap who?)

STIX looks at him—they exchange smiles.

STIX: Hey, wena!

HENRY [*chortling*]: Maak-a-kakkie . . .

STIX [*shaking his head*]: Faffa . . .

STIX parks off—playing with an orange—tossing it up, catching it—watching HENRY. A short pause.

STIX [*a new tack*]: Tell me something, Harry . . .

HENRY: Henry.

STIX: Henry. Tell me, Henry. Your brother. Why you looking for him?

HENRY: What d'you mean? He's my boet. I want to see him. [*Smiling confidently*] He's gonna sort me out. He's a businessman ... own boss. No-one's gonna fire him. No, he'll fix me up—one-time. You check—I've got this plan. Got my eye on this drilling rig. To drill water.

STIX: Water?

HENRY: Ja. I read this ad in the paper. There's a guy down in Klerksdorp. Two thousand rand down—you pay the rest off in installments.

STIX [*a beat*]: Your brother will buy this for you?

HENRY: Well, no—but we can—you know—make a plan. Maybe I work for him for a while. Maybe he gives me a loan. Maybe—I dunno—we'll see.

STIX: Uh-huh.

STIX gives nothing away. HENRY indicates the atjar.

HENRY: Hey, this stuff's quite nice, hey.

STIX: You like it?

HENRY [*mouth full, chewing*]: T's not bad.

STIX: Yes, atjar. Atjar is—er—is made from ... how you say?—locust. [*HENRY freezes*] Squash locust ... brains of sheeps ... [*HENRY looks ill. STIX guffaws*]: Aikona, man. Is okay ... I'm joking ... I'm joking ...

They share a laugh. STIX drops his smile.

STIX: What happens if you don't find this brother of yours?

HENRY: No, I'll find him. [*He tries to swallow*] Utcha ... ?

STIX: Atjar.

HENRY: Atjar.

STIX watches him carefully.

STIX: So. Mister Henry Help-U Card. You come now from where? Richards Bay?

HENRY: Huh. Dead loss. Kimberley, first of all.

STIX: Aha. Die Groot Gat. Big Hole. [*Laughs*] In your stomach is also the big hole, huh? Not for long.

HENRY wolfs down his food, swigs at the coffee.

HENRY: Listen, I owe you one, hey?

STIX: One what?

HENRY [*indicating the fare*]: No, I see you right.

STIX: What? You gonna pay me with your Help-U card, bra?

HENRY: No, no—I'm serious. Me—I don't scrounge off nobody. 'Specially ... 'specially ... you know—

STIX: Underprivilege ...

HENRY: I see them right. [*He lights up a cigarette*]

STIX [*mocking him*]: I'm very pleased to hear this, my bra—very pleased, because me, myself I was getting very worried . . .

HENRY: Soon as I find my boet, I fix you up.

STIX: Ja. I'm sure. A man with such a smart a suitcase as yours can fix up anyone. [*He lifts the New York paper bag*]

HENRY [*the penny dropping*]: Oh, no—my suitcase fell apart. I was getting off the train and it—sort of . . . splat! It was hellout old.

STIX: No problem. No problem. Maybe me, myself I can also do something for you. What is your fancy?

HENRY [*lost*]: Fancy . . . ?

STIX: What's your preference, bra? I get you one cheap. You want a lockbag? Sling-bag . . . back-pack? Briefcase-satchel-moon-bag . . . sunbag . . . star-bag . . . sporran . . . !

HENRY [*lost*]: Sporran . . . ?

STIX: I can organise. We codesa-desa the price. Jus' say the word. [*HENRY laughs out loud*] Hey, what's the matter with you? I'm offering you a good deal here.

HENRY: It's okay.

STIX: It's not okay, bra. You cannot walk around with a paper bag, even if it says New York. Shit is shit—doesn't matter what label you putting on.

HENRY [*smiling gauchely*]: You mad, man.

STIX: You the one who is mad, my bra. I make you a very sharp offer here. I know my job. I'm very good.

HENRY: Oh, ja? What you do?

STIX [*a beat*]: You don't know what I do? [*Aside*] Makwerekwere. [*A pause*] I'm a middle man.

HENRY [*a beat*]: What's that?

STIX: He's the man in the middle. There's the man on this side—there's the man on that side—there's the man in the middle. [*HENRY stares at him*] I sell things.

HENRY: You sell things?

STIX: I'm a businessman. People sell to me. I sell to other people.

HENRY: What do you sell?

STIX: Everything.

HENRY: Everything?

STIX: Anything. What you want?

HENRY [*smiling*]: Nothing.

STIX: Nobody wants nothing. Everybody wants something. You tell me just now, you want a . . . whatjoo-call . . . ?

HENRY: What?

STIX: For the water . . .

HENRY: Drilling rig?

STIX: I get you one.

HENRY: Where from?

STIX: Maybe I know somebody. This person, he knows somebody else . . .
HENRY: A drilling rig?
STIX: If there is one somewhere, you can get it.
HENRY: It's not for nothing, hey . . .
STIX: Nothing is mahala. You work for me, I make you rich.
HENRY: Me?
STIX: I make you rich.
HENRY: I work for you!?
STIX: What you say?
HENRY: Doing what?
STIX: Selling.

HENRY stares at him.

HENRY: You mad, man. I've never sold anything in my whole life . . . !
STIX: You can learn. Anyone can learn. People will buy anything . . . people will buy shit if you smile, wrap it up nice and do the right things.
HENRY: Uh-uh, no . . . that's not right . . .
STIX: You never bought shit?
HENRY: Never!
STIX: Nooit?
HENRY: Nooit . . .
STIX: Ja? And last night this guy sells you a kak Help-U card for four-hundred and eighty-five bucks . . . ?
HENRY: No, no—that was . . .

STIX grabs his arm—leads him to the merchandise.

STIX: Woza . . .
HENRY: What you doing?

STIX grabs a brand new toaster box.

STIX: Come. You sell me this toaster.
HENRY: Hey . . . ? Wha . . . ? It's not mine.
STIX: Don worry—come. Stand here. You in Mooi Street. This is Mooi Street. I'm walking down Mooi Street. You sell me that toaster.
HENRY: No, wait . . .
STIX: Okay. Now, Mooi Street—it's a busy road . . . one-way . . . all the cars are going that way . . . peak-hour traffic, right? . . . Lotsa' people on the pavement. There's a guy selling apples over there . . . woman selling snuff here . . . there's someone throwing up in the alley around the corner . . . you get the picture . . . ?
HENRY: Ja, no, but . . . hang on . . .

*STIX ignores him, positions himself some distance away and launches boldly into his
routine—in this case, a rap song—as he moves off down "Mooi Street."
(It could also be a tribal song, a shebeen song.)*

STIX [*moving and rapping*]: "Honking at the honey in fronta' you with the light on . . . she turns around to see what you was beepin' at . . . it seems the Summer is a natr'l affrodisiac . . ."

He peters out and turns to a dumbstruck HENRY.

STIX: Hey, mugu . . . ! Sell it to me!

HENRY: You don't want to buy this.

STIX: How do you know? Come. Stand here. When I go past—sell it to me . . . ! [*Over HENRY's protests*] Come, bra. Get the situation here. The cars . . . the people . . . the woman selling snuff here . . . the guy still 'round the corner, throwing up . . .

HENRY: But, wha . . . ? Uh . . .

He repeats the exercise, following the same routine. This time Henry makes a pathetic attempt to part with it.

STIX [*with feeling*]: "Honking at the honey in fronta' you with the light on . . . she turns around to see what you was beeping at . . ."

HENRY: Excuse me—um—do you want to buy a . . . ?

STIX is long gone.

HENRY: You didn't stop.

STIX: You didn't stop me.

HENRY: Hey? Ag, no—this is stupid, man.

STIX: Aikona. Is not stupid. Is stupid to buy a kak Help-U card for four-hundred-and-eighty rand . . .

HENRY: Hey, look—will you just forget about that now . . . ! That was robbery. It had nothing to do with buying or selling or . . .

STIX: Come. I'm teach you. You want to stay in Jo'burg, you must know these things . . .

HENRY: I'm not staying in Jo'burg. I hate Jo'burg.

STIX: Okay—you must beat Jo'burg.

HENRY: I don't have to beat Jo'burg. I'm not hanging around in Jo'burg. Soon as I got enough money, I'm going to go get that . . . I'm gonna go drill for water.

STIX: But you must get the machine. And to get the machine, you must first get the bucks. And this is how you get the bucks. Woza . . . woza . . . sell it . . .

HENRY: You not serious about this . . . ?

STIX: Yes, yes—come . . .

HENRY: This is a game, right . . . ?

STIX: Sell it to me. Come. Be sell, feel sell . . . you gotta feel the situation . . .

HENRY: Yes, I mean—no . . .

STIX: The cars . . . the people . . . the woman selling snuff . . . the guy in the corner still throwing up . . .

HENRY: Yes. Wait, I'm not . . .

STIX [*going for it*]: "Honking at the honey . . . !"

HENRY [*only slightly better*]: Excuse me—um—look at this lekker toaster . . . it's really nice . . . it makes four slices and pops up . . . ! [*He is unsuccessful yet again*] You not playing the bladdy game here, man . . . !

STIX: You not selling me, bra. [*Imitating HENRY*] "Excuse me, check this nice toaster . . . it can make four slices and the four slices pop out the top . . ."

HENRY [*grimly determined*]: Okay. okay. You in trouble, my boy. Try . . . come. Try again.

STIX [*enjoying himself*]: What . . . ?

HENRY [*shoving him*]: Come . . . come. Try again . . .

STIX [*allowing himself to be shoved*]: What . . . ?

HENRY: Let's go . . . come . . .

STIX [*beaming*]: You sure . . . ?

HENRY: Come on orready, man. I show you . . .

STIX: You sure . . . ?

HENRY: Come.

STIX is about to start—breaks off.

STIX: You got the picture, hey? The cars . . . the people . . . the woman in the . . . ?

HENRY: Look, are you going to . . . !?

STIX: Right-right-right . . . !

The procedure is repeated. This is the worst! HENRY grabs him and thrusts the toaster into his face with a selling technique that borders on battery.

STIX: "Honking at the . . . !"

HENRY [*grabbing him*]: Hey! Check this toaster! This is a fantastic toaster. It's cheap, man. It's got . . . ! You must buy this! This is wonderful . . . !

STIX struggles free, making a "time-out" sign.

STIX: Wait . . . ! Wait . . . ! Wait . . . !!

HENRY: What . . . ?

STIX: Take your hands off me, witgat!

HENRY: Ag, no, man—jislaaik . . . !

STIX: This is not selling! This is not . . . ! You can't sell to me like that. That is not selling. That is assault. That is assault with a traditional weapon!

HENRY: You don't want to buy this!

STIX: No. That's right. You must convince me that a toaster is the one only thing I must have.

HENRY: Why are we doing this?

STIX: I already tell you . . .

HENRY: I'm not doing this. This is . . .

STIX: You going to get this right.

HENRY: No, I'm not going to . . .

STIX: You must get this right . . .

HENRY: To hell with you . . .
STIX: Stand here. Kamaan . . . !
HENRY: Kak, I'm not going to do this anymore . . .

STIX slaps him—hard across the face. HENRY is stunned into silence. There is a brief moment of "anything could happen."

HENRY: Hey . . . !?
STIX: Come. Let me sell . . . to you. Okay? [*Gently taking the toaster from HENRY*] Come. Stand over there.

Like a little puppy, HENRY complies.

STIX: I'll stand here. You walk down the street . . . down Mooi Street. Come. Let's go.
HENRY: I don't want a toaster.
STIX: We will see . . .
HENRY [*with grim resolve*]: I'm not gonna buy it.
STIX: Come. Come. Walk down the road.

There is a brief pause. HENRY changes tack.

HENRY [*grimly*]: Okay. But you watch. There's no ways you going to sell it to me, boy—no ways . . .
STIX: Okay. We'll see.
HENRY: Are you ready?
STIX: Come. Go.
HENRY [*copying STIX's tune*]: "Hodgy at the . . ."
STIX [*stopping him*]: Hold it. Hold it right there. What's that there? What's that?
HENRY: What . . . ? Where . . . ?
STIX: Let me see your shoe. Lift your foot.
HENRY: What . . . ? Ag, no—they buggered . . .
STIX: What size are you?
HENRY: Wha . . . ? Hey . . . !? No, I gotta get some new ones. What you doing now, man . . . ?

STIX fetches a shoe box. HENRY is momentarily thrown.

STIX: Wait, wait. Have a look at these.
HENRY: No, no—it's okay—we . . .
STIX: Let's try. Sit down. Come . . .
HENRY: No, no, no . . .
STIX: These are the best, my friend. The girls are gonna go mad for you in these. The best . . . only the best. Imported from Italy. Made in Taiwan . . .

STIX leads HENRY back to his breakfast box and makes him take off his shoe. He slips on the new shoe.

HENRY: Stix . . .
STIX: How's that? What do you say?

HENRY flexes his foot.

HENRY: It fits. It's fine. [*He stands, trying it out—smiling now*] It's actually quite lekker.
STIX [*a beat*]: Five bucks.
HENRY: Five bucks!?
STIX: Five bucks—special price.
HENRY: Fantastic. You gotta deal.
STIX: Coevert!

*They shake hands and STIX goes into the double-handshake—Sowetan-style—
ending with hands extended, hip-height. HENRY misunderstands this.*

HENRY: No, no—I'll get you the money as soon as I see my boet. [*Turning away, admiring the shoe*] Wow . . .

*STIX puts the toaster back, and plonks down in his park-off place with his paper.
HENRY's back in "Mooi Street."*

HENRY: Hey. What you doing? Come. Let's go.
STIX: Where?
HENRY: What about the toaster?
STIX: What toaster?
HENRY: You s'posed to try sell me the toaster!
STIX: I sell you the shoes.
HENRY: But . . . you s'posed to sell me the toaster!
STIX: I made my sale, bra.
HENRY: But that's not the game . . . !
STIX: A sale is a sale, my bra. Lesson Number One.
HENRY: Jeepers . . . ! I don't believe this . . . ! [*Pacing about, as STIX laughs*] It's just talk, that's all it is. It's just talk-talk-talk. You worse than that bloke on the bladdy station, man. It's Crooks. Chancers. Snakes in the grass, man—whole lota' you . . .
STIX: Man does not live by bread alone . . .
HENRY: No, no—the whole town, man . . . every corner you turn there's another bladdy shark . . . ! [*Throwing off the new shoe, putting on the old*] You ask me if this place is different. It's different, orraight. You can't even . . . you can't even find this block of flats, because why . . . ? because they stolen the name off the front a' the building! What they want the bladdy name for . . . ? I come here last night, hey . . . I'm asking a bloke in the foyer downstairs if this is Cumberland Mansions—he's leaning against the door . . . he's pissing in the pot plant . . . !
STIX [*shocked*]: Wa ntlatsa yo . . . !
HENRY: He doesn't even stop! I ask him—is this Cumberland Mansions?—he just—waha-aaeugh . . . ! Sis . . . !

STIX: Haai! No wonder that tree is always dying.

HENRY: This morning—when you gone out—I check outside here, there's this big noise . . . they chopping up a sheep. On the stairs! All this blood and guts . . . and they . . . they selling it . . . in chunks! In big . . . chunks! Bladdy . . . sacrifices . . . !! No, I'm telling you—this place! As soon as I find old Steve and I got my money—I'm out of here, boy. I'm history. I get my rig. I go down to the farms and I deal with people you can . . . you can talk to. Straight talk. I get them their water—and they pay me my money. That's a living. That's a life. Not the way people live in this place! It's not right, boy. Uh-uh. It's not right.

STIX has been watching him for some time. His words are like stones—ice cold. He virtually spells them out.

STIX: Hey, wena. N'gubani gamalako?

HENRY: Wha . . . ?

STIX [*slowly*]: N'gubani gamalako? Wie is jy? What is your name? Ke-mangle bitso lehaho? (Zulu, Afrikaans, English, Sotho) [*He lets this sink in*] You must know the play. You are never the same thing twice . . . like a chameleon, you are what they want you to be, but—you make the sale. Lesson Number One. Sidewalking.

HENRY: Sidewalking?

STIX: Sidewalking.

HENRY: What's that?

STIX: That's how we live here in Jo'burg. Like the crab. [*He glides sideways*] Ghwak-ghwak!

HENRY: Crab?

STIX: That's how I got my place. Downstairs. 1988.

HENRY: Bull, man. You didn't have a flat here in 1988, man—none of you chaps did. You weren't even allowed in here, man. The only way you could get in the building was if you worked here.

STIX: Ja. That's why you sidewalk, you see. Sideways.

HENRY stares at him.

HENRY: Sideways?

STIX: Is how you walk when in front of you is the big, high wall—broken bottles on top. You can't go forward. You don't want to go back, so you—ghwak-ghwak—you sidewalk. Side-walking, bra. [*Dancing sideways*] The walk of the people. Stix' Walk. Stix Letsebe. That's me. Creature with the hard shell.

HENRY: I thought your name was Sipho?

STIX: Sipho for some. Stix for others.

He goes into reflective mode. HENRY watches him.

STIX: Huh. 1988. Top Gun Outfitters. Nice pay. Nice people. Nice holidays. The best part of it all—it's in Hillbrow. Haai—Hillbrow! The Strip. The Sunset Strip. Manhattan . . . ! [*Gear-change up*] Yei . . . ! I wake up one morning in the ghetto,

I say—no, no—aikona, uh-uh . . . ! Three hours to work. Three hours home. Three
hours to sleep. Aikona! Haai suka . . . ! [*Angrily, in the vernacular*] I was sick and
tired of this bladdy nonsense . . . ! Ek is die moer-in met die blerrie chandies . . . !
(I am furious with the bloody nonsense!) All over the place, I see signs—vacancies
. . . vacancies . . . vacancies! Furnished apartments! Rooms to let . . . ! [*In the vernacular*] I say—hey, fixed up—here we go! [*Back to English*] I put on my tie . . . my
Florsheim shoes—two-tone—ziya-sparkela . . . ! A dash of Brylcreem . . . and my
extra-special Colgate Smile—[*He smiles toothily*] I walk right straight up to the
door—[*Demonstrating*] Poem-poem-pa-doem-pa—tak-tak-tak . . . ! [*Bowing and
scraping*] Excuse me, madam—if the madam would be so kind—[*Flashing his
Colgate smile*] My name is Sipho Letsebe and I am enquiring about the possibilty
of unfurnished accommodation . . . [*Exploding in a high, squeaky voice*] "Voetsek!
Hamba! Go away . . . !" Hau. She didn't like me, that one. I try once more in Quartz
Street. "Goeie middag, meneer . . ." (Good day, sir) Goenk! [*The door is slammed*]
Try again in Kapteijn—[*He becomes the white landlady*] "I'm sorry, young man—
not to say we discriminate—but, this year we are trying Indians and coloureds.
Next year, we are trying blacks . . ."—But, madam—"Don't you understand Eng-
lish? I said NEXT year, we are trying blacks . . . !"—But, please . . . ! [*He mimes stone
throwing*] "Voetsek! Hamba! Go back to where you come from . . . !"
  HENRY [*smiling nervously*]: Voetsek . . .
  STIX: Ja. Didn't work. Not even the Colgate smile. These white people. No
sense of adventure. Too many brick walls with broken bottles on top.
  HENRY: So what you do?
  STIX: I say to myself—forget it, bra—the Boere have won. [*He swings around*]
And then it happens! OK Bazaars in Braamfontein—the shop next door! TV
in the window—six o' clock news . . . ! Mike Weaver arriving in South Africa to
fight Johnny du Plooy. Heavyweight Boxing Clash of the Titans! There it was
in full colour—the red carpet, Jan Smuts Airport. TV1, TV2, TV3—Topsport,
Supersport, M-Net—Bop . . . ! [*He becomes a white TV newscaster*] "Hello, Mike.
What do you think of South Africa?—Oh, you like it here?—Good. Lovely
to have you back again. Any time . . . !" [*He demonstrates a car pulling away*]
Vrrrroemm . . . ! [*Police car sirens*] Bee-boo-bee-boo—bee-boo-bee-boo . . . ! Police
Escort—ja, Police Escort . . . ! Bee-boo-bee-boo . . . ! Carlton—Sun City—cham-
pagne, blondes, brunettes, bikinis . . . ! I look at this, I say—aikona!—Horror-nary
White . . . !? Horror-nary White se moer, man . . . ! (Honorary White cunt, man!)
Time to change the tune, bra . . . ! Time for a little show biz . . . ! Time for some
side walking! I go to my boss at the Top Gun. I say—come, Mr Weinstein—come,
jong—emergency. I get a baseball cap—sharp jacket—USA—[*He indicates writing*] Yale—UCLA . . . ! Genuine Ray-bans—ten bucks! [*He sings*] "God Bless
America . . . !" [*"Sidewalking" along*] Poem-poem-pa-doem-pa—Abel Road. Accommodation. Apply Within. I sidewalk up to the front door—takka-takka-tak-
tak . . . ! [*He becomes the expansive American*] Howdy, ma'am . . . ! Gim-me Five . . . !
[*He gives himself five—slapping hands and so on*] Right on, right on, right on! My
name is Leroy Strawberry, and—as you can see—I'm from the US of A . . . ! [*Indi-*

cating his clothing] I'm a visitor in your bee-ooootiful country, and I'm lookin' for a place to stay . . . ! Hau! She looks at me. Her mouth is like so—[*Demonstrating a dropped jaw*] "Excuse me—are you a NEGRO . . . !?" You bet your cotton-pickin' Cincinnati Red Sox, ma'am . . . ! Eddie Murphy . . . ! Bill Cosby . . . ! Sammy Davis Junior . . . ! Louis Satchmo Armstrong . . . ! One-two-three—she's got the con-tract—"Sign along the dotted line, Mr. Strawberry . . . !" [*He "signs" while singing a spiritual*] "Nobody knows—the troubles I have seen. Nobody knows—but Jee-zuss . . ." I pay the deposit. First month—smokeless . . . ! The same afternoon, I say—hello Hillbrow—bye-bye the train . . . !

HENRY [*chuckling*]: Leroy Strawberry?

STIX: That's right, my bra. Gimme five!

STIX holds out a hand. HENRY tries to "give him five" and STIX pulls his hand away. They freeze.

STIX: Too slow.

Snap blackout. Johnny Clegg's "Jericho" as bridge music.
On lights up it is early evening and the flat is transformed. Another mattress is positioned near the boxes—another "living space"—signalling that HENRY is well and truly ensconced, and has been for some time.
STIX squats on the floor in a similar attitude to the one in which we first discovered him at the beginning of the play. He is working something out on a piece of paper—it is a crudely drawn map. He hums quietly to himself. Tap-taps on the map. Writes again. Gets up and paces about, checking his watch. Irritated, he returns to his map—tap-taps with the pencil—taps a tin mug, a plate. Pencil drum solo.
Presently, HENRY bursts into the room. He wears a suit and tie and is in a state of great excitement.

HENRY: Ta-ta-raaaah . . . ! Ha-haaa . . . ! [*He waves a wad of notes above his head*] Eight-hundred-and-fifty . . . ! Cash! Hell, it was so . . . like clockwork, man! Coevert! Gimme five! okay. I park the bakkie where you said, hey—where it says Customers Only, okay . . . ? I go round to the front. I'm standing outside and I'm scared, hey—I'm thinking, no—wait a minute—what if it all goes wrong? And then I remembered what you said . . . Just ask the question and take it from there. So, I go in and I look for the oke with the powder blue safari suit with six pens in his top pocket. Zabba-zabba . . . ! There he is. Right in fronta' me. Can't miss him. So I go up to the counter—exactly as you told me—"Excuse me, could you tell me the way to Crown Mines. I'm looking for Madala . . ."

STIX [*unimpressed*]: Mafuta.

HENRY: I know, I . . .

STIX: Mafuta. You say—I'm looking for Mafuta . . . !

HENRY ploughs on, nothing is going to stop him basking in the full glow of his moment of glory.

HENRY: Well, I said Madala and he still went along with it. So. We go outside
. . . I open up the bakkie . . . he takes out the radios—one-two-three . . . he gives
me the cash . . . there you go. Finish and Klaar . . . ! Didn't even count them, man—
[*Miming a soccer kick—STIX-style*] La-duuuuuuumaaa . . . ! Shoe! If Steve could
see me now . . .

STIX [*angrily*]: Mafuta. Not Madala. Is Mafuta!

HENRY: Ag, Mafuta—Madala—it's all the bladdy same. You should be pleased,
man. I just scored my sale. I just scored my first big sale . . . !

STIX: You must get it right.

The wind is a little out of HENRY's sails.

HENRY: Listen. You can be thankful it was me there and not you, hey. He
doesn't like you, that guy. He said so. He tunes me—where's the cheeky kaffir
today?

STIX [*quietly, in the vernacular*]: White bastard . . .

HENRY: I tell him you are taking the day off.

STIX: You tell him I sit here on my gat . . . !?

HENRY: What's wrong with you now, man? You should be thanking me for
scoring the sale!

STIX: How can I be thanking a stupid mugu who doesn't know the difference
between Mafuta and Madala . . . !? How can I be thanking a stupid mugu who runs
through the streets showing eight-hundred bucks for the whole world to see . . . !?

HENRY: I didn't run through the streets . . .

STIX is getting charged up now.

STIX: And what is this, my bra? What is this . . . !?

HENRY: What's it look like? It's a heater.

STIX: Is the goods, my bra. Is the merchandise. MY merchandise . . . !

HENRY: I was cold. What must I do if I'm cold? We got all these things just
sitting here . . .

STIX: Nothing is just sitting here. It moves in and then it moves out. This is
hard cash. Not something to play with . . . !

HENRY: I dunno what's the matter with you sometimes. You got all these . . .
these things. Why not use some a' them, man? You . . . you watch your soccer in
that shitty little shebeen down the road, when you got the best bladdy sets in
Johannesburg here . . . !

STIX: Business is business and pleasure is pleasure. Don get them mixed up. Is
Lesson Number One.

HENRY: Lesson Number One . . . ? Lesson Number One . . . !? When you
gonna get Lesson Number Two? It's nothing but talk . . . it's just talk-talk-talk . . .

STIX: I talk, yes. Sometimes you must listen.

HENRY: You talk about finding my boet . . . ! Everytime we go look for this
bloke who's s'posed to know where he is, he's not there . . . !

STIX: You always in a big hurry . . .

HENRY: Please! It's over three weeks now, my bra! It's like—ag, so what? Time means nothing to you okes . . .

STIX: You not happy with the bucks, bra? You rather go out in the street?

HENRY: Get one thing straight. I'm only doing this to help you out, hey . . .

STIX: You are helping me . . . !?

HENRY: Soon as I find my boet, we quits . . .

STIX: You are helping me? Mr. Help-U Card . . . !?

HENRY: Okay, so we helping each other . . .

STIX: What are we doing here—you and me?

HENRY [*a beat*]: No, it's okay. Los it . . . (Let loose of it.)

STIX: You work for me, my bra. You get a good deal. Fifty-fifty on what we sell. Accommodation—free of charge. Food—free of charge. Clothing—on the house . . . ! [*Indicating HENRY's suit*]

HENRY: Clothing? I didn't ask to wear this! Suit and bladdy . . . ! I'm not a fancy bladdy smart-arse, man!

> *He whips off his jacket, rolls it into a ball and hurls it to the floor.*
> *STIX has had enough.*

STIX [*matching his anger*]: Smart arse . . . !? Okay . . . ! Orraight . . . ! Go . . . ! Get out . . . !

HENRY: I'm not a bladdy . . . a bladdy . . . !

STIX: Finish and Klaar! Finito! Is finish!

HENRY: I mean—hell, man . . . jislaaik!

> *STIX picks up the suit, smoothes it out, puts it down. Returns to his*
> *piece of paper and pen.*

STIX: Leave the bucks. Leave the clothes. Take your shit and don't come back . . .

HENRY [*calmer now*]: You think it's easy, hey . . . ? I mean—you think it's a piece a' piss to take a . . . a whole buncha' radios in the back of a bakkie to a oke you never met in your whole bladdy life before and then . . . and then . . . ?

STIX: Hey—witgat . . . ! [*Shoving him backwards*] Something wrong in your ears? It's over for you, this job. No more Codesa-desa, you and me—Codesa's in its moer. Vat jou goed en trek, Van Vuuren! Hamba! Foggoff! (The deal's screwed. Just take yourself on a long journey, Van Vuuren! Go! Fuck off!)

> *HENRY stares at him. A stunned pause.*

HENRY: Okay. okay. okay. If that's the way you want it, then . . . then . . . okay. [*He backs away, looking about. Not ready for this*] If you want me to . . . okay. I mean—I help you out, hey . . . ? I sort of . . . hey? [*Indicating the boxes*] I go places you can never go and then you just . . . you just . . . hey? I mean—what've we been doing these last few weeks, hey? You mean to tell me now you just gonna . . . say bye-bye to three-and-a-half bladdy weeks of . . . of . . . of . . . hey?

STIX: Those trousers are my trousers.

HENRY: Hey?

STIX: You look on the inside—what does it say? [*Jerking a thumb at himself*] Man-About-Town.

HENRY: To hell with your bladdy Man-About-Town...! You want your...! You can stick your bladdy Man-About...! [*Hopping around on one leg, pulling them off*] I couldn't care less if they Pierie-Pierie Whatsisname...! [*He hurls them at STIX's feet*] Where's my pants...? [*He looks about, unable to find them*] Where's my bladdy...!?

STIX: They not your pants. They my pants. Your pants got a hole THIS big, my bra...

HENRY [*turning on him*]: Okay, so I say madala and not mafuta—big bladdy deal, man...

STIX [*folding the trousers*]: And it's Pierre Cardin, not Piri-piri Whatsisname...

HENRY: You gonna tell me that some...piss-face in a safari suit cares less if I say...ma-shoe-shoe or...ma-shwe-shwe or ma-ma-ma—whatever, man...!?

HENRY cuts a pathetic figure in his tartan underwear.

STIX [*in the vernacular, smiling*]: Hey, witgat, you look stupid in your underpants, jong...

HENRY: I mean—even I don't know what you charfing ninety percent a' the time, man. You hanna-hanna on at yourself in that stupid Fanagalo all the time and...and—what—I'm supposed to smell what you saying...?

STIX: Fanagalo...!?

HENRY: You talk to yourself one helluva lot, you know that? No, I'm serious. It's a major problem with you. People go to hospital for things like that.

STIX: Fanagalo?

HENRY: Zulu—Xhosa—whatever...

STIX: Fanagalo is white man's language. I speak Swahili.

HENRY: Bull, man.

STIX: You don't know Swahili?

HENRY: You should learn to speak English.

STIX: I thought all clever Dutchmen, they can speak everything...

HENRY: I'm not a Dutchman!

STIX: You a Dutchman, witgat. You the Afrikaner-Dutchman who runs around chasing the banana. And now—you slip on your banana! Hamba! Voetsek! Get out!

STIX leaves HENRY in no doubt that he is out in the cold. He stands room centre, a pathetic, broken figure.

HENRY: Stix...how can I...? Where can I...? I can't go out into the... [*as if in a dream*] I need some bucks for my rig, man...

STIX looks at him, does his best to stop himself from packing up, and then bursts out laughing, covering his eyes with his hands.

HENRY: What . . . ? [*STIX is in tears*] What's so . . . ?
STIX: Hey—please, my bra—put something over those legs. They hurting my eyes, man . . . [*He hurls the trousers at HENRY and staggers about—helpless with mirth*] You got whiter legs than Madonna, my bra . . .

HENRY stares at him. The prime poephol.

HENRY: Jusslaaik . . . ! Very funny, hey . . . !
STIX [*mimicking himself*]: Hamba! Voetsek! "Ag, please Stix. Don send me in the street . . ." [*Apologising, or trying to*] I'm sorry, my bra . . . those underpants . . .

HENRY picks up the trousers, unamused. He attacks STIX, whipping him. STIX ducks and dives, laughing again.

HENRY: Shit, you . . . bastard . . . !
STIX: Sunglasses . . . help . . . ! My eyes . . . !
HENRY: Having me on all the bladdy time . . . !

HENRY pursues STIX about the flat whipping and flicking at him with the trousers. STIX plays the "subservient black," pleading for mercy and laughing at the same time.

STIX: Please, my boss . . . ! I'm sorry, my boss . . . ! Don't hurt me, my boss . . . !
HENRY: Man-About-Town, se voet . . . ! (my foot) You shit . . . !
STIX: Eina-aaaa . . . ! Einaaa . . . ! [*He freezes and points off*] Behind you, Mashubane . . . !
HENRY [*swinging around*] Where . . . ?

STIX hurls a pillow at him and HENRY drops the trousers and catches it. He advances on STIX.

HENRY: Now you gonna get it, boy . . . now you gonna die a thousand deaths . . .

STIX does a kung-fu pose. HENRY clucks like a chicken. HENRY clubs STIX with the pillow a few times and STIX pretends he has been badly hurt.

STIX [*clutching his finger*]: Ow—eina . . . eeeh . . . !
HENRY [*concerned*]: What . . . ?

He approaches STIX to see what the problem is and STIX slowly uncurls his "hurt" finger—showing him the sign. They wrestle and struggle with each other, falling to the ground—a good natured scrap that clears the air.

STIX: Wait—don't tickle me . . . !
HENRY: Say you sorry . . . !
STIX: Don't tickle . . . !
HENRY: Say you . . . !

STIX: Aaaaah—sorry-sorry-sorry . . . !

HENRY: Ja, my friend . . . you must learn to play rugby. [*Cuffing him*] It's not fair, man . . .

They lie on the floor, out of breath, both laughing, sharing the moment.
STIX becomes "serious" again.

STIX: Mafuta.

HENRY: Mafuta.

STIX: Mafuta means fat and madala means . . .

HENRY: Old.

STIX: Old. Very good. Lesson Number One—Business is like soccer. You touch the ball with your hand in the penalty area—phhhsshht . . . ! One—down. [*He shoves the trousers at HENRY*] Put on your trousers. Man-About-Town cannot discuss business kaalgat.

HENRY [*putting them on*]: Bastard . . .

STIX [*getting up and going to his diagram*]: Okay. Now come. Sit. Tomorrow we do the Big One. I wait longtime for Pillay.

HENRY: Who is Pillay . . . ?

STIX: Pillay is not easy, my bra. He's always got five or six guys and you must be watching all the time.

HENRY: Which guys are these . . . ?

STIX: Pillay thinks because he's got these guys, he can Codesa-desa the price all the time. This time—he sees this white guy—he stops with the shit and he pays the bucks. [*STIX takes a pistol out of his table-box, placing it in front of him. HENRY just gawks at it*] Okay. Now. Listen carefully. You take the gun and the gun is in your pocket. Your hand is on the gun all the time . . .

HENRY [*nervously*]: Wait a minute . . .

STIX: What . . . ?

HENRY: No, no, no—hold it, hold it . . .

STIX: What!?

HENRY: I'm not messing round with any . . . guns . . .

STIX: Don worry. You won't need it.

HENRY: So why we taking it?

STIX: Insurance.

HENRY: Gsheesh . . . ! [*He paces about*]

STIX: Whatsa' problem?

HENRY: This is . . . this is heavy shit, man.

STIX: That's right. Is heavy bucks.

HENRY: I don't wanna get involved in . . . in . . .

STIX: In what?

HENRY: No, in . . . in . . .

STIX: Business?

HENRY: No, man . . . in . . . in . . . you know . . . ?

STIX: You already involved, my bra . . .

HENRY: Oh, no—! Uh-uh—no ways . . .

STIX: What you think you do with Sarel Safari Suit? You don't sell him ice-cream, my bra. Is Criminal Offence . . .

HENRY is shocked to the core.

HENRY: Hah! Listen. Don't get carried away, hey.

STIX: Who?

HENRY [*nervous laugh*]: Look. All I'm doing is . . . I'm . . . I'm helping you get rid a' some . . . some soiled goods, that's all . . .

STIX: Soil . . . ?

HENRY [*lying through his teeth*]: I'm helping you sort of . . . you know—move some of your factory sort of . . . rejects. [*Petering out*] Faulty sort of . . . shitty stuff.

STIX: This is the best, my bra. This is Number One Shit. You won't get better anywhere . . .

HENRY [*shutting him out*]: Okay. okay . . .

STIX: You know where this shit comes from?

HENRY: I don't wanna know, okay? You gave me this whole . . . you came with this . . . Operation Hunger thing, and let's leave it at that. Operation Hunger's fine by me.

STIX: What kak is this . . . ?

HENRY: Jeepers . . . ! [*He is struggling now, it's crunch time*] We all have to close our eyes sometimes and, okay—orraight—I admit it—right now, that's what I'm doing . . .

STIX: How can you close your eyes . . . ?

HENRY: Two thousand down, that's all it is . . .

STIX: Your eyes, they must be open . . .

HENRY: There's this bloke in Klerksdorp . . .

STIX: You think God's Eyes are not open . . . ?

HENRY: There's this . . . God!? What's this got to do with God . . . !?

STIX: You must KNOW what you do, and WHY you do it.

HENRY: Why are you doing this to me now . . . ?

STIX: I know what I do. Eyes open, bra . . . ! Open wide, all the time. I don't talk shit to my own brain . . . !

HENRY [*flustered, anxious, trying to block him out*]: There's this bloke in Klerksdorp. It's 2,000 down—that's all it is—and then you pay him off in monthly . . .

HENRY paces about, trying desperately to justify his decidedly dicey job-situation. STIX turns away—HENRY is after him like a dog-with-a-bone.

HENRY: You pay the deposit. You take the rig—it's yours—okay? And then you go round from place to place, drilling for water. And then—as the money comes in—you pay him off. You pay your . . . you pay your dues. It's honest work. Honest graft.

STIX [*in the vernacular*]: I'm wasting my time with this guy . . .

HENRY: Two-thousand rand. That's all I need. Once I got that, I can . . . I can start. I can get money in and I can . . . I can pay it back. I can pay you back. I can pay back whoever sort of . . . whatever sort of . . . I can work. I'm not scared a' work. [*Getting pretty het up*] It's hard work. It's helluva hard work . . . ! You slog your flippin' guts out, man . . . !?

There is a long pause. HENRY is spent.

HENRY: My own rig. That's all I want, man. That's all I . . . that's all I want.

Another pause. STIX toys with the piece of paper.

STIX: Okay. Come. Pillay . . .
HENRY [*quietly*]: What do YOU want?
STIX: I want to sell the stuff to Pillay . . .
HENRY: No, no, no—YOU! What do you want? You, yourself? For you? You got all this stuff . . . all that bucks in your ballas. What's it . . . what do you want?

STIX looks at him long and hard.

STIX [*matter-of-fact*]: I want to live, bra.
HENRY: No, boy . . . it's not right . . .
STIX: Take the gun.
HENRY: No, Stix, man . . . we been through all that orreadly, man . . . aikona . . . !
STIX: Hey, mfo—thatha!
HENRY: Those things got a mind of their own, jong . . .
STIX: If you don't take the gun, we say bye-bye to Pillay . . . ! Bye-bye to the bucks . . . ! Bye-bye to everything!
HENRY: I can't do it, Stix. I can't point that thing at somebody like I know how to use it . . .
STIX: What you going to use, white boy . . . ? Huh!? You going to stand there holding your cock!? Look outside, mugu! Look downstairs! Look out in the street . . . !
HENRY: There are guys who can . . . you're okay. You and . . . guys like Steve. Steve wasn't scared of guns, but then Steve wasn't scared of anything . . .
STIX [*angrily, in the vernacular*]: To hell with Steve now, you idiot . . . !
HENRY: You ask ol' Steve . . . you ask my boet what happens when you . . . hell, man—he's got some hair-raising bladdy . . . "Live by the gun—die by the . . ." shit, man . . . I gotta find my boet . . . I gotta find ol' Steve . . .
STIX: Steve . . . Steve . . . Steve . . . !
HENRY: No, I'm gonna find him. Just 'cos you don't help me, doesn't mean to say I'm gonna stand around here and just forget about . . .

STIX explodes. He can't take it anymore.

STIX: Steve is gone, my bra! Steve is finish! You won't see Steve no more— never again—so forget it . . . ! For-jet . . . ! For-jett . . . !! [*Thrown by his own outburst, he takes awhile to calm down. HENRY is stunned into silence*] Steve is on the Blue Train—pshweeow . . . !

HENRY [*incredulous*]: Blue Train . . . ?

STIX: Skokiaan. Purple Haze. First it was the coke. From the coke—to the kak! [*Vernacular*] Why did he do that, man. No, man, bra Steve . . . !

The depth of STIX's concern shocks HENRY.

HENRY: Hey, wait a minute . . . what're you saying to me here . . . ? You saying that you . . . ?

STIX walks away. The cat is out of the bag now. A pause.

STIX: Steve, he was my Brother. McQueen. [*Pause*] Steve and me, we work longtime together. [*Pause*]

HENRY: Where is he?

STIX [*recollecting fondly*]: In the lift. Nineteen-eighty-eight. He says to me, ja—Stix—you can sell a pair of Levi's and a three-piece suit, but can you sell a toaster . . . ?

HENRY: A toaster!?

STIX [*smiling*]: Work for me, I make you rich . . . [*Henry stares at him*] Man does not live by bread alone . . .

HENRY [*slow dawning*]: Of course—I shoulda . . . man does not live by . . . that was his favourite . . . he said it right here. Right here in this chair . . . [*He's just worked it out*] You knew him . . . !? You worked for him . . . !?

STIX [*wrily*]: Ja. Toasters . . . TVs . . . everything. But TVs are not enough for Steve—aikona! One day—psheeeow!—he's gone to Zimbabwe—and then it's Botswana. Week after—Swaziland. And all of a sudden, it's the cars . . .

HENRY: Cars . . . ?

STIX: BMW. Mercedes. Only the best. And now he's got this big operation . . . the cars are going out and the money's coming in.

HENRY: Wait a minute . . . stick around . . .

STIX: There are other guys. Guys I don't know. Plenty—[*Sniff, sniff*]—it's not the whisky anymore, it's the hard stuff. He moves out . . . gone . . . I hardly see him again.

HENRY: You trying to tell me he's running one a' those car-racket things . . . ?

STIX: Cars are nothing, my bra. It's the Jet Set that got him . . .

HENRY: Bullshit, man! You lie . . . ! My boet was . . . ! Steve was a . . . ! My boet was a . . . !

STIX: A businessman.

HENRY: A businessman, that's right . . . !

STIX: A Middle Man who wanted to be Top Man.

HENRY: Bull, man!

STIX: In the kitchen, you can get burn. Bad . . . !!

HENRY sits with his head in his hands. He knows this is true. A long pause.

STIX mumbles in the vernacular again, angry with the guy he fondly remembered as "McQueen."

STIX: I didn't want to tell you this, my bra. [*Vernacular*] Oh, God—why? [*English*] The day you walk in, it's like Steve's coming back. Small Steve. It's like the old times. The good times. Maybe if I can give something to you—in my heart, I can give it to Steve.

HENRY has had the wind well and truly knocked out of his sails.
He stares ahead of him, distraught.

HENRY: And you don't know where he is?

STIX: Nobody knows where he is. The last guy who saw him says, ja—he went long time ago to Mozambique.

HENRY mouths the word—like it's the other side of mars.

HENRY: Blue Train is . . . Blue Train is Meths . . . !?

HENRY gasps. There is a long pause.

STIX: Come, my bra. Let's talk how we do this job. We finish this job—maybe one or two more—you buy this water machine and you free as the bird.

HENRY [*miles away*]: Morgan Bay. We always went there for holidays when we were kids. There was this little road that led down to the beach . . . and Steve's got these shells. Hundreds of them. He makes a little gate kind of thing—toll gate kind of . . . boom. Everyone who comes down to that beach has got to stop. You want me to open the gate, sir—you buy a shell. Only 20 cents. I'll give you two for thirty cents, ma'am—special price. [*Laughing*] He got away with it too. People would stick their hands in their pockets and pay him. He'd open the boom and . . . through they'd go. Wasn't even his shells or his beach, but everyone would pay up and everyone would be happy. [*Pause*] He believed, you see. In himself. He just—puffed out his chest, made his voice kind of . . . all official-like and . . . looked like he was supposed to be there. Nobody ever asked him what he thought he was doing and he never explained why he did it. He just did it.

STIX: That's right, bra. He just did it. And now, we—we do it. Come, bra—come. Pillay . . .

HENRY: This place . . . ! This town . . . ! He should never of come here, man. This place is like . . . like poison . . . it's . . .

STIX: Is terrible. Come . . .

HENRY: The wrong crowd. He always got in with the wrong . . . bastards like . . . like . . . !

STIX: Pillay. Shits . . . !

HENRY: What d'you mean—Pillay? You, man . . . ! You!

STIX: Yei! Get it right, bra! He came to me . . . !

HENRY: But you were there . . . !

STIX: One Middle Man goes—another one comes . . .

Suddenly there is a ringing at the front door. The three long rings bring the
argument to a sudden, dramatic halt.

STIX [*quietly*]: Shit . . .

A pause. Three more rings. HENRY gives him a look to suggest they should pretend no-one's at home.

STIX: Not this time, my friend. This time, he breaks the door down.

STIX moves to the merchandise. Another three rings.

STIX: Ja, ja—I'm coming . . . !

HENRY snaps—shouting, angrily.

HENRY [*shouting*]: Bugger off, man! Voetsek . . . !
STIX: Shh! Uh-uh . . . ! Aikona . . . ! He hears you, then you must pay. All people staying here must pay.
HENRY: Bullshit! I'm not paying any . . . ! I've paid enough bladdy . . . spongers! Crooks! Con-men . . . ! [*He moves towards the front hall*] Fuck off—you parasite . . . !!

STIX struggles to restrain him—the rings continue.

STIX: Mugu—shaddap . . . ! That bastard will kill you for a fucken cigarette . . . ! Witgat . . . !
HENRY: That zot needs a stiff klap . . . ! I'll kick his fat arse all the way down the fucken stairs . . . !!
STIX: Voetsek, man . . . ! Sit . . . ! Sit . . . !! Sit . . . !!

He shoves HENRY back, grabs the toaster and moves off to the front door. For a second or two, HENRY does nothing. Then he gets up and begins getting together his things, dumping them into his "New York" bag.

HENRY: Not right, man . . . this is all . . . not right . . .

He stops, looks around, and lifts a pair of dripping black socks out of the wash bowl. He squeezes them out, sniffs at them and rolls them up, carefully—as if they were brand new Yves St Laurent.

During the following speech, STIX enters slowly. He staggers but HENRY does not notice. STIX moves gingerly to his mattress and slumps down.

HENRY [*trying to sing*]: "When she-e-epherds wash their socks-by-night . . ." Nursery School. [*He doesn't look at STIX*] You ever sing that . . . ? Primary School? [*Pause*] "Si-i-lent Night . . . Ho-o-ly Night . . ." [*Miles away*] "Sleep in Hea-venly Pee-e-eace, slee-ep in Hea-venly . . ." [*Pause*] I always thought that Liepies was somebody's name. You know? "Sleep in Heaven, Liepies . . ." I could never figure out what this Liepies bloke was doing in a song about Bethlehem. [*Pause*] And then, one year—one Christmas . . . standing next to Steve . . . it was like I was hearing it for the first time—[*Singing*] "Slee-eep in Hea-venly . . . Peace . . ." I s'pose it's just the way you hear it, hey? Until the day you hear it different. [*Pause*] You shoulda' told me, Stix . . . you should never have . . . you should've told me.

He finishes packing and approaches STIX. The room is quite gloomy now in the early evening twilight.

HENRY: Here's your cash. Here's your bucks. [*He throws the money on to the bed*] I don't owe you nothing.
STIX: You won't find him, my bra.
HENRY: We quits. It's over.
STIX: There is nobody, my bra—only me.
HENRY: We all square. Leave it alone . . .
STIX: Your eyes are open, bra. God's also . . .
HENRY: Ja. Ja.

HENRY moves to the door. STIX makes a sound—an odd sound of pain. HENRY stops, looks at him.

HENRY: Whatsa' matter?
STIX [*very quietly*]: Ai . . .
HENRY: Stix . . . ?

STIX has been working at dislodging a sharpened bicycle spoke from his stomach. He lets it roll across the floor.

STIX: Ah . . . !
HENRY: Shit, no, man—why didn't you . . . ? Stix . . . !
STIX: Is okay.

HENRY looks around for something with which to staunch the flow of blood. He grabs the nearest thing—a shirt from his bag.

HENRY: We gotta get you to the hospital . . .
STIX: Aikona . . . !
HENRY: You mad, man—we got to let somebody . . . !
STIX: Drink. Get me a drink . . .
HENRY: Drink . . . ? [*He runs around*] Stix . . . !
STIX: Drink . . . !
HENRY [*in a panic*]: Stix, listen . . . ! [*He grabs the Coke bottle*] We can't sit around here . . . !
STIX: Aikona . . . ! Whisky . . . !

HENRY digs around for the whisky, finds it.

HENRY: We gotta try find a doctor . . .
STIX: No. Nobody comes here . . . !
HENRY: You going to bleed to bladdy . . . ! It's a bladdy bicycle spoke, man . . . !
STIX: Stay here. Sit here.

HENRY [*helpless*]: Bugger it, man . . . !

HENRY puts the bottle to STIX's lips and Stix grabs him with his one free hand.
After a long swig, STIX perks up.

STIX: Siddown here. Is okay.
HENRY: Shouldn't we just . . . ?
STIX: Shh—I'm okay now . . .
HENRY: But it's my fault, man . . . !
STIX: Shhh . . . I'm okay . . . I'm . . . okay . . .

STIX smiles bravely and offers HENRY a sluk of whisky. HENRY hesitates
and then knocks back a large shot.

HENRY [*indicating the wound*]: How's it feel?
STIX: Is okay.
HENRY: For sure, it's okay?
STIX: Sure-sure. [*Shaking his head*] Stupid . . . stupid . . . break the rules . . .
HENRY: Somebody should arrest that guy.
STIX: Next time, I shoot him like a dog.
HENRY: Somebody should call the police . . .
STIX: No police. [*Pause*]
HENRY [*concerned*]: You sure you okay, Stix. Shouldn't we just . . . shouldn't we just . . . ?
STIX: Tell me about this water.
HENRY: What water?
STIX: You say you want this . . . machine . . .
HENRY: Oh, the rig?
STIX: Why you want this? Why is all you want?
HENRY: Why?
STIX: Why you want to go round with this?
HENRY [*a beat*]: Ever since I was a kid. It's all I ever . . . [*His voice fades out as he stares into the middle-distance*] To see those looks on the peoples' faces. People who've forgotten what . . . what water even looks like. [*Pause*] I grew up on the plots, you check, and every year this guy came around . . . towing this huge rig on the back of his truck. It was . . . it was like magic how he . . . he held this catty-branch in his hands and he'd walk . . . and he'd walk . . . and then he'd say—here—here it is . . . !
STIX: The water?
HENRY: Ja.
STIX: He found the water?
HENRY: Sometimes they'd tell him where they thought it was and they'd be wrong . . . but when HE said water was somewhere—water would be there orraight. And we used to watch him—all the kids from all around—watching him with that huge pipe going into the ground—gonga-gonga-gonga . . . ! Deeper and deeper, until . . . there it was . . .

STIX: Water?

HENRY: The farmers used to pay him and he'd pack up that rig. His tent. And then he'd trek off somewhere else. To some other place where people needed . . .

STIX: Water . . . I want this water . . . [*The life is ebbing out of him*] This is the water I want.

HENRY: Let's do it then, Stix. Los this stuff. (Get rid of this stuff.) We don't need it, man. [*STIX closes his eyes*] Look. Look. We sell the bakkie, okay? We go down to Klerksdorp and we find this oke. We ask him for the rig. Maybe we can . . . Codesa-desa the price a little bit. Maybe do a deal . . . It's a life out there in the Karoo, Stix—there's this . . . sky! You know that you're alive when you . . . Stix . . . ? Stix . . . !? [*STIX hums quietly, his eyes closed. HENRY looks about the room, pondering his future*] The sun goes down over the Karoo . . . and in the morning . . . in the morning . . . it comes up again . . .

STIX hums, a haunting tribal melody.

Lights fade to blackout. Music bleeds in.

Purdah

(1993)

Ismail Mahomed

Ismail Mahomed was born 29 May 1959 in Johannesburg and grew up on a sheep farm in Volksrust in the Transvaal. He trained as a math and science teacher at the Transvaal College of Education and later studied at the University of South Africa. He worked briefly in the teaching profession before turning full-time to issue-oriented, activist theatre. In 1987, he founded the Creative Arts Workshop (CAW) in Lenasia, Johannesburg's largest Indian community. The Workshop, run on private contributions without benefit of government or corporate sponsorship, offers classes in theatre, dance, voice, puppetry, and theatre production to adults and children and mounts at least six professional theatre productions annually. Mahomed's own compositions figure prominently among the Workshop's offerings. He writes what he calls "issue theatre," which deals with social topics such as racism, gender equality, and sexuality, and favors short, one-actor plays, because these can be most efficiently produced and toured to a variety of venues. The inspiration for Purdah *came first from the community workers who counsel battered women in Lenasia, and then from the story of Amina Begum, a 13-year-old Indian sold by her parents as a child-bride to a 56-year-old Saudi Arabian. The feminist themes of the play are linked to Mahomed's concerns over the Indian variety of Islamic fundamentalism that has become popular in some of South Africa's Muslim communities.* Purdah *has elicited condemnations and threats, although those conservative or fundamentalist Muslims who have seen it have generally agreed with its arguments and voiced surprise at the way its message has been distorted by its detractors. The more liberal Islamic community around the Cape Province has been very supportive of Mahomed's work.*

Purdah exemplifies well Mahomed's ability to turn monologue into theatre. One character speaks to the audience, but her presence is not reduced to a narrative voice. A degree of dramatic tension is elicited from the lived moments inserted in her narrative when she reacts again to the pains and pleasures she recounts and from her periodic transformation into her despotic tradition-bound aunt. Theatrical presence is established through interactions with props and the set. The woman's words do not simply flow from her mouth to the ears of the audience. They circle or are caught by the objects surrounding her. Her words draw her toward particular concrete things, making the story corporeal as her body comes into play with her physical surroundings. Her movements and actions lead, in turn, to the creation of tableaux among the props. Torn pictures, scattered sugar, and rearranged possessions leave a trace of the narrative that has passed through her body upon the scene she inhabits. This vivid rearrangement of the space gives the added ontological weight of theatre to her words. The story leaves an afterglow both in the marks made upon the objects in the scene and the performative exertions of her presence there.

Purdah *premiered at the Wits University Downstairs Theatre 14 February 1993 as part of student orientation at the request of the Islamic Student Association. From there, it toured to major theatrical venues such as the Natal Playhouse, the Market Theatre Laboratory, and the Grahamstown Festival, as well as being offered in matinee performances at private homes for groups of Muslim women. The original cast was:*

AYESHA: Aasifah Omar
Directed by Ismail Mahomed
Produced by Creative Arts Workshop

PURDAH (THE VEIL)
A ONE WOMAN PLAY

CHARACTERS

Ayesha: an eighteen year old Muslim girl who is both physically attractive and intelligent. As the play progresses, Ayesha caricatures her aunt: a grossly ugly, untidy and irritating woman with a strong Indian accent.

SETTING

A bedroom in a modestly furnished apartment with a window on the back wall.
Right stage: a dressing table and a small stool. On the dressing-table there are two framed photographs: one of a younger man and the other of an older man. In a drawer there is a Quraan and a hair-brush. Hanging over on one side of the mirror is a red embroidered bridal scarve.
Centre stage: a bed. Behind the bed (and out of sight of the audience) is a plate of stage blood. In front of the bed there is a wooden kitchen chair.

Left stage: a single seater couch on which a cuddly teddy bear rests. Over the back rest, there are denim jeans and t-shirts of the variety that teenagers like. Behind the couch there is a cardboard box (large enough to contain the teddy bear and the casual clothing). To the left of the couch there is a small table. On it there are school text books and a woman's handbag with a sanitary pad in it. About half a metre in front of the couch there is a Muslim prayer mat. On the mat there is a big sharp knife and two knitting needles.

THE TIME

It is early morning immediately after the first Muslim prayer.

COSTUMES

Ayesha is dressed in a white Hejab (a traditional Muslim dress which is loose-fitting and covers her almost completely: only hands, feet and face are unclothed.)

Scene 1

A pre-set position: In a dimly-lit stage, Ayesha is seen standing against the window and looking out. As the audience settles down and as the lighting intensifies, Ayesha turns to face and address the audience.

AYESHA: I've been awake all night. In about six hours time they're going to take me to court. I don't really care what they decide. As a woman they passed judgement on me the day that I was born. Being born a woman meant that I was destined to live a life with others deciding for me. [*Ayesha begins to move towards the audience very slowly*] The free will that God had bestowed me with was being denied to me by men assumed to be His vice-regents on earth. Look at me. I'm a prisoner within my own body. [*Ayesha finds a position behind the wooden chair. She raises her right hand as if testifying in court*] I swear to tell the truth . . . the whole truth and nothing but the truth. But . . . I refuse to plead guilty. [*In a fit of anger Ayesha throws down the wooden chair. Slowly as she recollects herself she resumes her position behind the chair.*] My lawyer advised me to plead guilty. I will not! I accept that I am responsible for killing my husband, but I bear no guilt feelings. If I had to live my life again, I would kill him again. [*Ayesha moves towards the dressing table. She passes her hand over the bridal scarf and then settles down on the stool.*] When I was born my father named me Ayesha. He chose this name because Ayesha was a powerful woman who converted to Islam. Despite being brutally assaulted by her brother, Ayesha defiantly stood up for the truth. [*Ayesha picks up the photograph of the older man.*] It's a pity that my own father did not live long enough to see his own Ayesha do the same. My father died two months ago after a serious heart attack. [*Holding the photograph close to her bosom*] I loved my father dearly but as each day passes and as I search for deeper purpose to my life, I realise that my love for my father was borne more by duty than by emotion. [*Puts the photograph into a drawer and then stares at her image in the mirror*] As a little girl I often saw my mum sit in front of the mirror of her dressing table. So many times, I saw her silently wipe away a tear that would escape from her eye and roll down her soft cheek. If I ever enquired about the reason for her sadness, her passive reply was always the same: "You won't understand."

Only as I grew older did I realise that this unbespeakable and sad mystery was to become a part of every woman. [*Ayesha strokes the wedding ring on her finger.*] There were those who chose to differ and break away but according to my mother, they were doomed to a life of disrespect and isolation. [*Removes the ring and places it on the dressing table next to the photograph of the younger man.*] I have never experienced greater isolation than in those years of my marriage. For me, being married meant that I was to be made both sacrifice and contributor to a relationship where only the other person had real choices. Exercising my own rights to happiness and choice in marriage meant that I was disobedient. [*Moves swiftly towards left stage and strains her body as if to eavesdrop into conversation in an adjacent room and then nervously continues her story.*] The first time I ever overheard my parents discussing marriage plans for me was a few weeks after my mother told my father that I was beginning to menstruate. My mother convinced my father to delay the marriage plans for at least a year or two. [*Moves to the table, looks into the handbag and removes a sanitary towel which she uncomfortably places into her panty.*] My first period was a nightmare. In our home, we never discussed sex or anything related to it. When I went to the bathroom, I just sat there staring at the blood between my legs. It was frightening. I once dreamt that I was evil with the devil inside of me. The devil was big and tall with a long white beard. He was dressed in a long white cloak and wore a big black turban on his head. The devil was mocking at me. He was trying to get inside of me. [*Flashback into the incident*] No! Leave me alone! Don't touch me! No! Go away! [*Dashes for the knife on the floor*] Don't come near me. I promise I'll kill you if you come near me! No! Go away! [*Drops the knife and runs to the bed where she covers her head with the blankets. Slowly, she dissolves into the present and continues her story as she sits on the bed*] When I awoke from my dream, I was still crying. My mother came rushing into the room. I told her about my dream. She lifted the blankets, my sheets were wet and soaked. I wasn't just menstruating but I had wet myself from fear. My mother walked me off to the bathroom where she gently washed me. From her handbag she took out a pad and placed it in my panty. She gave me a glass of milk and sent me back to my bed without any explanation about what was happening to me. [*Removing the pad from her panty and looking at it*] I spent the rest of the night constantly feeling the pad to see how much blood it absorbed. I thought that I was going to bleed to death. [*Throwing down the pad and like a little impish girl she dashes to sit on the wooden chair.*] The next day an elderly aunt came along and offered me my first lesson in sex education. [*Slowly, she transforms herself into a well behaved and disciplined girl.*] During this time I had to assume the quiet role of a non-questioning and listening student. I was warned that boys were evil and would want to touch me in bad places. Friendly boys would get me into trouble and if I was ever caught alone in the company of boys, I too would grow up to be evil and be disliked by everybody. Since nobody ever questioned the authority of this aunt, I too worshipped her wisdom. I began to look at the boys in my class with a strange kind of suspicion. I refused to talk to any of them, and if I was forced to have any kind of interaction with them which was enforced by the teacher, I would go home with biting guilt feelings. My first menstruation brought with it an endless complication of my life. [*She moves to the couch and pulls out a box. She places the teddy bear and school books in the box.*] At the end of that year, I was informed that I would no longer be allowed to go to school. My brilliant academic achievements did not matter. The cuddly dolls and teddy bears which added an interesting dimension to my room were removed and given to a younger niece. [*Places the casual clothes into the same box and places the box behind the dressing table*] The tops and trousers that I sometimes wore were removed from my cupboard and replaced by a whole new range of full length hand sewn dresses. [*From a drawer she takes out beautifully embroidered full length dresses.*] They were beautiful and made from the most delicate fabrics and adorned with the most impressive embroidery. I was told that I looked like a princess in these dresses. But what use is there in looking like a princess when her outer beauty hides the pain in her heart? [*Places the dresses back in the drawer. Removes the yashmak from her head. Passes her fingers gently through her hair. Becomes aware of her image in the mirror and then slowly draws the yashmak over her head*] I was made to realise that this shield that I wear over my head has to be my constant companion. That as a decent girl I was never to be seen with my hair uncovered. My character was being judged by whether I wore a yashmak or not! [*Pulls out the Quraan from the drawer, pages through it and then places it on the dressing table top.*] As a thirteen-year-old, I was already being burdened with the issues of morality and decency. I was abandoned to spend the rest of my childhood learning to cook and sew whilst most other girls my age were allowed to go to school and play outside till late. [*Outside the window, there are sounds of children playing a game. Ayesha becomes aware of the noise and dashes to the window. Slowly the sounds of the children fade*] I was only allowed to sit at my window and watch as the other children played outside. [*Walking away from the window*] If I ever questioned my fate, I was hastily reminded [*Assuming the caricature of the aunt*] "Rude girls like you won't get husbands!" [*Dissolving back into her own persona*] On the one hand I was being taught to see boys as objects with evil in their minds whilst on the other hand, I had to view every man as a potential husband. My only confidante was my own reflection in the mirror where like my mother, I would sit and have endless conversations with myself. [*Looking at her image in the mirror*] What a frightening image! [*Sits on the bed*] I hated Sundays. These would be the days when I would have to sit in my room dressed in extravagantly embroidered outfits and matching yashmaks. My parents would arrange for elderly aunts to bring their nephews as potential suitors. They would sit in the lounge with my parents and at appointed times, I was summoned into the room to serve tea to the guests. The whole experience was totally humiliating! I was being treated like an object for sale. [*Flashback into serving tea to the guests and then taking a seat to join the guests.*] The elderly aunt would gaze at me from head to toe and pose many questions [*Assuming the character of the aunt*] "Tell me, Ayesha-beti, how old are you? Hey ... ooh! Fifteen! Fifteen is very nice age for Muslim girl to get married. Ayesha-beti, you like to work in the kitchen? Your mummy says you make very nice biryani. Tell me, Ayesha-beti, I like the way you dress. You always dress like this? That's very nice. Muslim girls must always dress like this. This is very good for reputation." [*Agitatingly dissolving into her own persona*] Reputation! [*Assuming the character of the nervous suitor and then dissolving into her own persona*] The young man would sit and look at me embarrassingly as he stirred the sugar in his tea. I often sensed that the men who came with the prospect of taking me as their bride often trembled more than me. Had it not been for my mother, my father would have married me off to the first suitor that came along. In the two years since I had left school, I was able to turn down five proposals despite my father's continuous agitation that the first was wealthy, the second was handsome, the third was a relative. He knew the parents of the fourth and the fifth was the only son of his parents. When the sixth suitor came in search of his bride, the elderly aunt who was brought in to explain menstruation to me was brought in again. [*Assuming the character of the aunt*] "Tell me Ayesha-beti, what's wrong with you, hey! Why you being so fussy? Love? Ayesha-beti, love will come later in your married life. You know, your mummy didn't love your daddy when they got married. You know, Ayesha-beti, if you continue to be so fussy, everybody will say there's something wrong with Ayesha-beti and that's why she doesn't want to get married. You know Ayesha-beti, because of you, all of us here will get a bad name! All of us here! [*The aunt turns to Ayesha's father*] Hey, Ebrahim-bhai, don't listen to this rubbish daughter of yours. You just make Bismillah and get her married!" [*Dissolves into Ayesha's persona. She goes to kneel on the prayer mat raising her hands in the traditional way of prayer which she then rubs over her face*] After prayers that evening, my father informed me that he already decided that I was to get married. [*Rises from the prayer mat and goes to the photograph of the young man on the dressing table*] When my father decided to marry me off to you, I could neither love nor hate you. [*Crumbling the photograph*] I hardly knew you at all! [*Places the bridal scarf over her yashmak and goes to sit on the bed*] Later that night, all our relatives came to visit us. I was dressed in my finest outfit and had to sit in my bedroom with elderly women who passed their time talking about the trials and tribulations of being a busy housewife. The men sat in the lounge drinking tea and discussed their businesses. The other young girls of my age had to be in the kitchen on their best behaviour so that some aunt may notice them as potential brides for her nephew. [*Moves to the table, picks up the bowl of sugar, places a pinch of sugar in her mouth, stands over the prayer mat and spills the rest of the sugar on it*] The long and dreary evening finally ended with everyone greeting me and placing the customary pinch of sugar in my mouth. As each pinch followed the other, I wondered what sweetness there was in such a bitter life experience. [*Kneels down over the sugar and with her finger writes the figure three in the pile of sugar*] When all the guests had left, my mother informed me that I was now engaged. My father told me that the wedding would be in three months time and then he retired to his bed. I was only fifteen years old but I was about to be married off to a man whom I had only met once. His only conversation with me was "No, thank you" to the tea that I was serving. [*Picks up the crumbled photograph of the younger man*] I was allowed to keep this photograph of him in my bedroom. As the weeks passed, everyone told me how lucky I was to be marrying such a wonderful man. Wonderful ...! [*Agitatingly tearing the photograph and then assuming the character of the aunt*] "Hey Ayesha-beti, come here! Come sit down here! What is wrong with you, hey? You know, Ayesha-beti, Ahmed is a good man. He has a good job. He's a computer operator. You know, how many women will want to marry a man like that, hey! Ahmed earns a good salary. Fatma-bhai, just talk some sense into this girl's head. She doesn't know what she's doing. Ahmed is a religious man. He won't flirt around with other women!" [*Dissolving into her own persona*] My father was a religious man. That didn't stop him from flirting with other women. Despite Ahmed possessing all the qualities that everybody spoke about to me, Ahmed was still a stranger. Besides, how could I as a fifteen year old girl with barely any education relate in a marital or coital relationship with a man who was ten years my senior? As the wedding day approached, our home was a hive of activity. All my aunts were busy making a beautiful trousseau for me. The young girls would be baking. The men would smoke cigars in the lounge and at every opportune moment shout out to one of the girls to bring in a cup of tea. Outside little toddlers would play games of "mummies and daddies" and their innocent enactments of domestic relations fuelled my anxiety even further. As a child, I always imagined myself as a beautiful bride at a romantic wedding. My white gown was long and flowing and I was being fussed around by many bridesmaids. My groom was a prince and he promised to take me from this world to another one of eternal make believe. [*Moves to the dressing table and picks up the wedding ring which she places on her finger*] I still don't understand why the ring on my finger was given to me by his best man! I've learnt many times that dreams don't come true. On my wedding day, I wore a simple red dress and again, I sat in a room crowded with elderly women. [*Moves to prayer mat and sits in the traditional prayer position*] This time, the men were at the mosque and I was being represented at my own wedding ceremony by two uncles. An hour later, the men returned from the mosque and the same two uncles informed me that I was now Ahmed's lawful wife. [*Ayesha begins to gently weep in her palms*] Other brides are happy on their wedding day. It was only on the evening of my wedding that I really met my husband for the first time. The elders served us with the celebratory cocktail made from rose water and syrup and then [*Going to sit on the bed*] ushered us into the bridal room. I was terrified about what was to follow. My greatest anxiety remained for the morning when my in-laws would scrutinise the bed-sheets for blood stains. This would be my only testament to being a virgin bride. [*Sensually caressing a pillow*] The first week after our wedding was full of bliss. I would spend the days being fussed about by my in-laws and their relatives. I was inaugurated into the family and later into the kitchen where

I was to become the family slave. The only time that I was allowed to be alone with my husband was when we shut the bedroom door at night. Ahmed had a tremendous appetite for sex. Our nights were spent with him exercising his prowess at sexual acrobatics and then dozing off to sleep. I was left unfulfilled but I feared to express this to my husband lest he think of me as being forward. I quietly assumed that happily married lives were composed of sexually satisfied husbands and wives who only fantasised about orgasms. [*Nonchalantly putting down the pillow*] After a fortnight since our wedding, I first began to appreciate my menstruation. During this time, Ahmed would avoid sex and I was able to give my exhausted body a moment of rest. Yet, at the same time, I could not understand Ahmed's coldness towards me. I thought that during this break in sexual activity, we would have time to communicate with each other. Instead, Ahmed chose to sleep on the floor. When I enquired the reason for this behaviour, he explained that menstruating women were unclean. [*Getting off the bed and coldly staring at the pillow*] His reply was etched in my mind. After my menstruation, when he tried to engage me in sexual activity, for the first time I was beginning to feel a sense of resentment towards him. For one month since our wedding day, we were able to share nothing! I felt a deep sense that Ahmed was using my body for his own sexual gratification. I needed to express my resentment through denying myself to him. I began to make excuses like: "I'm tired . . . I have a headache . . . my body is aching." No matter how hard I tried to conjure up excuses, I always gave in at the end. This little exercise would only result in Ahmed becoming more vulgar and abusive towards me. Only once did I try to physically resist and Ahmed . . . [*Flashback into being assaulted by Ahmed and then slowly dissolving into the present*] As the weeks progressed, I learnt from other wives that it was not unusual to receive a beating. That one was to accept it as part and parcel of wedded bliss. [*Pause*] After eight weeks, Ahmed took me to visit my parents. My father and Ahmed spent hours discussing the tenets of religion. My mother and I worked quietly in the kitchen preparing the evening meal. Somehow, I knew that between our silence, my mother shared my unhappiness. Yet, under the power of my father she felt helpless to intervene. As I left my parents' home that evening, I felt a deep sense of remorse at the blossoming relationship between my father and his son-in-law. I felt angered that my father was becoming increasingly blind to the widening divide between father and daughter. I was beginning to view everyone as a suspect for my unhappiness. When I decided to confide my unhappiness to my mother-in-law, she chided me for being spoilt and overly demanding. Later that evening, she reported my confession to Ahmed and she watched unhesitatingly as Ahmed . . . [*Flashback into a violent assault. Ayesha falls violently over the bed as she drags herself across to her prayer mat begging Ahmed for forgiveness, her face and hands are covered in blood. As Ayesha is on the prayer mat she dissolves into the present*] Despite all the hiding that I was now becoming accustomed to, I still felt sorry for Ahmed. I saw him as the victim of the same society that caused my unhappiness. Men in our society are groomed to be strong and powerful and a disobedient wife is a product of his weakness. I began to assume the same facade that my mother was so good at putting on—that one needed always to put on a happy face and that tears were to be absorbed into the silence of one's heart. I accepted that this was my fate. If my mother had bravely accepted her lot in the eighteen years of her abusive marriage to my father, how could I deny my own after only two months of marital bliss? [*Moves to the dressing table as she looks at her image in the mirror, her hands move sensually to her belly*] Anyone could tell that my silent acceptance would be shortlived. I became extremely anxious when I did not have my monthly period. Pregnancy . . . the thought shot through my head like a bolt of lightning. I spent every opportune moment praying that this wasn't true. As much as I thought that perhaps this baby would provide me with the insurmountable companionship and happiness that I so longed for, there was always the fear that my baby would grow up to be a girl . . . subject to the same misery as most women in our society. I did not want to bring a girl into this world knowing that she may curse me the same way that I sometimes curse my own mother. On the other hand, my in-laws were placing increasing pressure on us to honour them with a grand-child. [*Goes back to the prayer mat, picks up the knitting needle and caresses it*] Approximately seven weeks have passed since my last period . . . [*Flashback: Slowly pushes the needles under her dress and screams painfully as she aborts the foetus. She collapses over the prayer mat. Slowly regains her composure*] When I awoke, a pair of masculine hands gently caressed my forehead. Was it Ahmed? Or, was it just a dream? There was no need for me to explain my ailment to my doctor. He knew that I had stupidly aborted my baby. Instead we spent the hour talking about my unhappiness. Before I left his surgery, he made me promise that I would never attempt to abort my baby on my own. I made him pledge that he would not utter a word of this to my in-laws, my parents or even to my husband. [*Moves to sit on the wooden chair*] My in-laws sent me for two weeks to my parents home to recuperate. I began to have increasing difficulties trying to fall asleep. I began to have nightmares of babies choking and screaming for help. One night I dreamt [*Stands on the chair and replays the incident as she relays it*] that I was in a cemetery encircled by the graves of little babies. They were all girls. I tried to run but I couldn't get out of the cemetery. [*Sounds of crying babies*] One by one, more crying babies began to rise from their graves. They were soaked in blood. The babies joined hands and formed a barricade around me. They began to move closer and closer to me. I tried to run but I could not escape. Then, the baby who was bleeding the most came forward and she placed a white rose in my hands. One after the other, all the others followed. [*The crying dissolves into laughter*] There was something very strange about the way they went back to rest in their graves. The babies weren't crying any longer and the blood. . . . it just disappeared. The white roses that the babies gave me . . . there was something unusual about them too. Not a single stem had a thorn on it. [*The laughter fades into silence. Becoming aware of herself standing on the chair, she slowly goes back to sitting on the chair*] In the two weeks that I spent recuperating at my mother's home, Ahmed visited me once. We spent most of the time with him telling me how difficult his mother was finding it trying to cope with all the housework. Her arthritis was severe. There were times that I wished that her arthritis would spread to her jaw. This would be the only way to keep her from her endless nagging. Yet, I often wiped this thought from my mind for fear that if she were to become completely bed-ridden, and that in attempting to nurse her, she might just bite the hand that feeds her. [*Despondently going to sit at the dressing table*] Five months have passed since I have shared any kind of sexual intimacy with my dear husband. I've come to realise that romantic marriages are only found in dreams and in story books. When I look at other married women, I know that behind their smiles rests volumes of agony. Yet, when I see their beautiful homes with antique furniture and rolling gardens, with healthy children and husbands who are seen at their sides all the time. I too, want to be like them ... in beautiful dresses and attractive hairstyles. I want to run in the fields and feel the wind blowing through my hair. Even if I was given this freedom for one day in a year, I wouldn't mind waiting for twelve months just to cherish it again. [*Outside there is laughter of children. Ayesha dashes to the window to have a look. As she does so, the children play a game singing "Ms Johnson had a baby." Ayesha becomes aware of the baby that she had aborted and slowly moves away from the window to the dressing table*] Just before our first wedding anniversary, my mother-in-law began to express fears that I may not be able to bless her with a grand-child. At social functions she spent much time pointing out other girls ... prospective second brides for my dear husband. When I expressed my shock to Ahmed about his mother's intentions, he clearly pointed out to me that under Islamic law he was entitled to have four wives. I accepted his reply with an angry disbelief. Yet, I consoled myself in thinking that if this were to happen, I would not be alone in my agony. His four brides could each offer the others a shoulder to cry on. While Ahmed went out scouting for the bride who would satisfy his mother, I had to sit at home. When people enquired about me, he simply told them that I chose to stay in purdah. While Ahmed was away, I began to silently play a game of my own. I found escape in my fantasies. My youthful mind would conjure up romantic sexual liaisons with some of Ahmed's best friends. One day, when Ahmed and his mother had gone visiting, one of Ahmed's best friends came looking for him. Ridwaan came to look for Ahmed but found me instead. As he sat in the lounge waiting for Ahmed whom I knew would be away for three hours [*Flashback: Ayesha sensually undresses and recreates a passionate moment with her having an orgasm.*] His surprised eyes focused on my body and then slowly, his one hand rose and stroked my breast. The other passed gently through my hair pulling me closer to him. His soft and delicate hands went all over my body and soon, we were both lying on the carpet, breathing in unison ... my fantasies have been realised. For the first time in three years since my first sexual experience, I am now able to experience an orgasm. I feel no remorse or guilt about this secret sexual encounter with a man who was a stranger to me but my husband's best friend. Besides, how could a man whose only conversation with me was "no thank you" to the tea that I was serving, make him any less of a stranger? In the weeks that followed, Ridwaan and I met clandestinely to share the joyous beauty of intimacy. I no longer minded that I hadn't experienced a sexual orgasm with my husband. Then, one day, Ahmed came home and he pointed . . . he pointed out his prospective second bride to his mother. The old woman was elated. I wasn't sure whether I should feel angry or envious. [*Flashback: Frustratingly, Ayesha wraps herself in her Hejab. She picks up the knife and moves to sit on the prayer mat. She raises her hand as in prayer and then attempts to slit her wrists. As she does so, the children's laughter rings outside. Ayesha hides the knife under the bed and dashes to the window. The children outside sing "Here comes the bride." As song fades, dissolves into the present.*] Outside the children were playing a wedding game. All the bride's maids carried bouquets of roses. Only the bride carried a bouquet made from thorns and sharp twigs. Just as the bride was about to reach the altar, the boys came out to play in the streets. Their laughter and mockery forced the children to abandon their game. [*Ayesha goes to sit on the bed; sensually she picks up the pillow and caresses it*] That night, I waited naked in bed. As Ahmed undressed, I marvelled at his athletic body. I invited him to me. His body was warm. I could feel his heart throbbing against my breasts. I looked into his eyes. There was a gentleness that was being suppressed by this horrible society into which we both needed to fit. Then as he began to thrust himself inside of me [*Flashback: Ayesha caresses the pillow as if it were Ahmed, panting sensually and then slowly her hands reach to under the bed from where she removes the knife and plunges it into the pillow. Dissolve into the present*] Ahmed and I were still lying in the coital position but he was dead! I couldn't care less. Our marriage had never been alive. I watched as the blood covered his body and then flowed over his head and his beard. The blood flowed between our legs and soaked my white bed sheets. I began to sweat as I thought about the nightmare I told my mother about when I first began to menstruate. [*Cleaning herself as she moves back to her mirror*] My father died from a heart attack when he heard what I had done. My mother, she was there when the police came to pick me up. My two uncles who represented me at my wedding forbid her from seeing me or speaking to me. As the police took me away I turned to look at my mother. A tear silently rolled down her cheek. The elderly aunt who advised me to marry comforted my mother-in-law telling her that she knew that I was bewitched because as a little girl, I always played in the sunset with my hair untied. [*Goes back to stand behind the wooden chair as if testifying in court*] My lawyer is my husband's best friend. He posted bail for me and he got this apartment for me. He has also helped me to enroll at a correspondence college so that I may complete my matric. For the first time in years, I am able to feel a sense of control over my life. His name is Ridwaan. [*Goes to the dressing table, picks up the Quraan and returns to sit on the chair as continues to tell her story*] I am not afraid to tell my story. I will tell it again to the magistrate in court. I am eighteen years old and I am about to be condemned as a murderer. I am not afraid. I will tell my story again because I want the truth to be unveiled. [*Pages through the Quraan*] I am a sinner. I have sinned. I sinned when I aborted my baby. My relationship with Ridwaan may not be right. I am a sinner but I believe in a God who looks upon me with eyes of mercy. My God doesn't shun sinners. My

God knows that I am a victim of other people's injustices. In studying this book, I have discovered that in the eyes of our creator, women are no less equal than men. My God has given my dignity back to me and yet when I look at other women and I sense the pain in their hearts, I pray that when their husbands read the same Quraan that I do, they would realise that our God frowns upon the way that they have brutalised their women.

END

Crossing
(1994)

Reza de Wet

Reza de Wet was born in 1955 in Senekal, a small town in the Orange Free State. She majored in English and Drama at the University of the Orange Free State (an Afrikaans institution) and went on to post-graduate study in English literature at the University of Cape Town, University of South Africa, and Rhodes University. As an actress, she worked with the experimental unit of the Performing Arts Council of the Transvaal and the Market Theatre. Her first play, Diepe Grond *(1985), was the first Market Theatre production of an Afrikaans play and was praised for ushering in a new style and intensity of drama in Afrikaans. She is one of only three Afrikaans playwrights whose work is regularly shown at the Market Theatre, with critical accolades from the liberal, nonracialist media in South Africa. She has also written two plays in English (which argue for the universality of the hypocrisy and repression she explores in her Afrikaans plays) and recently translated* Crossing *for the Cape Performing Arts Board. She has won more major South African awards for her writing than any other South African playwright (including Athol Fugard). She has recently completed* Drie Susters Twee *(Three Sisters Two), a response to Chekhov's play, set during the Russian Revolution.*

Afrikaans theatre established its own insular tradition of melodramatic domestic realism from the 1930s onward. Typical of this tradition was a complete disregard of the Black majority in the country and a combative relationship toward the urban, Anglo centers of economic and political power. Even the Anglos, however, were often ignored in favor of dramas sealed within the Afrikaans community, aimed at articulating a sense of national ethnic identity. De Wet takes up this tradition of Afrikaans theatre but turns it against itself. She transforms the sexual repression typical of Afrikaans drama into a hypocritical veneer over a pulsing, incestuous sensuality. The sentimental melodrama that earlier Afrikaans playwrights used to imbue domestic scenes with a heroic, national stature she inflates to lurid gothic spectacle animated by an ironic postmodern fascination with kitsch. She reduces the Afrikaners' interest in their own national historical narrative to a necrophilic obsession with the dead, an unsavory, dysfunctional form of ancestor worship and spirit possession. Rather than draw strength from the past, her characters are haunted by unquiet ghosts. The more desperately the characters try to exorcise the ghosts, the more intensely they are possessed by them.

Crossing is the third and most somber play in a trilogy dealing with theatrical themes as well as restless specters and incestuous obsessions. In this aspect, it moves well beyond the concerns of Afrikaans drama to a more general interest in creating a script that tests the transformative mimetic powers of the actors and that examines the attractions of theatricality from a feminine perspective. To make the issues of theatricality more visible, de Wet makes them strange by focusing on the stage presence of an itinerant hypnotist and his assistant, the seductive spectacle of a hunchback, and the transformations of a puritanical spirit medium. The feminist perspective in the play is articulated through the interactions of the three women and by making the one male character more an object of desire than an agent of action.

The Afrikaans version of Crossing *(Drif) premiered at the Grahamstown Festival 4 July 1994 with the following cast:*

HERMIEN: Wilna Snyman
SUSSIE: Mary Dreyer
MAESTRO: André Roodtman
EZMERELDA: Michelle Scott
Directed by Marthinius Basson

The English version premiered at the Nico Arena Theatre, Cape Town, 22 October 1994 with the following cast:

HERMIEN: Diane Wilson
SUSSIE: Mary Dreyer
MAESTRO: André Roodtman
EZMERELDA: Jana Botha

CROSSING

CHARACTERS

HERMIEN—respectively thirty and fifty years old. Tall and gaunt with colourless hair. Her appearance changes during the course of the play and this will be indicated in the script.

SUSSIE—respectively thirty and fifty years old. Shorter than Hermien with a promiment hump. She has full lips, large eyes, and long hair. Her appearance changes during the course of the play and this will be indicated in the script.

MAESTRO—between forty and fifty years old. A tall man with dark hair and deep piercing eyes. He has a strong magnetic presence and a deep seductive voice. He wears a black tailcoat and black pants and at the start of the play a cloak and a top hat.

EZMERELDA—a fragile, doll-like young girl with an abundance of ringlets tumbling over her shoulders and down her back. Her eyes are large, her cupid-bow mouth is red and there are two red patches on her cheeks. She is wearing an elaborate, light-coloured dress extremely low-cut. Her dress and her shoes are too big for her. She wears a string of "jet" beads. At the start of the play she wears a traveling cloak with a hood.

THE SET

The parlour of the large house on the bank of a river in the north of South Africa. It is a generous room. Front left there is a bay window with faded velvet curtains drawn across it. Upstage right is a door leading to the bedroom. Upstage left in the back wall there is an arch leading to the entrance hall. There is a landing in front of this arch and three steps leading down to the parlour. Left, centre stage, there is an ottoman, angled slightly towards the audience. Middle, centre stage, there is an upholstered armchair angled towards the ottoman. Front stage, extreme left, there is a small desk and a chair. On the desk there is a paraffin lamp. Right centre, there is a round table covered with a floor-length cloth and a hanging lamp above it. At the table there are two chairs with ornately carved backs. On the table there is an oblong tin with a lid. Against the back wall there is a sideboard and above the sideboard hangs an oval portrait of two, nearly identical, pale female faces. On the sideboard there is a silver tray containing two glasses and a decanter filled with sweet wine. All the exits and entrances to the kitchen, the floor above and the front door, are made through the entrance hall arch. A large grandfather clock can just be glimpsed in the hall. In front of the arch on the landing, there is a marble graveyard angel. The angel is seen from the side with its wings unfolded behind it.

PERIOD

The play takes place in the early spring of 1910 and 1930.

EFFECTS

The characters should be so pale that their faces appear almost mask-like. Sensitive orchestration of the sound effects is of the utmost importance. Slow fade up. The paraffin lamp above the table as well as the one on the desk are burning. For a few moments only the soft rushing of the river can be heard. HERMIEN is sitting at the desk. She is wearing a dark, late-twenties dress. Her greying hair is confined in a tight bun. There are dark shadows under her eyes and her lips are pale. She is writing with a scratchy pen and seems to be making sums. From time to time strong gusts of wind can be heard in the trees. After a while the bedroom door opens slowly and SUSSIE appears. She is wearing an ankle-length flannel nightgown and a woollen shawl with long fringes. Her greying hair is confined in a tight plait which hangs over one shoulder. There are dark shadows under her eyes and her lips are pale. For a while she is motionless and then she moves slowly, as if in a trance, towards the table. HERMIEN sees her and starts. Then HER-MIEN puts down her pen and moves slowly and soundlessly towards SUSSIE. She touches her lightly. SUSSIE starts.

HERMIEN: I thought you were sleep-walking again [*Moves back to the desk*]. What's the matter with you? You look as if you've seen a ghost. [*Writes*]

SUSSIE: [*Quietly, distracting*] I had a dream and then I woke up. Now I can't get back to sleep.

HERMIEN: [*Writing*] It must be the wind in the trees.

SUSSIE: No, it's the dream. I can't quite remember it and yet . . . I can't seem to forget it.

HERMIEN:[*Writing*] You mustn't let dreams disturb you. Of course I'm not talking about visions and premonitions. They are an entirely different matter. There! Now our books are in order. [*She shuts the heavy book*] I do hope I'm not getting a headache. When I work with figures I always get a headache. [*Getting up*] Maybe some sweet wine will help. You can pour me some if you like.

SUSSIE: [*Moves to the sideboard*] What about me?

HERMIEN: If you like. But only a little.

SUSSIE carefully pours sweet wine into the glasses. She fills the glass for HERMIEN and pours a very small amount for herself. The sound of happy laughter upstairs.

HERMIEN: Listen. How happy they are!

SUSSIE: [*Takes a small glass of sweet wine to HERMIEN*]. In the bedroom you can hear them very well. They're just above us.

HERMIEN: [*Taking the glass*] Is that how you spend your time? [*Takes a sip*] I've always thought as much. That you eavesdrop on our guests and peep through keyholes.

SUSSIE: How else must I see them? [*She licks the last drop of sweet wine out of the bottom of the glass*].

HERMIEN: Keep your nose out of other people's business and your eyes to yourself.

SUSSIE: [*After a silence*] Can we look at our mementos? [*Silence*] Please?

HERMIEN: It's very late. The clock has just struck. It is a quarter to eleven.

SUSSIE: Not many, only three or four.

HERMIEN: [*Smiles*] Oh, very well then. At least it'll take my mind off the figures. [*HERMIEN and SUSSIE sit at the table*]

SUSSIE: [*Pushes the tin towards HERMIEN*] You can start.

HERMIEN: [*Opens the lid and rummages in the tin. She picks out a large round button. SUSSIE stretches out her hand and takes the button. She rubs it between thumb and forefinger. SUSSIE touches all the objects that are taken from the tin with a true sensual delight*] Marthinus Johannes.

SUSSIE: Blonde, with corduroy trousers.

HERMIEN: His eyes were closed.

SUSSIE: We couldn't open them.

HERMIEN: No, we couldn't.

SUSSIE: [*Looks at the button*] All the buttons were still on his shirt.

HERMIEN: He was stiff.

SUSSIE: [*Stretches her arms out in front of her*] With his arms stretched out in front of him.

HERMIEN: [*Satisfied*] No one ever fetched him.

SUSSIE: Every Sunday in the summer I put flowers on his grave. [*Throws the button back in the tin. Pulls the tin towards her and rummages excitedly. She takes out a pocket-watch on a chain. Swings it gently from side to side*]

HERMIEN AND SUSSIE: [*Together*] Stoffel Gerhardus!

HERMIEN: [*Clapping her hands together*] That's quite right. He was almost old. Balding with a grey beard.

SUSSIE: His eyes were wide open and brown.

HERMIEN: But dull.

SUSSIE: [*Looks at the watch*] His pocket-watch stopped at half-past ten. [*Shakes the watch*] There's still water inside. [*Holds it next to her ear*] I can hear the water.

HERMIEN: [*Takes the watch from SUSSIE*] Now it is my turn. [*HERMIEN rummages and takes out a leather pouch*]

SUSSIE: Lukas Stephanus! [*Opens the pouch and shakes it. Two round river stones roll out onto the table*] These two river stones we found in his pocket. [*Knocks the stones together rhythmically*] His eyes were open and blue and he was young. The current was so strong it had torn off all his clothes.

HERMIEN: Washed away his shoes. Yes.

SUSSIE: There was a deep cut across his cheek and a wound in his thigh.

HERMIEN: We had him for only one day and then they came: Pa, Ma, all the brothers and sisters. The wailing! A whole choir. [*Puts stones back into the pouch*]

SUSSIE: I dried his hair, fair hair that curled around my fingers.

HERMIEN: Yes. I wish we could have kept him. [*Puts pouch back into tin*] Come on then. One last one.

SUSSIE pulls the tin towards her and takes out a long string of "jet" beads.

HERMIEN: No! Please! [*Takes the beads from SUSSIE and puts them back into the tin*] I don't want to remember her. She'd been too long under the water. [*Deep sigh*] The poor misguided fools. I warn them but they don't listen. Always in a hurry. Too eager. Too greedy.

SUSSIE is dreamily pensive and not paying attention to what
HERMIEN is saying.

HERMIEN: And when the river is in full flood they must get through! What more can I do? I can only do my best. Only my best.

SUSSIE: Can you remember the one with the small fish in his pocket? The pocket was filled with water and the little fish was swimming around and around.

HERMIEN: [*Without interest*] Yes, I remember. [*Shakes her head*] When we were small all they wanted were river diamonds. Shining under the lamp. Yes, I remember. Stars, the men called them. Stars under water, stars in the sand. Now it's river gold but nothing's changed. Scabby hands, dirt under their nails. They search and sift and weigh on tiny scales. They're consumed by diggers' fever. Now gold and then diamonds but nothing has changed. Now and then, one and the same.

A service bell tinkles.

HERMIEN: [*Jumps up*] It's them!

SUSSIE: Let me go. Please.

HERMIEN: You!

SUSSIE: Yes, me.

HERMIEN: The poor young couple on their wedding night! Do you want to give them a fright?

SUSSIE: I only wanted to see what they look like. I've only seen you, Ma, dead people, Maestro . . .

HERMIEN: How many times have I warned you not to mention that name in this house? [*Silence*] You know you must keep out of sight and not alarm the guests. [*Loudly*] I'm coming! Oh, before I forget. He wants his tailcoat brushed down. Do it now or you'll forget. [*Takes a tailcoat from the back of the chair and picks up a clothes brush from the seat of the chair*]

HERMIEN gives the tailcoat and brush to SUSSIE. SUSSIE takes them reluctantly. HERMIEN exits. SUSSIE starts brushing the jacket. Then, slowly, she brings it towards her face and inhales with sensual pleasure. She rubs her cheeks against the fabric. She starts brushing again, slowly and rhythmically. She bends back and lays the jacket on top of her, folding the arms around her neck. Her eyes are closed. Her brushing becomes more and more rapid. She gives a stifled cry and drops the clothes brush. The sound of approaching footsteps. SUSSIE quickly hangs the coat over the chair. She looks furtively over her shoulder and then puts her hands deep into her coat pockets.

HERMIEN: [*Entering*] They only wanted me to fetch their plates. [*Looks at the clothes brush*] And what's the brush doing on the floor?

SUSSIE: [*Quickly takes her hands out her pockets*] I dropped it. Sorry.

HERMIEN: You're so clumsy. Poor thing, what can one expect. You should see them. [*Sits down slowly*] How happy they are! I peered over his shoulder and then

I saw her. Sitting in the chintz chair in front of the fire, wearing a white nightgown with pink ribbons. Her hair is long and loose and her eyes are shinning. The room smells of lavender and violets. On the dressing table there is a silverbacked brush. [*Smiles*] I'm so glad I could warn them before they tried to cross the drift.

SUSSIE: Perhaps later . . . he'll brush her hair.

HERMIEN: Yes, perhaps he will.

Wind howls.

HERMIEN: Listen. There might be another storm. And the river is already so full.

SUSSIE: I'm afraid of the wind. Do you remember when the wind tore the roof off? The whole house groaned and rocked. All the candles and lamps were blown out and the rain ran down the walls.

HERMIEN: And the time when all the orange trees in the orchard were blown over with their roots in the air. Right up in the air.

SUSSIE: Or when the big black bluegum tree burst through our window.

HERMIEN: [*Sighs*] Yes. A storm is coming. We nearly died of fright that night. You were covered by the leaves.

Wind howls.

HERMIEN: [*Listens*] But even if there's no storm, it'll still blow green lemons from the trees, break the shutters or smash birds against the windows. But one thing is for certain. It is bringing more rain. I could have told you yesterday. I had pains in all of my joints. Just listen to the wind rushing through the poplars. [*Moves to the window and opens the curtains*] Thin cloud covers the moon.

SUSSIE moves toward HERMIEN and stands behind her.

HERMIEN: You mustn't look! Do you want to see your own reflection? [*Firmly closes the curtains*]

SUSSIE: And why not? The only mirror in the house is very small and cracked and I only see my face in it.

Pause. HERMIEN looks back at SUSSIE.

SUSSIE: Am I so monstrous?

HERMIEN: Enough of that. [*Sighs*] Yes, our heavy task begins again. Tomorrow we must go over the nets and the hooks.

SUSSIE: I'm so tired of lifting heavy wet bodies out of the water. I'm tired of dragging them all the way up the hill. Tired of digging graves. Sometimes it takes two days.

HERMIEN: And why should you complain? The earth is always soft after the rain.

SUSSIE: But there are lots of stones.

HERMIEN: [*Sighs*] I know. I know it's not easy.

SUSSIE: Why don't we just leave them where they are?

HERMIEN: That is not how our mother brought us up. You know it is . . .

HERMIEN and SUSSIE: [*Together*] Our sacred duty.

HERMIEN: [*Stands behind SUSSIE. SUSSIE mouths what HERMIEN is saying as though she knows it by heart*] Surely you know what happens to the poor souls who drown and are never found. Who have to lie for ever and ever in the dark depths of the river among willow roots and crabs. No one knows of them. No! They are utterly lost. They don't get a decent burial [*Indicates towards the window*] with their Christian names on a cross. They know no rest but wander the earth until the last day! Is that what you want?

SUSSIE: I don't care! I wish I could go away! Far away! Where there's no water. Where there are no corpses!

HERMIEN: And where would that be? The people would point and stare.

SUSSIE: Be quiet! Just be quiet! I don't want to hear any more!

SUSSIE moves towards the bedroom door. As she reaches the door there is the sound of ghostly heart-rending sobbing.

SUSSIE: It's her.

HERMIEN: Yes it is. I'd quite forgotten about her. That's because she appears only once every five years. [*Sighs*] We must do something. She'll disturb the guests. And if they notice anything, tongues will start wagging, you can be sure of that. You know how people are. They would rather cross a drift when there is a flood, then spend a night [*sarcastically*] in a haunted house.

SUSSIE: But we've tried three times.

HERMIEN: We must silence her or at least calm her down until the guests are asleep. Did you read the full list of names I gave you last time?

SUSSIE: Yes. Every name.

HERMIEN: Did you read them slowly or did you gabble?

SUSSIE: I read them slowly.

HERMIEN: Did you pronounce them properly?

SUSSIE: Yes, I did!

HERMIEN: There is no need to shout!

SUSSIE: [*Hisses*] Yes, I did.

HERMIEN: And loud enough? Or did you mumble?

SUSSIE: [*Very quietly*] Loud enough.

HERMIEN: Then I really cannot understand it. If what you say is true . . .

SUSSIE: Are you accusing me of lying to you?

HERMIEN: [*Silence while she glares at SUSSIE*] If what you say is true, then we must think of what else to do. [*Sudden irritation*] The others are always so relieved to give us their Christian names. To be called to by their full names. Then we put their names on the crosses and there is peace and quiet once and for all. But of course there are those who have forgotten their names.

More heart-rending sobbing.

HERMIEN: [*Sarcastic*] I must say tonight she's particularly sorrowful. [*Qui-

etly] It gives me the shivers to think of her. No one would have known her. She'd been under the water for far too long.

SUSSIE: [*Whispers*] Yes, it still gives me nightmares.

HERMIEN: I know. Then you scream in your sleep and wake me up. [*Sighs*] Oh well, we have to do what our mother taught us. I believe in keeping my nose out of other people's business, but it can't be helped. You need to question her. She might remember something that can be of use.

SUSSIE: But it takes a long time.

HERMIEN: I know! Believe me I know. And it tires me out. For days afterwards I'm not myself. But what else can we do?

SUSSIE: Maybe it won't even work.

HERMIEN: The last time we were very successful. You must remember Pieter Joachim. He couldn't remember his name. Five times he manifested and each time it was the same. But when you questioned him he spoke of the storm and of the flood and of the drift he tried to cross. And just before the water closed over his head, he saw a vision of his dear mother calling to him: "Pieter Joachim! Pieter Joachim!" [*Matter of fact*] Then we put his name on his cross and we never heard from him again. But remember her full name. Nothing less will do.

SUSSIE: I know. I know.

HERMIEN: And be very careful not to scare her. Don't let her see you from the side.

SUSSIE: [*Tearful*] Why must I do everything?

HERMIEN: And what about me? Do you think it easy for me? My gift is a heavy and terrible burden but I inherited the gift and there is nothing we can do.

SUSSIE: Yes, you inherited everything. Mother's gift, her house, her pearls. And I only got a trunk of clothes I can't wear.

HERMIEN: That's only because they won't fit over your back. You can hardly blame our mother for that.

SUSSIE: She never liked me.

HERMIEN: You only imagined it. But this is not the time. Come on, we have work to do. It is getting late.

SUSSIE: Why did I have to stay in the bedroom when there were guests? She came to fetch you, with your hair braided and your best dress and locked the door behind her.

HERMIEN: How should I know? It happened such a long time ago.

SUSSIE: And why could only you go to school?

HERMIEN: I used to teach you everything I learned.

SUSSIE: Why could you go and play with little friends but I never could?

HERMIEN: I was your little friend. You didn't need anyone else.

SUSSIE: It's because of the way I look! I know it! As if it's my fault. But we know whose fault it really is, don't we?

HERMIEN: Please. Not that again.

SUSSIE: Yours! Yes, yours! When we were together in our mother's womb, you stabbed me with your big sharp bones. You crushed me with your long thin feet. My soft, tender bones were mangled and bruised.

HERMIEN: I've told you that I don't want to hear it again.

SUSSIE: Because it's the truth! And you know it! [*Cries and puts her hair in front of her mouth*]

HERMIEN: [*Gets up and sits next to SUSSIE on the ottoman. Strokes her hair tenderly*] There now! I've always been good to you haven't I? I make gooseberry jam and I stroke your hump when it aches.

SUSSIE: It's only that it's always been . . . Hermien this, and Hermien that . . . But no one ever heard of me. No one even saw me.

HERMIEN: Believe me, that was all for the best. But we are happy together, aren't we? Like our mother and tante Katie?

SUSSIE: [*Soft. Desperate*] Yes. Yes. Just like our mother . . . and tante Katie.

HERMIEN: [*Tenderly strokes her hump*] There . . . there . . . that's better. All over now. We've always slept together in one bed and one day, like them we'll lie side by side for ever and ever. [Gestures towards the marble angel] With the same gravestone at our head. That is why I told him to make two. One for our mother and tante Katie and one for me and you. So you see, there's no need to cry Sussie. [*Dries SUSSIE's tears with a small, white handkerchief that she takes from her sleeve*] I'll always look after you. Yes, always. That is better. No more tears. Come along now, we have work to do.

SUSSIE: I'm tired. I want to go to sleep.

Heart-rendering sobbing.

HERMIEN: And I have aches and pains. I know it's very late. [*Sighs, shakes her head*] But of course they have no sense of time. None at all. Come on. We only need her name and then we can get some rest.

SUSSIE: Yes. I'm sick of her wailing. I hope this will be the last time.

HERMIEN moves to the desk and blows out the lamp. SUSSIE moves to the table, climbs on a chair with difficulty and turns down the lamp above the table.

HERMIEN: Not too much. [*Moves towards the table*] At least there are no rowdy diggers tonight. But we mustn't waste any time. If it starts raining, they'll stumble in here, wet and bedraggled, demanding strong spirits of one kind or another.

SUSSIE gets off the chair, then takes the two small glasses back to the sideboard and places them on the tray as before.

HERMIEN: [*Sits down slowly. Sighs and drops her head in her hands. Sudden gust of wind. She looks up.*] Hurry up! We must begin.

SUSSIE sits at the table with HERMIEN. The rest of the stage is now in darkness and there is only a circle of light on the table. During the "seance" scene, the howling wind becomes more noticeable.

HERMIEN: I really hope they don't ring the bell. And please, if you want to cough or sneeze, clamp your hand over your nose and mouth.

SUSSIE: I know.

HERMIEN: And if you want to . . . go you'd better do it now.

SUSSIE: No, I don't want to.

HERMIEN: Very well then, let us begin. [*The clock strikes*] Wait. Let the clock strike first. [*They sit motionless while the clock strikes 11*] Well then . . .

HERMIEN stares straight ahead. She puts her arms on the table with her palms facing upwards. After a few moments her eyes close. They flicker. She starts breathing slowly and deeply and does this for quite some time. Slowly she opens her eyes. Now HERMIEN is EZMERELDA. It is a complete transformation. HERMIEN/ EZMERELDA is nervous and tentative. Her voice is rather high and childish. She looks about her with fear and uncertainty.

SUSSIE: [*Quietly*] Don't be afraid.

HERMIEN/EZMERELDA: Did you wake me up?

SUSSIE: Were you asleep?

HERMIEN/EZMERELDA: Yes. And . . . I was dreaming.

SUSSIE: What were you dreaming?

HERMIEN/EZMERELDA: I dreamt that I was flying in a swarm of big black birds. Their wings beat the air and they flew around and around. [*Silence. Intertwines her fingers and looks down at her hands. Softly*] I'm glad I've woken up.

SUSSIE: Could you . . . perhaps tell me . . . who you are?

HERMIEN/EZMERELDA: [*Scared*] Who . . . I am?

SUSSIE: What your name is?

HERMIEN/EZMERELDA: My name . . . my name . . . [*Drops her head, starts crying softly*]

SUSSIE: It doesn't matter.

HERMIEN/EZMERELDA: [*Crying*] I can't remember. I can't remember.

SUSSIE: Don't cry.

HERMIEN/EZMERELDA: I'm cold [*Shivers*] so very cold.

SUSSIE gets up, takes off her shawl, moves to HERMIEN/ EZMERELDA and gently puts the shawl around her shoulders.

HERMIEN/EZMERELDA: Thank you.

SUSSIE: [*Sitting again*] Tell me if you can remember anything. Think carefully.

HERMIEN/EZMERELDA: [*Shakes her head*] Everything seems so . . . far away. I can only remember my dream.

SUSSIE: [*Gentle and encouraging*] Think. Think back. Maybe you'll remember what happened . . . just before you went to sleep.

HERMIEN/EZMERELDA: [*Lifts her head and moves her head from side to side*] I don't remember anything, I really don't. [*She freezes and looks at the lamp above the table with wonder. Slowly she looks down at the table and touches the tablecloth*] I remember the lamp . . . I remember the tablecloth . . . I think . . . I've eaten at this table.

SUSSIE: But are you sure?

HERMIEN/EZMERELDA: [*Happy*] Yes! I remember! [*Frightened*] Who's that crying outside?

SUSSIE: No one. Only the wind.

HERMIEN/EZMERELDA: Yes. I remember the wind.

SUSSIE: You were busy telling me how you had a meal at this table.

HERMIEN/EZMERELDA: And somewhere . . . [*Looks up*] up there . . . people were talking and singing.

SUSSIE: It must have been the diggers.

HERMIEN/EZMERELDA: And you were here! Yes! [*Very happy*] I know you!

SUSSIE: Me!

HERMIEN/EZMERELDA: You looked almost the same. [*Looks around*] And . . . there were two other people in the room. A man and a woman.

SUSSIE: What did the woman look like?

HERMIEN/EZMERELDA: She was bony and ugly.

SUSSIE: My sister! Hermien.

HERMIEN/EZMERELDA: [*Frightened*] What's that?

SUSSIE: I've told you. It's the wind.

HERMIEN/EZMERELDA: No, it's something else. Something that frightens me.

SUSSIE: You must be hearing the river. The water washing over the stones.

HERMIEN/EZMERELDA: [*Softly*] Cold . . . deep . . . dark water. [*Gives a cry*]

SUSSIE: But don't be afraid. You're in here with me, you're safe.

HERMIEN/EZMERELDA: Yes. I'm here with you.

SUSSIE: [*Visibly agitated*] Now tell me . . . about the man. You said there was a man.

HERMIEN/EZMERELDA: Yes. [*Lifts her head as if she can see him*]

SUSSIE: [*Urgently*] What does he look like? Tell me!

HERMIEN/EZMERELDA: He's tall. I have to look up at him. He wears a cloak and a high black hat. His hair is dark and wet . . . his eyes . . . are deep . . . [*A heartfelt cry. Rising from her chair*] I'm here Maestro!

Sharp intake of breath from SUSSIE.

HERMIEN/EZMERELDA: I'm here! [*Looks sad. Sits down and turns her head away*]

SUSSIE: Yes . . . Yes . . . Maestro . . . I've never forgotten him . . . he's the only man I've seen . . . Maestro . . . then you must be . . . what is it again . . . a strange name . . . Espranza! No, that's wrong. It was something else. Now I know!

HERMIEN/EZMERELDA and SUSSIE: [*Together*] Ezmerelda!

SUSSIE: And you're Ezmerelda. I'm so sorry that I didn't recognise you.

HERMIEN/EZMERELDA: [*Sad. Her head dropping*] But . . . it's not my real name.

SUSSIE: Never mind. Everything will turn out well in the end, you'll see. Think again. Think back. Try and remember.

HERMIEN/EZMERELDA: Yes . . . I remember . . . [*As though she is living what she describes*] A carriage with two horses . . . I'm sitting close to him with my head on his shoulder. The night is very very dark. The coach rocks from side to side in the rain in the howling wind. We stop next to the road and wait for the storm to pass. Everything shakes and trembles. There is a light and then darkness. Light and then darkness. Maestro gets out to look at the horses. I'm afraid in the coach. When he comes back, his hair is wet and water runs down his throat. The rumbling gets louder. The whole coach creaks and rattles. I cry and he holds me close. I put my arms around his neck and press my head against his chest. I can feel his heart beating but I can't bear it. He rocks me and kisses me on my eyelids. First on the one . . . then on the other. The rain grows softer. The thunder moves farther away. We drive on but it's uphill and the mud is thick. We see a light on the hill and a sign hanging from two chains. Maestro shouts to the coachman to stop. He gets out and holds a lantern in front of the sign. He reads it out: "Beware! Do not cross the drift when the river is in flood. Find refuge here. Bed and board."

SUSSIE: Our sign.

HERMIEN/EZMERLEDA: Then Maestro says that we must stop there for a bit and the coach drives through a big iron gate.

SUSSIE: Our gate.

HERMIEN/EZMERELDA: We drive down a narrow road and stop in front of a house. The house is dark, but not quite! Somewhere, right up there, we see a light.

SUSSIE: I remember the diggers gambled all night.

HERMIEN/EZMERELDA: We get out. My shoes sink into the mud. My train's heavy and wet. Maestro tells the coachman to mind the horses. He lifts me in his arms and carries me to the steps. He kicks against the door and cries: "Open the door!"

HERMIEN AND THE VOICE OF MAESTRO: [*Together*] Open the door!

The lights fade. In the darkness the sound can be heard of someone kicking against a heavy door. The sound is loud and resounding. The sound of the wind is slowly faded out. The sound of the river grows slightly louder.

MAESTRO: [*In the darkness. Off*] Open the door!

For a moment the stage is illuminated by a flash of lightning.

MAESTRO: [*As the lights come up, MAESTRO enters with EZMERELDA in his arms. He is carrying a lantern*] Is there anyone here? Please answer. Is anyone here?

The sound of muted thunder.

EZMERELDA: [*Snivels*] Not a living soul!

HERMIEN: [*Calling from the bedroom*] Please wait! I will be with you presently!

MAESTRO carries EZMERELDA to the ottoman, bends forward as if wanting to put her down gently, then suddenly drops her.

EZMERELDA: Oh! You've hurt me! [*Tearful*] Why did you do that?

MAESTRO: [*While he takes off his cloak and drapes it over a chair*] You are heavy and I am tired. [*He hangs his hat over the angel's head*]

EZMERELDA: I think something is broken. [*Moans*]

MAESTRO: [*Lifts the lantern which throws light patterns over the floor and against the walls*] Not a bad place.

EZMERELDA: Maybe it's my back. Maybe my back's broken.

MAESTRO: [*Puts down the lantern, crosses to the ottoman*] Then you will have to be carried around like a rag doll. [*Bends over her. Strokes her arms. Softly, with his face near hers*] I would have to do everything for you. Dress you . . . and undress you. Wash you . . . and put you to bed. [*Puts his hands under her dress*] Can you . . . feel that?

EZMERLEDA: Yes.

MAESTRO: [*Moves his hand further up her legs*] And . . . that?

EZMERLEDA: Yes.

MAESTRO: Are you sure?

EZMERELDA: Oh yes.

MAESTRO: [*Gets up quickly*] Then it can hardly be serious. [*Moves to the window and looks out*]

EZMERELDA: You said you would be gentle. You said.

MAESTRO: Did I?

EZMERELDA: Yes. And you promised.

MAESTRO: It must have slipped my mind.

EZMERELDA: You promised. [*She cries*] You know you did.

MAESTRO: [*Quickly to the ottoman. Sits and holds Ezmerelda.*]

The room is illuminated by lightning.

EZMERELDA: [*Her head against his chest*] I'm so cold. And hungry.

MAESTRO: [*Playing with her hair*]

EZMERELDA: [*Whining*] I said I was cold and hungry. [*Sniffs*]

MAESTRO: [*Grabs her hair and pulls her head back*] What did I tell you?

Muted thunder.

EZMERELDA: I . . . can't remember.

MAESTRO: I told you to stop whining and snivelling. That is what I said is it not?

EZMERELDA: Yes yes . . .

MAESTRO: Never mind. [*He kisses her neck*] In a short while we will be there. I will carry you up the stairs. Candles will burn in the bedroom and I will lie you down. With your hair spread over the pillow. And then . . . we will tell each other all our secrets.

EZMERELDA: Yes. Oh yes. [*She embraces him*]

*HERMIEN enters. Her hair is no longer grey and she is wearing
a plain victorian dress with a train.*

HERMIEN: [*At the bedroom door. Clearing her throat*] I'm glad to be able to give you refuge on such a night, Meneer. You did close the door behind you? The wind blows leaves and pods into the house.

MAESTRO: I did, kind lady. I am so sorry that we took the liberty of entering uninvited, but I did knock.

HERMIEN: Well you are lucky, Meneer. [*Lights the lamp on the desk*] Earlier this evening a strong gust of wind broke the lock. If you hadn't come in, I might never have heard you.

MAESTRO: I am most deeply sorry that we have to disturb you at the dead of night.

HERMIEN: Not at all, not at all. I am grateful that you're safe. I only hope you didn't cross the river. [*Moves to the table*]

MAESTRO: No, dear lady. We came from the west. [*Blows out his lantern*]

HERMIEN: You must be wet and cold, Meneer. [*Stands on a chair and lights the lamp above the table*]

MAESTRO: Food and wine! That will make us feel much better.

HERMIEN: Of course. [*Gets off chair. Moves to the sideboard*] There is still some roast chicken and half a bottle of wine. [*Puts the matches in the drawer and closes it*] I'll stoke the coals and your food will soon be hot.

MAESTRO bows formally. HERMIEN exits to kitchen.

MAESTRO: [*Commandingly*] Take off your cloak. [*Helps EZMERELDA to take off her cloak. Takes her hands and rubs them between his own*] Like two frozen little birds.

EZMERELDA: [*Frightened*] What's that! That terrible rushing sound!

MAESTRO: Only the river coming down.

EZMERELDA: I've always been afraid of water.

MAESTRO: There's nothing to be afraid of. [*Holds her*] Don't I always take care of you? [*Caresses her face with his lips*]

HERMIEN: [*Off*] Luckily the oven was still warm. [*Appears in the arch carrying a tray. Clears her throat. There is half a bottle of wine and two glasses on the tray. She puts the wine and the glasses on the table and the tray on the sideboard*]

MAESTRO: How splendid. Let me pour. Will you partake?

HERMIEN: No it is much too late for me, Meneer.

The room is illuminated by faint lightning.

HERMIEN: I hope this storm has passed. It was terrible while it lasted. And an owl was blown against the window.

MAESTRO: [*Pours two glasses of wine and gives one to EZMERELDA*] Drink this down and it will make you feel warm.

The bedroom door opens. SUSSIE stands in the door. She is wearing a long white nightgown and an embroidered Victorian shawl with long silk fringes. Her long hair is loose. The shadows under her eyes are gone and her full lips are red.

SUSSIE: I . . . heard voices.

HERMIEN: [*Quickly crossing to SUSSIE. Hissing*] Can't you see? We have guests!

SUSSIE: You're hurting me!

MAESTRO: I am so sorry. Did we wake you up?

HERMIEN: My sister's had a bad dream. She's going back to sleep.

SUSSIE: I don't want to sleep anymore.

HERMIEN: I told you! We have guests.

MAESTRO: But the lady is most welcome in our midst. The more the merrier.

HERMIEN: It's very good of you I'm sure, Mneer. But my sister needs her sleep.

MAESTRO: What a pity.

SUSSIE: She's lying! My sister doesn't want anyone to see me. That's the truth!

HERMIEN: What nonsense!

MAESTRO: And why would that be?

SUSSIE moves forward. She stops. She turns slowly to the side. She takes off her shawl. Her hump is grotesquely visible under her white nightgown. She turns her face away. HERMIEN gives a soft cry and clamps her hand over her mouth. MAESTRO looks without saying anything. SUSSIE slowly turns her head and looks at him.

MAESTRO: I see. [*Carefully moves towards SUSSIE. Puts his hand out gently and touches the hump. SUSSIE pulls away*] But . . . didn't you know?

SUSSIE: Know what?

MAESTRO: That you have wings in there.

SUSSIE: Wings?

MAESTRO: Yes. Wings. But very tightly folded. Perhaps one day soon they will burst through the hard cocoon of flesh and bone. And then you will spread your wings. Large, rushing wings with feathers of many colours.

HERMIEN: That is a very pretty little story, Meneer. But my sister's not a child any more. She knows she is deformed.

SUSSIE drops her head.

MAESTRO: [*To SUSSIE*] It is your choice, Juffrou. If you do not wish to believe me . . . [*He shrugs*]

SUSSIE looks at MAESTRO. For a moment there is an intense contact between them.

MAESTRO: [*Half stumbles. Then sits down. Suddenly very tired*] I . . . am really very hungry.

HERMIEN: The food must be ready, Meneer. Sussie, seeing you're up, go and fetch the food for the guests.

SUSSIE looks reluctant and moves towards the kitchen.

HERMIEN: [*Sits*] You must be very tired, Meneer?

MAESTRO: Oh dear Mevrou, we are. We have been travelling all day.

EZMERELDA: We've been travelling all year! [*Tearful*] We've been travelling for many years!

HERMIEN: And where are you going, Meneer?

MAESTRO: To the diggings on the river bank a little way upstream.

HERMIEN: So you were going to cross the river?

MAESTRO: That is so, Mevrou. Apparently the drift is not far from here.

Muted thunder.

HERMIEN: Yes. Right in front of the house at the bottom of the hill.

MAESTRO: How fortunate.

HERMIEN: Even if the early rains have upset your plans, don't be despondent. I have a nice room for you with a good view of the river.

MAESTRO: Thank you very much, dear Mevrou, but we will only stay for a short wile. We are expected.

HERMIEN: But, Meneer, you dare not! The river is in full flood! Surely you can hear it!

SUSSIE enters with a fully laden tray. She puts the food on the sideboard and proceeds to lay the table.

MAESTRO: There is nothing to fear.

The clock strikes a quarter past eleven.

HERMIEN: That's what they all say, Meneer! Listen to me! You'd be in mortal danger! Tell him Sussie!

SUSSIE: Yes! It is true.

HERMIEN: There are rapids and cross-currents and whirlpools to suck you under.

EZMERELDA: I'm scared.

MAESTRO: You have nothing to fear.

HERMIEN: Listen to the rushing water! Listen to the stones rolling on the river bed!

EZMERELDA: I'm scared! I'm scared!

MAESTRO: Be quiet!

HERMIEN: You're a fool just like all the rest.

MAESTRO: [*Suddenly friendly*] Enough of this unpleasantness. I can see the food is on the table. [*HERMIEN sighs. MAESTRO leads EZMERELDA to the table. EZMERELDA sits where HERMIEN/EZMERELDA sat during the "seance" scene. SUSSIE dishes up. She is shy and, from time to time, she glances furtively at MAESTRO*]

MAESTRO: It looks delicious. You can fill my plate. [*Laughs*] I'm as hungry as a wolf. But not too much for her. She eats very little.

HERMIEN: You say you are on your way to the diggings. If I may say so, Meneer, you hardly look like a typical gold prospector.

MAESTRO: This is quite true. [*To SUSSIE, who puts a plate in front of him*] Thank you. I am no prospector. [*Pushes the end of his serviette into his collar*] Oh dear lady, what an oversight. [*Gets up*] Let me introduce myself. I am MAESTRO, the celebrated hypnotist. [*Bows formally and sits*] I practice the art of hypnosis. [*He starts eating*]

HERMIEN: [*Very formal*] I am Juffrou Hermien and this is my sister Sussie.

MAESTRO: [*Gets up again and bows formally*] I am pleased to make your acquaintance.

SUSSIE looks at him furtively and puts a plate in front of EZMERELDA.

HERMIEN: And I suppose this is Mevrou Maestro?

MAESTRO: Oh no. This is my assistant, Ezmerelda.

HERMIEN: And you travel alone together?

MAESTRO: Don't forget my coachman. [*Opens Ezmerelda's serviette and pushes the end of the serviette down the front of her low-cut dress*]

HERMIEN: Come on Sussie! [*Indicates that SUSSIE should join her on the ottoman. SUSSIE sits next to HERMIEN. They both fold their hands on their lap and they watch as MAESTRO eats voraciously while EZMERELDA pecks at her food*] Excuse me. I don't quite understand, Meneer. What is it exactly that you do? What is this ... [*Looks inquiringly at SUSSIE who whispers in her ear*] ... hypnosis?

MAESTRO: Dear Mevrou, a strong force flows through me. I am only the instrument. But I am a very particular kind of hypnotist. I make all dreams come true. [*Continues to eat voraciously*]

SUSSIE: Are you a magician?

MAESTRO: A magician! [*Laughs*] How amusing. As I said, I make dreams come true and that is why we travel from diggings to diggings. Everyone there searches so feverishly and few find what they are looking for. But for a small fee [*Smiles and wipes his mouth*] their dreams can come true. [*Jumps up, moves to the landing. Elaborate gesture*] Usually the small hall is filled to capacity. [*He pauses dramatically*]

Far-off sound of an accordian being played upstairs and a sad song being sung by the diggers. For a while everyone listens.

MAESTRO: [*After a silence, irritably and loudly*] Usually the small hall is filled to capacity. My entertainment is extremely popular. I call someone to come forward. [*Takes out his pocket-watch and quickly moves down to the ottoman. He stands behind SUSSIE and swings the pocket-watch slowly from side to side in front of her, while she watches wide-eyed. SUSSIE turns her head away. MAESTRO returns to the landing*].

EZMERELDA sees the memento tin on the table and picks it up.

MAESTRO: When they are hypnotised I say: "Stroll a little way down the river. See how the sun shines on the water. Now take up your pan and get to work. Today may be your lucky day."

EZMERELDA opens the tin and takes out a button.

HERMIEN: [*Jumping up*] Put it back at once! [*Quickly to table, closes box and then puts it on the desk*]

MAESTRO: She meant no harm! Look how upset she is. She is very sensitive you know.

HERMIEN: These are our most treasured possessions. Our mementos, Meneer.

HERMIEN sits down on the ottoman again. EZMERELDA wipes away her tears.

MAESTRO: [*Very irritated*] Now where was I? Where was I?

EZMERELDA: [*Tearful, prompting*] This may be your lucky day . . .

MAESTRO: Oh yes! This may be your lucky day. Then he starts shovelling in dirt.

HERMIEN: And where do you find the dirt, Meneer? Do you provide it?

MAESTRO: It is not really there, Mevrou. They can see whatever I tell them to see.

HERMIEN: Goodness me.

MAESTRO: And they sift and feel among the small stones. Then I say: "Look! A nugget as big as an egg." Then—and it differs from person to person—they start laughing and screaming or dancing and some run around in circles. And so I give to each who pay the fulfillment of a dream.

HERMIEN: [*Covertly glances at SUSSIE*] How interesting I'm sure. And what does your assistant do?

MAESTRO: [*Sits down at the table*] The poor diggers see so few fine ladies. And she is always a feast for the eye. Oh yes, she is a great draw card. She has a trunk filled with beautiful clothes. Tell them Ezmerelda, tell them about your clothes.

EZMERELDA: I don't want to.

MAESTRO: Come on!

EZMERELDA: [*As if reciting*] There are lots of lovely things. Hats with feathers and bows. Lace parasols. Dresses made of silk and velvet. White, lavender and rose. Pretty shoes, everything to choose from . . . [*Turns her head away*]

HERMIEN: What's wrong?

MAESTRO: Go on!

EZMERELDA: But they're not my clothes. They belong to Ezmerelda.

HERMIEN: What do you mean?

EZMERELDA: All the Ezmereldas before me. They wore these clothes too. I see their stains on the dresses and I smell the sweat under the arms and their musty underclothes. The nightgowns smell of their bodies.

MAESTRO: [*Laughs*] It's not as bad as that.

EZMERELDA: The shoes are too big for me. [*Gets up and illustrates*] Look. The sleeves are too wide and I keep tripping over the train. [*Stumbles and falls on the ground*]

The diggers stop playing and singing.

MAESTRO: Too big is surely better than too small? [*Getting up and stretching*] And now I would like to sit back in that easy chair if I may.

HERMIEN: If you like.

MAESTRO takes one of the chairs from the table and turns it around. He takes EZMERELDA by the wrist and wrenches her up from the floor. He pushes her onto the chair. He lifts her head and arranges her hands in her lap. She looks wide-eyed and dazed. He sits down luxuriously in the easy chair.

MAESTRO: And of course she takes part in the entertainment. The Ezmerelda section of the entertainment is extremely popular. It usually comes at the end and everybody stays for that. She looks breathtakingly lovely and when she appears on stage the crowd cheers. Her cheeks and lips are red and she wears one of her loveliest dresses and feathers in her hair. I take her hand and she makes a small bow and smiles. [*Bows and smiles with a gentle feminine grace. He is not imitating EZMERELDA but seems rather to be embodying her*] Everyone whistles and claps. Then she lies down and I hypnotise her. It has become very easy for me to hypnotise her. I only have to click my fingers. [*Clicks his fingers*]

EZMERELDA's eyes close. Her head drops to her chest and she breathes deeply.

MAESTRO: As you can see. [*Clicks his fingers again*]

EZMERELDA wakes up and looks startled.

MAESTRO: And then I say: "You are getting younger and younger. You are sixteen, you are ten, you are five, you are three." Yes that is where I usually stop. You should see her. She is quite adorable. She giggles and lisps and sucks her thumb.

HERMIEN is clearly shocked.

MAESTRO: I usually choose a few who are fortunate enough to play with her.

HERMIEN: What on earth do you mean?

EZMERELDA: Please! Please! Don't say any more!

MAESTRO: Well, let me see now. They stroke her hair, tickle her under her chin, pinch her cheek, put her on their laps and throw her into the air. That makes her squeal with delight.

HERMIEN: But this is surely no life for an innocent young girl.

EZMERELDA is sitting with her hands over her eyes.

HERMIEN: [*Sympathetically*] How did it happen, you poor child? How were you beguiled into becoming an assistant to this man?

EZMERELDA: I . . . can't remember.

MAESTRO: What she means is that she does not wish to remember. [*Laughs*] I don't suppose you have more wine dear lady?

HERMIEN: [*Coolly*] Unfortunately not.

MAESTRO: Unfortunate indeed.

The sound of raucous laughter upstairs. Everybody looks up and listens.

MAESTRO: [*After a few moments leans forward. Confidentially*] It was an early spring evening the same as this one. There was also a storm. [*Dramatically*] I see a small flickering light through the lashing rain. I follow a narrow winding road. I stop in front of a desolate little hovel.

EZMERELDA: No! You promised! [*She flings herself at him*] You said you would never tell it again! Never ever again!

MAESTRO: [*Grabbing her wrists*] Come on. It will amuse the ladies. [*He flings her down onto the floor next to his chair*] I knock and a fat slut opens the door. At first she is suspicious but I give her a pound and she invites me in. The hovel is dingy and the chimney smokes. The fat slut calls to her daughter to make me some food. [*Looks at EZMERELDA. Softly*] Her daughter comes in. She wears a shawl over her nightgown. When I've finished eating the fat slut sends her daughter to bed. Then she makes me a feather bed in front of the fire and also goes to bed. [*Plays with EZMERELDA's hair*] I wait a little while and then I slowly open the daughter's door. The fat slut is snoring in the next room. The girl is lying on a narrow bed in front of the window.

HERMIEN is clearly shocked. SUSSIE sits motionless,
her eyes riveted on MAESTRO.

MAESTRO: Stealthily I move closer. I put my candle next to her bed and I look at her. [*His head droops onto his hand with gentle feminine grace*] Her cheek rests on her palm and her other hand lies on her breast.[*He places his hand on his breast, his eyes closed. His lips part slightly. He seems to be asleep. He does not imitate EZMER-ELDA but seems to embody her. Opens his eyes, suddenly*] I lift the threadbare blanket and get into the bed next to her.

HERMIEN: [*Jumps up*] That is enough!

MAESTRO glares at her and she sits down as though she has no volition of her own.

MAESTRO: A cold breeze blows her hair against my cheek and outside the long grass sighs like the sea. I undo her buttons and caress the pale crescent of her breast. I touch the small hollows of her back. She sighs and turns her head. Her lips are slightly parted and the candlelight washes into her mouth. I put my finger lightly between her lips. They are warm and swollen. I feel the wet soft tip of her tongue. I kiss her on her eyelids, first one, then the other. I brush her temples with my mouth. [*Softly with his mouth against EZMERELDA's temples*] I whisper. I whisper . . . and she dreams. [*EZMERELDA draws her breath in sharply. MAE-STRO laughs. Stops, bends over and strokes her arms*] And she dreams. What does she dream? [*He lifts her hair kisses her in the nape of the neck*] What . . . does . . . she . . . dream?

EZMERELDA: I can't remember. Please . . . I can't remember . . .

MAESTRO: Yes you can. [*Seductively, with his lips against her hair*] What are you dreaming? [*Slowly*] What . . . are you dreaming?

EZMERELDA: [*Rather automatically with staring eyes*] I dream that I wake up. I turn my head and I see him next to me. His eyes are half-closed, glinting under his lids. I sit up and bend over him. He lifts his head and flickers his tongue . . . [*Slowly she touches the hollow in her neck with her forefinger. Falters, drops her head*]

MAESTRO: [*Kneeling behind her, grabbing her by her shoulders, prompting*] "My head feels heavy" . . .

MAESTRO and EZMERELDA: [*Together*] My head drops against his chest. I am afraid and I hide my face under the pillow. When I look again he is standing at the foot of the bed. He puts his hands under the sheet. Under my nightgowns. He strokes my thigh. He pulls me towards him with my arms above my head. My arms feel heavy. My head falls back. [*EZMERELDA seems slightly confused as though she had just woken up*]

HERMIEN: [*Getting up*] It's late. I think we need some sleep.

MAESTRO: And I knew you were dreaming. Your eyelids flickered and you moaned. I knew you would remember the dream.

EZMERELDA: Yes, I did. When I woke up I remembered. [*Gets up*] And I was . . . ashamed.

MAESTRO: That's a lie. [*Lunges at her*]

HERMIEN gets a fright and sits down. After a while she gets up again.

MAESTRO: [*Catches EZMERELDA and pulls her down onto the ground*] When you remembered the dream that was not shame. The hot blood scorched through your veins.

HERMIEN: Stop this! Stop this at once!

MAESTRO: [*With extreme violence*] I am sick and tired of your lies!

HERMIEN gets a fright and sits down.

MAESTRO: [*Bitterly, laughing*] Of course you believe everything she says. But I want you to listen carefully. We will get to the bottom of this. For the rest of the night I slept in front of the fire. When she saw me early the next morning she blushed. I'm right am I not? When she bent over the hot stove I kissed the nape of her neck. Did she cry out? Did she slap me? No. She trembled lightly and sighed.

EZMERELDA drops her head.

MAESTRO: Why so quiet dear heart? After that I knew it was decided. When I offered the fat slut sixteen pounds for her daughter's services she accepted it gladly. And the daughter? Did she wail? Did she beg? No! She never even demurred but climbed into my coach without a word. Am I right or not? And what do you have to say for yourself?

EMERELDA bites his hand. He roars with pain. She writhes out from under him and jumps up.

EZMERELDA: I wish I'd never seen you.

MAESTRO: Is that so?

EZMERELDA: I wish I'd stayed at home. I should have said, "No, I'll never go. Never. Not over my dead body!"

MAESTRO: [*Suddenly sympathetic*] You poor little thing. Then you would have still worn braids and fed your ma's chickens.

EZMERELDA: Yes. I would have.

MAESTRO: Oh to think what I have deprived you of. [*Lifts her chin*] Look at me. Look at me.

EZMERELDA lifts her head and looks at him.

MAESTRO: If I'd gone away for ever would you have remembered me, would you have thought of me, or would you have been quite satisfied with your fat ma and your chickens?

EZMERELDA: [*Despairingly*] I would have forgotten you. I would have.

MAESTRO: [*Strokes her cheek*] While the fat bitch counted her money you stood there in your blue dress at the window. And I looked at you. My eyes . . . touched you everywhere. You could feel my eyes touching you. Could you have forgotten that? My eyes caressing you as they are caressing you now. Your wrists . . . your mouth . . . your hair . . .

EZMERELDA looks at him. She gives a soft cry and flings her arms around him.
MAESTRO presses her to him, lifting her slightly with one arm around her waist.
Her feet don't quite touch the ground and he takes a few steps, carrying her.

MAESTRO: As you can see. [*He pushes her away. She stumbles*] She is not under duress!

EZMERELDA sobs.

HERMIEN: [*Puts her arms around EZMERELDA*] You are certainly no gentleman, Meneer.

MAESTRO: Not?

HERMIEN: I am sorry to say, but you have no breeding.

MAESTRO: [*Without interest*] You're quite wrong, Mevrou. I come from a very old family. Oh I see my dear assistant has not eaten all her food. There are still two drumsticks and two wings. If you can add anything, anything at all my coachman will be deeply grateful. He must be dying of hunger poor fellow. Of course I am prepared to pay more.

HERMIEN: [*Coldly*] You don't have to pay for the meal, Meneer.

MAESTRO: And why not?

HERMIEN: I don't want to make money out of my guests. The small fee for the room is only to cover our costs. I am here to give warning against the dangerous water. I also have . . . other duties. But these don't concern you.

MAESTRO: But you are an angel of mercy!

HERMIEN: No, I am only doing my duty.

MAESTRO: No. No you are a wonderful person! A most excellent person, Mevrou. [*Kisses HERMIEN's hand*]

HERMIEN: [*Draws her hand away*] I don't want any thanks.
MAESTRO: And Ezmerelda? Why do you not show your appreciation?
EZMERELDA: [*Bows*] Thank you very much.
HERMIEN: [*Flustered*] Come on Sussie, help me to clear the table.
MAESTRO: Ezmerelda can help you. She would be glad to help you, wouldn't you dear heart?
EZMERELDA: [*Unwillingly*] Yes.
HERMIEN: Well if it's not too much trouble . . .
MAESTRO: Not at all. Not at all.
HERMIEN: Well . . .

EZMERELDA gets up rather unwillingly and starts clearing the table. Loud noises and the sound of furniture being overturned can be heard from upstairs.

HERMIEN: Drunk again! It is always the same. [*Exits into hall, loudly off*] Stop that! Stop it at once!

HERMIEN enters. They all listen until everything is quiet. Sudden laughter from upstairs.

HERMIEN: [*Sarcastically*] My but they are in high spirits tonight! [*To EZMERELDA*] You seem to have finished in no time at all. Now if you will help me, we can take everything through.

HERMIEN and EZMERELDA off. The clock strikes half-past eleven.

MAESTRO: [*Sits next to SUSSIE and takes her hand in his*] I was just thinking . . . you and your sister have been so good to us and without expecting anything in return. To show my gratitude I would like to give you something.
SUSSIE: A gift?
MAESTRO: Yes in a manner of speaking. Something that only I can give you. [*Glances at her hands*] You have such lovely hands. Delicate and pale.
SUSSIE: I . . . don't often go outside. I hardly ever go out into the sun.
MAESTRO: That is as it should be. A lady's skin should be delicate almost transparently thin. You should see the blood under the skin.
HERMIEN: [*Off*] Milk and rusks make you sleep much better . . .

MAESTRO lets go of SUSSIE's hand. HERMIEN and EZMERELDA enter from the hall. HERMIEN puts food wrapped in cheesecloth on the table.

MAESTRO: I was just telling your sister that in order to show my gratitude, I would like to give you something.
HERMIEN: That is really not necessary.
MAESTRO: Oh but it is. [*Gets up, moves to the landing. Bows*] I, Maestro, will present a short entertainment. [*Holds out his hand*] Come now Ezmerelda, we shall begin with you.
EZMERELDA: It's very late. I'm tired.
HERMIEN: This is really totally unnecessary, Meneer.

MAESTRO: It is my pleasure, dear Mevrou. [*To EZMERELDA*] You wish to show your appreciation or not?

EZMERELDA: [*Pouting*] I don't want to.

MAESTRO: Come now. You are being disagreeable.

EZMERELDA: No.

MAESTRO: How dare you behave like this? I am deeply ashamed of you.

EZMERELDA: [*Snivelling*] I'm tired. I'm very tired. [*She gets up slowly and seems to be unsteady on her feet*]

HERMIEN: Surely you can see the young juffrou is exhausted. Look at her! Dead on her feet! And it's getting very late.

MAESTRO: [*To EZMERELDA*] Very well. As you wish. Who else wants to join me?

SUSSIE: I do!

HERMIEN: [*Takes SUSSIE's hand firmly in her own. SUSSIE attempts to get up but HERMIEN holds her back*] Sit Sussie! I am telling you to sit down!

MAESTRO: I assure you there's nothing to fear.

SUSSIE tries to get up but HERMIEN pulls her down.

HERMIEN: No! You can't go! You can't dabble in this hypnosis! We know nothing about it!

MAESTRO: Then this is a chance to find out, dear Mevrou. And believe me you will not regret it. All your wildest dreams can come true. If you wish for sumptuous clothes, they will appear at once.

HERMIEN: Vanity. I do not hold with such things.

MAESTRO: What about a feast; game, lamb, tarts and cream cakes . . .

HERMIEN: I've eaten, thank you, Meneer.

MAESTRO: [*To SUSSIE*] And what about you, Juffrou? What do you desire?

SUSSIE: [*Pulls free of HERMIEN and runs up to the landing*] To go away! Far away from here! To see other places!

HERMIEN: Oh! So, our mother's home is not good enough for you any more!

MAESTRO: Then we shall go on a journey. More swiftly than breath you will float out of the window higher and higher . . . the river will be a writhing snake . . . and the house too small to see with the naked eye . . .

HERMIEN: What rubbish!

MAESTRO: Perhaps you wish to go to the sea? In the wink of an eye you are there . . . Walking down the narrow sand path, glinting in the moonlight like a shallow stream . . . and there it would be . . . infinite reflection of the night sky . . .

HERMIEN: This is quite enough!

MAESTRO: Or in a dense forest? In the liquid green light under the high arches of trees . . .

HERMIEN: I said it's enough!

MAESTRO: Just say where and I Maestro will take you there.

HERMIEN: Sussie! Listen to me!

MAESTRO: [*Formal*] I must ask you to be quiet. This is a very delicate matter!

Before each performance I always say: "Dames and Here (Ladies and Gentlemen), silence is of the most utmost importance. Even if you only wish to cough or sneeze, I must ask you to leave the hall."

HERMIEN: So, you're telling me to be quiet! And in my own home!

SUSSIE: Please! Please! Do what he says!

MAESTRO: Look! [*Takes out pocket-watch*] Look at my watch. [*He swings the watch from side to side. SUSSIE watches and in spite of herself HERMIEN follows the movements of the watch as well. Then she shakes her head vigorously.*]

HERMIEN: Stop [*Rising*] I say stop!! [*Rushes up the stairs*] I warned you didn't I? [*Grabs SUSSIE by her arm*]

SUSSIE: Please! I want to!

HERMIEN: No!

SUSSIE: I beg of you!

HERMIEN: I said no!

SUSSIE: I'll do anything. I'll repair the nets by myself even when my fingers bleed. I'll never complain again even when I dig a grave for two days!

HERMIEN: For the last time no! Over my dead body!

SUSSIE: Please! I beg of you! [*Falls on her knees*] Please! Please! Please!

HERMIEN: Get off your knees! Have you lost your senses! Get up! [*Pulls SUSSIE up by her hair*] I said get up! And behave yourself! [*To MAESTRO*] Do you see what you've done! And all because you wanted to fool my poor deformed sister with your trickery!

MAESTRO: [*Cold fury*] Trickery! Is that what you call it? Ha! Cut and dried! Cut and dried. Oh yes, I know your kind! Everything is always cut and dried. You will never understand. Never. How I pity you. You miserable creature.

HERMIEN is clearly shocked.

MAESTRO: But I must control myself. After all, this is only a waste of time. [*Puts away his pocket-watch. To SUSSIE*] I am deeply sorry, dear Juffrou. [*Moves to table, picks up the food in the cheesecloth. Small bow*] Please excuse me. [*Exits rapidly. Sound of the heavy front door opening and closing*]

There is a few moments silence. SUSSIE is on her knees with her face buried in her hands. HERMIEN still has her hands in SUSSIE's hair. HERMIEN pushes SUSSIE away. SUSSIE falls and lies with her head in her arms.

HERMIEN: What a hideous man! [*To SUSSIE*] And what possessed you? Have you no shame? [*To EZMERELDA*] I'm so sorry for you. Bitterly sorry. Such a monster! And when I see how he treats you!

EZMERELDA: Yes. He often gets angry. Then he scolds me.

HERMIEN: Poor child.

EZMERELDA: And sometimes he hurts me.

HERMIEN: How terrible.

EZMERELDA: He never allows me to rest. He drags me from one place to the other. I am so . . . tired.

HERMIEN: I am sure you are!

EZMERELDA: And then all the performances. Candles and lamps shining in my eyes. And all the men looking at me.

HERMIEN: How horrible!

EZMERELDA: And the noise. Clapping, whistling and stamping! [*Touches her temples*] It always gives me a headache. And they smell of rancid sweat and dirty clothes.

HERMIEN: Oh!

EZMERELDA: And sometimes they touch me. They touch me . . . everywhere.

HERMIEN: But this is terrible. What would your poor mother say? Come now. Don't cry. [*Strokes EZMERELDA's hair*] Let me dry your tears. [*Dries her tears with a small white handkerchief which she takes out of her sleeve*] I'll help you. Yes, I will. Trust me child. I'll save you from the clutches of this man. Let me think . . . there must be a way . . . Tell me, speaking of your dear mother, you must be very homesick?

EZMERELDA: [*Tentative*] Yes . . .

HERMIEN: But that is the answer to our problem! I must help you to go back home where you belong. Surely you'll be happy to see your home again?

EZMERELDA: It's funny . . . I can hardly remember my home. [*Happy*] I remember the chickens. [*Sad*] But I wonder if I would still know my home. If I'd still know it if I saw it.

HERMIEN: Of course you will. East west home is best. And your mother! She'll be quite overcome to see you again. Think how happy she'll be when she opens the door and there you are! She'll take you in her arms and press you to her bosom. [*Wipes away a tear*] Forgive me but I feel deeply moved.

EZMERELDA: Yes . . . my ma. [*Glad*] I'm sure I can remember her! She is a big woman and smells of rancid drippings!

HERMIEN: You'll be so happy! You'll forget . . . your unfortunate past. Your life will go on as if nothing's happened.

SUSSIE gets up.

HERIMEN: Yes! I'll take you to the nearest station . . . I'll make you egg sandwiches . . . I'll buy you a ticket and put you on the train . . . I'll wave until the train disappears behind the silo.

EZMERELDA: [*Uncertain*] Yes . . .

HERMIEN: But then you must tell this hideous man. You must tell him that you want to stay with us.

EZMERELDA: I don't know . . .

HERMIEN: You poor thing. I suppose you're afraid of him. And who could blame you? Then there is only one thing to do . . .

SUSSIE moves to the bedroom door.

HERMIEN: [*To SUSSIE*] Have you no manners? Don't you say goodnight to our guest?

SUSSIE remains motionless.

HERMIEN: [*To SUSSIE*] But go! Get out of my sight! [*Strokes EZMER-ELDA's hair*] I'll speak to him.

SUSSIE exits to bedroom.

EZMERELDA: No . . .

HERMIEN: Yes it is probably better if you tell him yourself.

EZMERELDA: I . . . don't really know.

HERMIEN: There is really no time to shilly-shally! Tell him and make it very clear!

EZMERELDA: I'm not really sure . . .

HERMIEN: But surely you don't want to stay as you are? Have you no mind of your own?

EZMERELDA: It's only . . . sometimes he's very good to me . . .

HERMIEN: Oh I see.

EZMERELDA: Yes he is.

HERMIEN: I can hardly believe that.

EZMERELDA: It's true. [*Dreamily*] Very good.

HERMIEN: The man has you in his power! [*Shakes EZMERELDA*] Wake up! Come to your senses!

EZMERELDA: Let me go! What are you doing to me! I'll tell him! He'll be very angry with you!

HERMIEN: I can hardly believe my ears! Do you want to stay with this repulsive monster?

EZMERELDA: He isn't a monster! He isn't! He isn't! What do you know?

MAESTRO appears on the landing. EZMERELDA runs to him and embraces him passionately. She turns her head and looks triumphantly at HERMIEN.

MAESTRO: [*Pushes her aside*] Fortunately the rain has stopped. [*Picks up his cloak*] The ground is still quite soggy but the air is crystal clear. And so my coachman and I have decided to continue our journey.

HERMIEN: Surely you don't mean to cross the drift?

MAESTRO: Most certainly. We have to get to the other side.

HERMIEN: But the dangerous flood water. I've warned you haven't I?

EZMERELDA: Listen to her! I'm afraid!

MAESTRO: [*To EZMERELDA*] Put on your coat. [*He puts on his cloak and his top hat*]

HERMIEN: You must listen to me! You're in grave danger! Listen! Please, Meneer!

EZMERELDA: I'm trembling . . .

MAESTRO: We are leaving! And there is nothing more to be said!

HERMIEN: Then you face certain death!

MAESTRO: And where is your sister? I wanted to see her before we left.

HERMIEN: You are a fool! Go and look! [*Points towards the window*] Look out there!! Look at the rows of graves and white crosses!! The last resting place of those who wouldn't listen!

EZMERELDA: [*Crying*] I'm afraid! I don't want to go! It's so dark outside ... and listen to the rushing water! I'm afraid of water!

MAESTRO: It is because of her! With her prophecies of doom!

HERMIEN: Yes, possibly I am only making the situation worse! I will go to my room. You can talk about it on your own. [*HERMIEN moves towards the bedroom*] I can only hope and pray that you will make the right decision but ultimately it is your choice. [*Turns around at the door*] I have warned you over and over again! I have done my best! I have done everything that is humanly possible! I sacrifice myself but nobody ever listens!! [*Exits banging the door behind her*]

EZMERELDA: I don't want to go. I'm scared! I'm scared!

MAESTRO: [*Sits. Suddenly exhausted*] Yes, yes, yes! You are always scared or tired or cold. I know.

EZMERELDA: That's not true!

MAESTRO: Yes it is. [*Silence. Drops his head into his hands*] The same lament. Just like all the others.

EZMERELDA: I'm not like the others! [*Sobs*] I'm not!

MAESTRO: At the beginning I'm always so glad because I think I have found someone to go on my journey with me. Someone to hold through the long nights in all the desolate places. And I won't have to be alone any more. Not so ... utterly alone. [*Short silence*] But then it starts again. You always want something every moment of the day. Food, clothes, or love ... and if you don't get what you want then you look at me. Always looking at me. Even in the dark. And every time the loneliness becomes more and more unbearable. I am consumed with longing. I burn with loneliness. [*Lifts his head and looks at EZMERELDA*] I show you visions of strange places and other times. In one moment you live many years. You drift weightless or lie in a perfumed garden half-hidden under rose petals and jasmine. Or you sing like an angel and see your song unfurling like a golden feather. And at night all night you lie in my arms with my breath against your hair. That is what I give you. But no! That will not do! What you want is a warm bed, a bowl of soup and a thick slice of bread! That is not life! That is death!

EZMERELDA sobs.

MAESTRO: I should have left you with the fat slut and the chickens. Yes, that is what you all are. Soft and simple-minded. Maybe I need a real woman. A real woman with blood in her veins. [*Short silence. Sudden thought*] A woman ... like Sussie!

EZMERELDA: Sussie!

MAESTRO: Yes! Sussie! I immediately sensed that she is a warm-blooded passionate woman. Did you see how her eyes shone when she looked at me? How her whole body glowed?

EZMERELDA: But she is misshapen!

MAESTRO: [*Excited. Gets up*] Her unusual proportions are simply another sign of her exceptional nature! She is different from other people! She wishes to be free of her day-to-day existence. She finds it narrow and soul-deadening. Like me, she wishes for life and more life! Yes . . . such a woman will be a true assistant. You can stay here if you wish. I will take her with me.

The clock strikes 7a quarter to twelve.

EZMERELDA: [*Desperately*] But the clothes won't fit over her hump!

MAESTRO: I shall have an entire trunk of new clothes made for her. To reveal her exceptional attributes.

EZMERELDA starts crying bitterly.

MAESTRO: Stop crying. I have already told you you can stay.

EZMERELDA: But you said you loved me.

MAESTRO: Yes, of course. That is what I always say over and over again. It is what you want to hear, is it not?

EZMERELDA: And you said forever and ever. [*Sniffs*] Isn't that true?

MAESTRO: Yes, I know. I always say that to please you.

EZMERELDA: [*Cries*] And now you want her and not me!

MAESTRO: Oh stop snivelling!

EZMERELDA: What will I do without you! What will become of me!

MAESTRO: Here it starts again. I should have known. The same refrain!

EZMERELDA: I'll go with you if you want me to! Even if it's dark outside! Even if the water's deep!

MAESTRO: Did I not say you could stay? [*Smiles*] Soon my new assistant and I will be on our way. And this time . . . everything will be different. [*He moves towards the stairs*]

EZMERELDA: [*Clings to his legs. Sobs*] Please, please don't leave me! Please! I'm nothing without you! Oh please!

MAESTRO: [*Pushes her away*] Very well then! Come on! We have a long way to go! [*Moves rapidly to the landing*]

EZMERELDA: [*Still on her knees*] Maestro!

MAESTRO: [*Turns around*] Yes?

EZMERELDA: You must say it.

MAESTRO: Say what?

EZMERELDA: You haven't said it today: "Ezmerelda, I love you."

MAESTRO: Ezmerelda! Ha! You are all the same. Ezmerelda. At first you are all Ezmerelda. But in time you all become . . . Johanna Gertiena again or . . . Petronella Magdalena or [*Gesture*] what is your name? It has slipped my mind. Of course [*Gesture*] Maria [*Laughs*] Maria Elisabet [*Laughs. Picks up the lantern and moves to the hall arch. EZMERELDA gets up and stumbles after him*]

MAESTRO: [*Off, sarcastic*] Maria Elisabet! [*Further away*] Maria Elisabet!

EZMERELDA exits. The resounding sound of the heavy front door closing. For a moment the stage is in darkness while the sound of the rushing river can still be heard. The sound of soft rain is faded up.

HERMIEN/EZMERELDA: [*In darkness. Softly. With wonder*] Maria Elisabet . . .

Lights slowly up. The lamp throws a circle of light on the table. The rest of the stage is in darkness. As during the "seance" scene, HERMIEN and SUSSIE are sitting at the table. They are dressed as they were at the beginning of the play. HERMIEN is wearing SUSSIE's woolen shawl over her shoulders.

HERMIEN/EZMERELDA: [*Softly*] Maria Elisabet.
SUSSIE: [*Leans over and takes HERMIEN/EZMERELDA's hands between her own*] Yes.
HERMIEN/EZMERELDA: [*Joyously*] Maria Elisabet! [*Very slowly her eyes close and her head drops onto her chest. SUSSIE pulls away her hand and SUSSIE's whole attitude changes at once*]
SUSSIE: [*Watches HERMIEN for a few moments*] HERMIEN! [*Very loudly*] HERMIEN!!
HERMIEN: [*Starts. Her head jerks back and she opens her eyes*] You nearly frightened me to death!
SUSSIE: I'm sorry. [*Turns aside. Smiles to herself. Looks radiantly happy*]
HERMIEN: I really don't feel very good. Not quite myself. Quite lightheaded. I have a stiff neck and my throat is parched. She seems to have had a great deal to say.
SUSSIE: Yes. She . . . said a great deal.
HERMIEN: Tell me were you successful?
SUSSIE: Yes.
HERMIEN: So she remembered her full name?
SUSSIE: Yes.
HERMIEN: Oh thank heavens! Now we'll be relieved of her unquiet spirit. By the way, what is her name? [*Sighs*] Oh never mind. Help me up. I've been sitting for a long time and now my leg has gone to sleep. You can tell me tomorrow.

SUSSIE helps her to get up and holds her arm.

HERMIEN: I'll have to walk a little to get the life back. [*She walks in a circle with SUSSIE holding her arm*]
SUSSIE: She said she'd been here. That she'd been here before.
HERMIEN: Well it is no wonder we didn't recognize her. She'd been under the water for far too long. Oh well that feels better. I think I might sit again. [*HERMIEN sits on the ottoman. SUSSIE lights the lamp on the desk*] Did she mention when?
SUSSIE: [*Bending over the map. Tenderly*] She was here with Maestro. The hypnotist.
HERMIEN: That monstrous man. As though I'll ever forget him. [*Sighs*] Poor little thing. I remember her well. Pretty and sweet-natured. Yes, I knew she was in

grave danger. I wanted to save her from him. I remember now I wanted to send her home. But it was far too late. He had her in his power. Then they left with the river in full flood. There was nothing I could do. Sometimes . . . I feel so tired. What is the use? [*Sighs*] I ask you. [*Wipes away a tear with a small white handkerchief she takes from her sleeve. Suddenly bitter*] And what happened to him? We never found him. But then monsters like that always survive.

SUSSIE: [*Softly*] Yes.

HERMIEN: You must put her name on the cross without delay. She might be calm for the time being but she won't go away until it is all over and done with.

SUSSIE: Yes.

HERMIEN: [*Watches SUSSIE*] What is wrong with you? You look . . . funny.

SUSSIE: It's nothing.

HERMIEN: What are you trying to hide?

The rain suddenly becomes louder.

HERMIEN: Listen! That's what I was afraid of. [*Shakes her head*] The rain is early this year. Yes the winter is over. [*Sighs*] I enjoy the winter. To sit in the sun. To crochet or knit. To rest. Oh, what am I thinking? [*Points upwards*] I must warn them at once. They must not leave tomorrow as they'd planned to do. It would be most perilous. [*Gets up. Notices the shawl around her shoulders*] And why am I wearing your shawl?

SUSSIE: It was for her. She was cold.

HERMIEN: [*Takes off the shawl and drapes it over the chair*] Yes, poor thing, she was half-frozen. [*Sighs, moves quickly to the hall arch*] I'll be back soon. You must get some rest. [*Exits*]

SUSSIE remains motionless for a while. Then she gets an expression of joyous abandon on her face and throws her head back. She sighs deeply. She gets up slowly and moves towards the window. Far off the sound of HERMIEN's knock on the door. SUSSIE remains motionless in front of the window and then she opens the curtains. She stands back and looks at her reflection in the dark window. She undoes her plait. She closes her eyes and lays her cheek against her hair.

HERMIEN: [*Off*] And the same to you!

SUSSIE looks at herself one more time and then closes the curtain. She goes back to the ottoman and sits in the same place.

HERMIEN: [*Off. Closer*] Now those are sensible young people. [*Enters. The rain becomes softer. In her one hand HERMIEN is holding a small muslin parcel*] It is five to twelve! No wonder I'm so sleepy. [*Happy*] They immediately realized the danger. Thank goodness. They'll stay until it's safe. [*Moves to the desk*] Yes, sometimes it is all worthwhile after all. What a consolation. [*Puts the small parcel down on the desk*] He was so thankful the dear young man. He gave me a piece of wedding cake to show his gratitude. [*Opens the muslin parcel*] Look how pretty.

SUSSIE: [*Gets up*] Let me see!

HERMIEN: With small white roses.

SUSSIE: [*Stands next to HERMIEN*] Yes, it's lovely.

HERMIEN: Unfortunately I don't have a sweet tooth.

SUSSIE: Will you give it to me? Please.

HERMIEN: If you like. But you mustn't eat it at this time of night. You'll get heartburn.

SUSSIE: [*Folding the muslin*] I won't eat it.

HERMIEN: [*Blows out the lamp on the desk*] Well, let us go to bed. Tomorrow our work begins again. We have to look over the nets, the ropes, and the hooks. We must also order some more crosses, don't forget. We're almost out of them. [*Turns*] Come on now.

SUSSIE remains motionless with the piece of wedding cake on her palm.

HERMIEN: You're not going to eat it at this hour are you?

SUSSIE turns her head away.

HERMIEN: Don't tell me . . . but surely it can't be! Sussie, do you intend putting that piece of wedding cake under your pillow?

SUSSIE drops her head.

HERMIEN: You know it is only for young normal girls who wish to dream of their prospective bridegroom. Who could you possibly dream of? Who would ever marry you? You must accept things as they are. There's nothing else to do. [*Sighs*] Poor, poor Sussie.

SUSSIE: That's not my name!

HERMIEN: Well! It's always been good enough for you until now! [*Coldly*] If it's all the same to you, I am going to bed.

A loud rushing sound.

HERMIEN: Do you hear that?

SUSSIE: Yes.

HERMIEN: It is the river bursting its banks. How terrible. [*Sighs*] Well, we should get some sleep. Who knows what awaits us tomorrow. [*Moves towards the bedroom. Turns head*] And why are you still sitting there? Turn out the lamp and come to bed.

SUSSIE: You go.

HERMIEN: Well, just as you like. [*Exits banging the door behind her*]

The lamp throws a circle of light on the table and the rest of the room is in semi-darkness. SUSSIE is only dimly seen as she moves to the armchair and picks up the shawl. She moves to the table. When she gets to the table she puts the cake down carefully and hangs the shawl around her shoulders. Her movements are slow and dreamy. She sits on the chair occupied by HERMIEN/EZMERELDA during the "seance" scene. Her palm rests on the wedding cake. For a few moments she sits motionless and only the ceaseless rain can be heard.

SUSSIE: [*After a silence. Dreamily*] I don't have to sleep because I am dreaming already. [*Silence*] I dream ... of the rain ... I dream ... of the big house with all its rooms ... with all the doors ... and all the windows ... I dream ... of a coach drawn by two black horses ... the coach is getting closer and closer in the rain ... through thunder and lightning and sheets of rain, the coach is getting closer. [*Silence while she listens*] The horses' hooves are muffled by the damp ground but I can hear them.

The sound of a coach approaching.

SUSSIE: Everything is dark ... There is nothing but a thin white feather of smoke rising from the chimney ... a man gets out of the carriage ... he wears a cloak ... the cloak glistens from the rain. ... [*She gets up slowly. She undergoes a subtle transformation and almost seems to embody MAESTRO*] Now he is in front of the great door ... he pushes against the door ... the door opens.

The sound of a heavy door opening. The wind blows leaves through the room.

SUSSIE: He stands at the door ... he sees her at the table under the lamp ... she doesn't look around but she knows he is there ... she feels his eyes on her ...

The clock strikes twelve.

SUSSIE: [*Speaking over the striking clock*] His eyes touching her hair, her temples, her wrists. [*She suddenly becomes soft and more feminine and completely herself*] Her throat. [*She pulls a button off her nightgown*] She hears his voice. [*She pulls the memento tin closer*] Softly, softly murmuring. [*She opens the tin and drops the button into the tin*] "Ezmerelda ... Ezmerelda ... Ezmerelda ... I have come for you ..."

She closes the tin, gets up slowly. She turns her head and looks towards the hall arch. Then almost like a sleepwalker she moves towards the hall arch. The wind blows SUSSIE's hair across her face and her shawl flaps behind her. Slowly she climbs up the stairs and exits.

After a while there is the sound of a heavy door closing. The wind stops blowing through the house. For some moments, only the rushing sound of the river can be heard, then there is the ghostly and heart-rending sobbing as before. While the sobbing is heard, the lights fade very slowly to black.

Ipi Zombi?
(1998)

Brett Bailey

Brett Bailey was born in Cape Town in 1967. He studied drama and English literature at the University of Cape Town and, in 1990, began experimenting in various forms of street performance and community theatre projects: a medieval street theatre spoof, township happenings, dada cabarets, an expressionist spectacle in the middle of the Karoo lit by truck headlights, a passion play with the "Coloured" community of Nieu Bethesda. After traveling up the east coast of Africa and on to India to study meditation, in 1994 he returned to the Cape Province to teach acting and scriptwriting and to mount even more ambitious community theatre projects. In Hermanus he pulled together a cast of 170 from a wide range of cultural and ethnic groups (Blacks, Coloureds, hippies, yuppies) for the local Whale Festival. In 1996, he began studying Xhosa culture with traditional teachers in the Transkei. This experience has led to his creating several plays that combine performance elements from sangoma rituals with other forms of experimental theatre to create highly original and unique forms of theatre. He has established a theatre school in Grahamstown where he incorporates trance elements (often with the assistance of sangomas) in the training of actors.

Ipi Zombi? *began to develop when Bailey traveled to Kokstad to investigate an outbreak of witchcraft hysteria. The previous year, twelve boys had been killed in a minivan crash, and rumors began to circulate that witches had caused the crash and had enslaved the souls of the boys. The stories split the community along religious lines between the Christians and the traditionalists. The lack of strong adult authority figures in the community, the legacy of high school–age activists in the anti-apartheid movement, and the unresolved grief over the loss of the boys created an extremely volatile atmosphere in which several women were murdered by mobs for witchcraft, the bodies of the boys could not be buried, and sangomas tried unsuccessfully to call up the souls of the boys and calm the anger and fear in the community.*

In response to the Kokstad incidents, Bailey wrote and directed Zombie *for the Grahamstown Fringe Festival in 1996. The production used a cast of sixty local residents, including six sangomas and a church choir. It marked the largest participation of local Blacks in the Grahamstown festival to date and won acclaim for both the strength of performances and the power of the spectacle. Over the next two years, Bailey reworked and restaged the play several times in different communities with different performers, bringing it back to Grahamstown for a main stage production at the festival in 1998 under the new title* Ipi Zombi? *Zakes Mda called the play "a work of genius that maps out a path to a new South African theatre that is highly innovative in its use of indigenous performance forms."*

Bailey weaves indigenous performance forms (church choirs, sangoma chants and trance movement, secular dances, comic caricature) with a number of important trends from the Western theatrical tradition. He complicates the didactic theatre tradition of presenting the moral choices of individuals within particular social situations by mixing in elements of community theatre, in which the actions of large groups of people replace the actions of individuals and in which actors represent their own lives rather than the abstracted, exemplary lives of imagined characters. He creates enticing spectacles of color, movement, and sound to seduce and please the audience, then throws in dadaistic anti-aesthetic elements that make the audience ill at ease with its passive, privileged position as uninvolved observers. He infuses the theatre with ritual elements that make it seem sometimes a sanctified refuge from the violent outside world and sometimes a scene of dangerous possessions, in which the violence outside reaches a disturbing spiritual concentration. The play as a whole has a dreamlike structure of condensed and contradictory impulses that illuminate the complexities of both township life and the strange cultural practice called theatre.

Although clearly disturbed by the persecution and murder of innocent women accused of witchcraft, Bailey does not indulge in comfortable gestures of moral superiority such as one finds in Arthur Miller's The Crucible. *He does not take seriously the charges of witchcraft, but he does take seriously the belief in magic and spiritual possession that lie behind such charges. Rather than simply condemn unjustifiable acts of violence, he seeks to explain the circumstances in which such violence arises. He wants to show how terrible fears and bereavement can become an evil force, how people struggle against or are seduced by this force, and how wishing to remain an unaffected spectator at such scenes of affliction raises its own moral questions.*

IPI ZOMBI?

SET

Ipi Zombi? is played in three-quarter round, the way any African ceremony would be performed. The floor is covered in dry cow dung, and surrounded by grass mats on which the performers sit, sing, play music etc. Several drums, other instruments and crates containing props and costumes share these mats. The space is lit mainly by candles. A fire in a sawn-off drum burns centre, though this is later moved off. At the back is a three-tiered stack of rostra—brightly painted and decorated with bones, crucifixes, animal heads, live chickens in a cage, and other paraphernalia. On top of this structure stands a huge old cupboard spangled with fragments of mirror. This structure brings to mind a vast "voodoo" altar, and is used extensively as an acting platform. A tall white box covered in a sheet stands just in front of the "altar," containing one of the performers (INTOMBI 'NYAMA) to be revealed later.

CAST

Fifteen in all: "The Natives" are presented as a roughly-hewn troupe of roving performers from the hills of rural South Africa, with the NARRATOR as their leader—many of them play several roles in the show with the help of larger-than-life costumes, which they pull over their hessian shorts and bras. All are covered from head to toe in white clay—an indicator of sacred people amongst the Xhosa. INTOMBI 'NYAMA (Black Girl) is styled as a special guest star from the Johannesburg metropolis—a gaudy, endearing black transvestite.

MUSIC

Most is drawn from sacred "shamanic" ceremonies in the rural hills of the Eastern Cape Province, though lyrics have sometimes been adapted to fit the context, as have those of the hymns. One of the songs is based on a 60's piece from Mali. The cast plays several drums, marimbas (African xylophones), rattles, antelope horns, etc.

THE PLAY

When the audience enters the cast are sitting in a ring around the perimeter of the arena on mats and are wrapped in blankets, facing inwards, heads down, singing softly "Zitshothina, sifela ethongweni" (we die in our dreams). Three figures—school boys—sit unmoving on the rostra like altar figures. NARRATOR tends a central fire, moves around slowly checking candles, showing audience in, "preparing the space."

NARRATOR: Hey we are the pride of the Eastern Cape, we are the pride of this place—we The Natives, we entertainers, we who are telling you this story, this *IPI ZOMBI?, sitshothina,* a story of this province; we who are travelling from village to village, from town to town, while others are afraid, locked up in their houses, believing their televisions, and outside the wild spirits of the forests are possessing the people, killing each and everybody in the streets, in the taverns, even in their beds. Hey this country is struggling. These are the hungry times: the rich are eating the poor, the dead are eating the living, even the roads are eating the children. My friends, we bring wonderful stories to you in these strange times in this land of ours, we tell you the stories from the heart of the country, we The Natives, we Real Live Blacks! JA! *Balele, balele, balele . . .*

[*Cast soars into "Zitshothina, sifela ethongweni"*]

People, bantu, tonight we are telling you a terrible story, the most hungry story, a story of something bigger than all of us, a story about something worse than you can imagine, about something that eats people bones and everything, and what is making it even more terrible is that it is a true story—ja—from Bhongweni Township, not even six hours drive from where we are tonight, not even three years ago from this night. A taxi crashed and twelve boys were killed, and this hungry thing came out of the forests that night and into the town to eat. For two months it grew fat there, turning the people against each other, making children to kill their own mothers, and eating the people of that town. This is a story of these times, this is a story of this province: IPI ZOMBI?

NARRATOR removes sheet from tall box and reveals the black-painted head and shoulders of INTOMBI 'NYAMA, resembling an African carving standing on a pedestal. Moving only its lips the statue speaks as if entranced.

INTOMBI 'NYAMA: The day the birds came, it started. I watched them and I knew it was coming. They came over from the forest in flocks, flock after flock after flock, black birds like I'd never seen before, flying so quietly and blocking the stars . . .

The old man was in his yard, and he was shaking his head, shaking his head at the small boys:

"Yoh, yoh, yoh! When we were boys those birds wouldn't dare to do a thing like this—passing above us like that, and we boys just sitting there and not even beating them! What kind of boys are there these days? If only I could be a boy again . . ."

They came from the forest, all night they came—flying, flying . . .

The old man said there would be great feasting, but me—I knew it was the end of the world . . .

Exit. A sickening thud of huge cow-hide drum, singers rise up on knees wailing traditional sangoma chant.

SINGERS:
Abazali bam, abazali bam,
Bayalila, bayalila . . .

ABAZALI BAM BAYALILA (MY PARENTS ARE CRYING . . .)

STEVE and KROTCH, the two bloodied schoolboys in white shirts, red ties, and long red socks, sitting on the altar, address the audience directly; a third bandaged and silent youth sits between them. The three singers are arrayed in a group to one side wrapped in blankets; they move into mechanical weeping action on cue.

STEVE: Ja, you know, it was late and we were coming back from Durban—fifteen boys.

KROTCH: At that time I was almost dreaming, then I heard a big noise and we just fell.

STEVE: I tried to scream: *"Imoto iyawe!"* and the taxi bounced on the ground and then it went down the hill and everybody was screaming.

KROTCH: When I woke up I just saw the taxi going round and round, I don't know what happened, then I woke up in the hospital. It's all because the driver was fast asleep.

STEVE: No, the driver was not fast asleep, the driver was drunk.

KROTCH: *Hayi,* he was tired.

STEVE: No, no, no—

KROTCH: He was tired.

STEVE: No, no, no, I was sitting next to him. He was drunk. I don't know how I survived, but somehow I got out of the taxi.

KROTCH: Who is the one who pulled me out?

STEVE: It was me.

KROTCH: Ja, *ne?*

STEVE: Ja, actually I don't know how I pulled him out, it was so dark—I pulled him by his feet.

KROTCH: Hey thanks man thanks, 'cos I was confused.

STEVE: Ja you know, I was so scared. The kombi was upside down—upside down! I crawled to the dashboard to try and pull another body out. The other guys were all dead then.

KROTCH: Where was I at that time? Was I sleeping?

STEVE: You were unconscious at that time.

KROTCH: *Yoh!*

STEVE: Ja, now I'm remembering . . . as we went off the road I saw fifty females in front of the taxi, just watching, with no clothes on, naked, undressed—

KROTCH: *Yoh!* How did you know there were fifty?

STEVE: Because I'm brilliant. I managed to count them—actually it was plus-minus fifty.

KROTCH: And tell me why you didn't shout to warn us, so we could see those witches?

STEVE: It all happened so quickly, you see. I shouted internally—inside myself. I was fascinated at that picture of the fifty women, and then the taxi went over the edge and I went out of my mind!

KROTCH: Even there in Durban my friend Xolani said his mother was wanting to kill him.

STEVE: Who?

KROTCH: Xolani. He said it. His mother is a witch. Hey, Xolani. Xolani! [*shaking the silent youth between them, who slumps over*] Is Xolani dead?

STEVE: Yes, he died with the others.
KROTCH: Oh, how could these mothers kill so many?
SINGERS:
Abazali bam, abazali bam,
Bayalila, bayalila . . .

Enter GOGO and FAZI, elderly women in Xhosa traditional dress—long orange shirts, turbans, huge strap-on gourd breasts—played by men in drag. They join their boys on the altar.

GOGO: *Yoh, wena,* what's wrong with you, huh?
STEVE: We had a crash grandmother.
GOGO: A crash, where?
FAZI: Oh my boy! Where does it hurt, where does it hurt? *Thixo wam* (my God), my son is alive!
GOGO: Tell us Steve, tell us what happened!
STEVE: You could just hear bones breaking—the others are all dead: twelve of them.

Enter MAMBAMBA, haggard and dressed in black drag.

MAMBAMBA: Where is my son Xolani? Have you seen my son Xolani?
BOYS: Xolani is dead!
MAMBAMBA: Oh my son, my son . . .
SINGERS:
Abazali bam, abazali bam,
Bayalila, bayalila . . .

The three mothers prance around the arena.

GOGO: Tell me what happened. Tell me everything.
KROTCH: It was so dark and the driver was sleeping.
FAZI: Sleeping! Driving the car asleep?
STEVE: No, no, no, he was not sleeping, he was drunk.
FAZI: The driver was drunk?
KROTCH: *Hayi* he was tired, my *bhuti.*
FAZI: Drunk? Tired? What is happening here?
SINGERS:
Abazali bam, abazali bam,
Bayalila, bayalila . . .

The three mothers prance around the arena. Enter doctor in a lab coat and big spectacles.

GOGO: Doctor. Doctor! Our sons have had a terrible crash!
DOCTOR: Ja, actually I was the first one there after the ambulance, and the bodies were all there on the side of the road covered in these blankets but there was no blood—twelve dead boys and no blood—and then I felt the pulse of one but it

was dead, but when I lifted up the blanket the face it was shaking like this shaking like this . . .

ALL: Shaking like this . . . shaking like this . . .

GOGO and FAZI: *Hawu 'madoda!* (Oh man!)

STEVE: It must be these witches.

GOGO and FAZI: *Amagqwira!* (Witches!)

STEVE: Yes, I saw fifty witches standing at the side of the road.

MAMBAMBA: Oh let's go and kill them, let's go and kill them!

KROTCH: I was so dizzy at that time. Steve saw everything.

GOGO: Tell me my boy, what did they say to you?

STEVE: They just smiled at me. All of them just smiled.

DOCTOR: *Thyini*, it seems to me you were all drunk.

STEVE and KROTCH: No, no, no—

FAZI: Hey, *wena*, my son does not drink!

DOCTOR: You don't know the children of today!

KROTCH: And one of them cried: "Xolani! Xolani! I want to kill you!"

MAMBAMBA: Oh my son, my son.

KROTCH: It's her! She was there at the crash. She is a witch.

MAMBAMBA: I'm not a witch, I'm not a witch.

FAZI: *Hamba* Satan!

MAMBAMBA: I'm not a witch, oh I'm not.

KROTCH: He was my best friend.

MAMBAMBA: Oh my God!

GOGO: Hey, why did you do this to our children?

FAZI: Why are you blackmailing us?

MAMBAMBA: Nobody likes me, where must I go, what must I do? Oh!

GOGO: I'm going to phone the police and tell them Mambamba was there—she is a witch.

MAMBAMBA: I'm not a witch, oh I'm not.

GOGO: Hey, *thula wena*, shut-up, shut-up, I'm trying to phone. [*into cell phone*] 9–1–1

ALL: Tring-tring . . . tring-tring . . . TRING-TRING!

COP: [*speaking into a vintage red telephone receiver*] Eh . . . hello!

GOGO: Hello, is that the police station?

COP: Eh, yes, this is Sergeant Ndindwe speaking.

GOGO: Okay, we have a big problem here—some witches have killed our sons.

COP: What? I do not understand what you are saying to me. Explain it carefully.

GOGO: Explain *yonke into ngendlela.* (Explain everything that happened.)

COP: *Ewe.*

GOGO: They were coming from . . . what? Where? Where?

FAZI, STEVE, KROTCH: *eThekweni.*

GOGO: Durban! Durban, they were coming from Durban, and as they reached that that that sharp curve, the kombi just fell, and they saw Mambamba flying on a loaf of bread with the other witches—fifty of them!

COP: *Yoh, yoh, yoh!* Where are the boys now?

GOGO: There are only five left, the others are all dead. Please you must come now and catch these witches, we need justice!

COP: Okay, I'm coming! Bee-bah bee-bah, bee-bah, bee-bah—

SINGERS:

Abazali bam, abazali bam,

Bayalila, bayalila . . .

Together COP, GOGO and FAZI form a little train—the police car—and chase Mambamba about the stage and then off. School boys wailing in the background. Enter SENTI—student leader in school uniform—in shock; mounts an up-turned cooldrink crate, centre, halts the singing and addresses the audience as schoolkids.

SENTI: Brothers and sisters. Students of Karl Malcomess, we are shocked today because of what has happened to our friends, our comrades, our brothers in arms. These news are a shock to me. They were young, they were innocent, they were promising students. As your student leader I promise you we are going to do something about this. We have allowed these things to happen for too long. We are going to come together. We are going to finish this thing!

ALL: bee-bah bee-bah . . .

Exit SENTI. Re-enter the "witch-hunt."

COP: We've got her!

FAZI: She is a witch.

MAMBAMBA: I'm not a witch, I'm not a witch.

GOGO and FAZI: You are!

MAMBAMBA: I'm not . . . *She* is a witch! [*Pointing into audience*]

ALL: Huh! [*All peer into audience in dread*]

MAMBAMBA: And that one!

ALL: Huh!

MAMBAMBA: And even that one!

GOGO: Oh, this place is infested—call the doctors! Call the doctors!

Intlombe (divining ceremony)

Rise up three sangomas (witchdoctors) dressed in their distinctive white attire with rattles, beads, sticks etc. They dance slowly in a tight ring around the central fire, leading the cast in the chant "Zilila ngantoni izinyanya zam?" (Why are the Spirits crying?)—which calls their spirit up inside them, enabling them to divine and to see sources of evil. Footstamping, drums, and whistles. At the climax of the dance one of them on her knees brays her prayers to her ancestors while another dives amongst the audience and retrieves evil talismans—a goat skull bristling with pins, a bottle of oily liquid. They rush it to centre and doctor it with potions and smoking herbs. The NARRATOR takes the charms from them and ends the ceremony.

NARRATOR: [*Punctuated by chants of agreement from The Natives*] My friends, now of course we can not say that witches were not involved in this thing—in our communities there are many women using witchcraft: maybe they want power or they have jealousy for your money or your family or your good luck. White people and even many blacks laugh at us, they think we are superstitious, but there are many things they do not know with their science, and also there are many things they do not know that they do not know. Sometimes a woman is putting some poison there at your gate, and this thing will burn you when you are walking past every day. Then your feet are swelling until you cannot walk, and no doctor can help you, even the *sangoma* or the prophet is helpless. Or the witch is sending these these these short men to poison you while you sleep, and the doctors say: "*Thyini!* Look at these crystals we are finding in your stomach," and nobody knows how they were getting there.

The sangomas found many of these things [*Indicating the talismans located by the sangomas*] hidden in people's houses in this town we are telling you about. This is a true story! These things have power for our people, you believe it or not.

But there is something bigger than that, something that brings a fear inside people, like a dirty thing so they look at their neighbours and say to each other: "she is the one" or "he is the one." This is a story about this thing, this thing that is all around us, just waiting to come inside.

But now, the trouble really started one week after the crash when a small girl, only eleven years, told some things to her friends. People, please welcome our special star to act this character . . . INTOMBI 'NYAMA! [*A moment of panic as she doesn't show*] *Iphi* Intombi 'Nyama?

WOMEN: [*Sitting in a row on the rostra in gaily coloured plastic skirts, call*] Intombi 'Nyama!

BOYS IN THE CUPBOARD

INTOMBI 'NYAMA: Hi! [*Played as an urban superstar in drag: pearls in her dreadlocks, plastic ball gown, diamante jewellery etc. Greets everybody, introduces herself in Xhosa, explains that she plays the role of the young girl, Malaksa, who first started the zombie rumours. Then mounts an old big bass drum, centre to take the part, speaks in dreamy tones*]

You know, when our friends were killed it took my breath away.
WOMEN: Aaah . . .
INTOMBI 'NYAMA: When our friends were killed it took my breath away.
WOMEN: Aaah . . .
INTOMBI 'NYAMA: My God, it was silent. As silent as the stars.
Have you ever lost a friend?
It was the quietest time of all.
And I wondered to myself, who would do such a thing?
And then I wondered, who would kill so many?
I remember our friends, with eyes like the stars,
Why? Why did she close their eyes?
I wondered all these things in that silence . . .

*Clatter of drums, marimbas, percussion, and the women bounce into dance
and song around the arena.*

WOMEN: [*Chanting*]
   If you are afraid of the dark, if you hear a bump in the night,
   You better be staying inside if you wanna be staying alive.
   They will catch you in your pyjama, they will eat you for their supper.
   Zombies looking for food. Ipi zombi up to no good.
INTOMBI 'NYAMA: And then I dreamed of a big *mielie* field,
   and all those long green leaves waving,
   waving in the wind—
WOMEN: waving in the wind
INTOMBI 'NYAMA: A strange dream for a small girl, a small girl like me—
   waving in the wind like long green tongues,
   and whispering
WOMEN: whispering
INTOMBI 'NYAMA: words to me
WOMEN: words to me
INTOMBI 'NYAMA: telling me secrets,
   calling my name . . . *mtla mtla mtla, mtla mtla mtla*
   I feel the wind, I feel the wind
MEN: [*Chanting*] Boys in the cupboard calling her name, boys in the cupboard
calling her name.
INTOMBI 'NYAMA: And then a bird says to me:
WOMEN: "*Yiza sisi, yiza* (Come, sister, come)—I'll show you everything."
INTOMBI 'NYAMA: A little bird, so I go . . .
MEN: Boys in the cupboard calling her name, boys in the cupboard calling her
name.
INTOMBI 'NYAMA: And the snake by the river is eating his children,
   eating his children with his big snake mouth,
   eating his children with his big snake mouth,
   eating his children with his big snake mouth . . .
   Huh! It's coming from my grandmother's cupboard!
   Oh, it's coming from the cupboard of *makhulu*! [*She dashes up the stairs of
   the altar to the cupboard*]
WOMEN: [*Chanting*] If you are afraid of the dark,
   If you hear a bump in the night,
   You better be saying your prayers,
   Or you'll be crying the tears.
   They will take you home to their mother,
   She will make you into their brother.
   It makes the tears run out of my eyes,
   Makes the tears run out of my eyes.

INTOMBI 'NYAMA: Ssh. [*Listening at the cupboard doors*]

Oh—human voices . . .

Ewe, ewe, Oh—they are hungry grandmother, the boys are hungry

Oh, they are thirsty grandmother, crying for water . . .

Oh they say "why, grandmother, why are we here?

Why, grandmother, we want to come out,

We want to come out, we want to come out,

Oh we see snakes, grandmother, snakes and frogs,

It's cold in here, cold and dark,

Oh I'm hungry, open the door,

Where's my mama, open the door . . ."

MEN: [*Chanting*] Boys in the cupboard calling her name, boys in the cupboard calling her name.

WOMEN: [*Chanting*] If you are afraid of the dark,

If you hear a bump in the night,

You better be staying in bed

Or you'll be losing your head.

She'll cut off your tongue with a knife,

You'll be dead the rest of your life.

Zombies looking for food,

Ipi zombi up to no good.

Extended chant with all women jump-dancing around in a ring singing at the audi-ence with heads thrown back and hands up-raised. INTOMBI 'NYAMA loses it and wanders down into the centre of the ring clutching her head. Dance/song ends.

NARRATOR: [*Leaping into the arena*] Intombi 'Nyama and the Natives!

INTOMBI 'NYAMA: Oh, you make me feel so special!

A cheer and all off except NARRATOR and INTOMBI 'NYAMA.
Stage is set for funeral.

INTOMBI 'NYAMA: My friends, hey we are proud to have you here to come and enjoy our performance, to listen to this terrible story—you make us very strong. And we have worked very hard to make this drama great for you—we even went to the mountains for two weeks to find the Spirit of this play. You think there is no Spirit, you think we are not working with the Spirit. You think the Spirit of Africa is dead because everybody is wanting the hungry Spirit of America inside them? *We* are making the spirit strong, *we* are bringing it to you. So you are not coming here by accident—something, maybe even your ancestors, brought us all together tonight. Also to our sponsors: we thank you very much that you helped us to do this work in these hard times. *Enkosi bhuti.* (Honored brother.)

NARRATOR: Now, I hope you are following this story? It is 15 October 1995, and we are on the sports field of Karl Malcolm High School with five thousand people and twelve coffins . . .

DEVIL with long red fork rises up through trapdoor, creeps on and stabs NARRA-TOR in the arse, he flees. DEVIL begins the falsetto introduction to "Nkosi sihlangene" in angelic tones, summoning up PRIESTS with a pitch of her fork.

THE FUNERAL

PRIESTS: We are gathered here today to bury our sons, in the name of our Lord Jesus Christ, amen.

The choir sweeps into hymn—Nkosi sihlangene—there's a great flourishing of white robes. The two PRIESTS don bright gowns under a vast umbrella, and the solemn choir all in white and sunglasses bear a coffin on high. An angel (played by INTOMBI 'NYAMA) lights altar candles. Priests take up position on the grand old big bass drum—after chasing DEVIL from it—with the umbrella towering above them. DEVIL crouches malevolently on the coffin. Choir gathers in pyramid formation on the altar.

PRIESTS: *Masevaleni amehlo.* (Let us close our eyes.) Let us pray.

All pray simultaneously in loud lamenting Xhosa.

PRIEST 1: [*PRIEST 2 gives Xhosa translations after each phrase*] Brothers and sisters, today we are sad, we grieve for the sons we will bury today; but listen to me, do not weep, do not weep: for *God* has come for our boys. *He* has come for our sons. He shouted their names and they answered His call. Be proud of your sons. They were hand-picked by God. They were called by the Lord. He said:

PRIEST 2: "Come to me. Come to me. I need you. I have work for you. I have a job for you in Heaven."

PRIEST 1: "Yes Father, yes Father, yes we are coming to Jerusalem, Father, we will come when ever you call us." And they went! Yes, they went. They gave up their lives to work for the Lord. Be proud of your sons. Their spirits are alive, alive in Jerusalem!

Three women break into hymn—Halleluiah—move forward with framed portraits of their deceased sons, kneel at the coffin where they place the portraits and then return to join the choir who sing the chorus.

WOMEN: Oh no my son, now you've left your mother
    You go to heaven and your mother weeps
    Yes a mother suffers, yes a mother's crying
    For the boy is killed and what can I do?
    Hosanna—hosanna . . .
CHOIR: Halleluiah, halleluiah . . .
WOMEN: Oh no no my son, your mother's crying,
    Now you live with God and what can I do?
    All my dreams are dying, mother suffers,

And my heart is dead and what can I do?

Hosanna...

CHOIR: Halleluiah, halleluiah...

PRIEST 2: But, let us learn from this lesson. Let us learn from this lesson. I say to you, I ask of you: are *you* prepared? Are *you* ready? For *your* time will come too! Yes your time will come! What are you hiding there in your closet? What are you doing there in the corner? NO! It's no good, it's no good...for the Father knows!

Enter three BOYS: SENTI, ZOL, FIRE. Confer at the coffin.

PRIEST 2: And the Father sees! He knows what you are doing. He sees what you are hiding, and He does not approve! He will punish you! Repent, I say repent, before it is too late. There is no escape!

Choir explodes into rousing hymn: "iNceba yavela!" (Mercy is coming!) BOYS into stomping "train dance," whistles blasting as they invade the funeral.)

PRIEST 1: Brothers and sisters...

SENTI: [*Imploring*] People, listen to me. This is not true. The spirits of our brothers are not alive and in Heaven. Their spirits were stolen before they could even reach Heaven. Stolen and made into slaves by our mothers. Stolen and locked up in the dark.

PRIEST 1: Oh! Beware of Satan. [*Drumbeat starts ominously, and choir erupts into panicky shifting dance*]

PRIEST 2: Beware of Satan.

PRIEST 1: For he is alive.

PRIEST 2: He is alive amongst us.

PRIEST 1: He comes when we are weak with grief.

PRIEST 2: He takes us when we are sad and angry.

PRIEST 1: He comes up like a snake through the floors of our houses.

PRIEST 2: He comes into our hearts and turns us against one another.

PRIEST 1: Beware of Satan. Trust in the Lord.

PRIEST 2: Pray to God now!

SENTI: And did the witches pray to God when they killed our brothers? Where was Jesus that night on the side of the road, and where is God now when our brothers are made into zombies?

FIRE: Open up these coffins 'bafundisi and show us the meat—the meat they want us to bury!

Choir screams, slowly raising black umbrellas.

PRIESTS: Oh the demons are in the house of the Lord!

FIRE: You can't bury this meat 'bafundisi. We the *abafana* must first find out who is responsible for this thing. We will save our comrades. And if you try, if you try to bury this meat we will burn this town. *Sizakuyitshisa!* (We will burn it!)

Choir rhythmically opening and closing umbrellas in synch, hooting with horror—the umbrellas make the eerie sound of big wings beating, to the delight of dancing DEVIL. Priests driven from their citadel, which is quickly taken by SENTI. FIRE and ZOL open coffin—inside, a shrouded human form, animal bones, and feathers. Choir screams and umbrellas burst open as a shield against the evil. Kudu horns wail. SENTI speaks in emotionless, hypnotic tones over the steady pulse of the drum. As he speaks, weaving the audience into his web, the choir cranes forward to gasp and ogle in horror at the contents of the coffin.

SENTI: *Yiza, jonga* (come and look), this is what they have done to our brothers. Look, these were your sons—now there is just meat. Come and see the meat. Come, look. These are not boys. Look, now they have beards. Have you ever seen boys with beards before? Look at their gray faces. Look at their long nails.

Don't be angry with us, we want your sons to rest in peace. She has stolen their souls and put bones in their heads, and cut off their tongues to make them her slaves, and you Christians say "do not question the ways of God"? Is this the ways of God? Must I sit here and wait for my turn?

WOMEN: [*Into Halleluiah hymn again*] Oh no my son, listen to your mother your brothers work in the house of God
A mother suffers, yes a mother's crying
Let your brothers sleep six foot underground.
Hosanna—hosanna . . .

CHOIR: Six foot under the ground, six foot under the . . .

SENTI: Where are our friends? You can not hide them forever. We will bring the witchdoctors from the mountains, they will bring our brothers back to life, they will show us who you are and then you will pay. We want a clean society.

FIRE: *Asheshe . . . asheshe . . . asheshe . . . shona!* (a war cry)

ALL: *Ziphi izitshixho? Ziphi izitshixho?* . . . (Where are the keys?) [*Stripping off gowns, throwing them down trapdoor, and advancing onto stage and to their instruments. Women run screaming, pursued by the DEVIL*]

THE FEAR

Brief burst of percussive song "Bulala abathakhati" (Kill the witches) and five BOYS in school uniforms muster in agitation.

ZOL: Kubo! Kubo! I am the son of Blood and the son of Anger. Hey, *bafana*—do you hear me?—I ask you young men—What is going on in our town of Bhongweni?

BOYS: What are you saying? What are you saying?

ZOL: Our brothers are in her grandmother's cupboard. She said it: —her grandmother—that Mrs Magudu—she's keeping our brothers in her cupboard.

BOYS: Even us too—we saw them—washing her taxies—our dead brothers.

ZOL: Where?

BOYS: There—at her house—washing the taxies—our dead brothers.

ZOL: When?

BOYS: Last night—and when we called them—they ran away.

ZOL: OH! That Mrs Magudu—that Mrs Magudu! Why does she hate us?

BOYS: She hates us because we are young—and she is too old—and we love her daughter!

ZOL: OH! That Mrs Magudu—that Mrs Magudu! Why does she hate us?
BOYS: Its the jealousy.—The jealousy.—The reason of the jealousy.
ZOL: OH! Kubo! Kubo!

*Percussive leap into "Bulala 'bathakathi." MRS MAGUDU runs onto arena
and is barked at by savage boy-dogs.*

ALL: *Bulala—bulala 'bathakathi!*
Bulala—bulala 'bathakathi!
SENTI: Comrades, order! This is a very serious matter. We must do things in
a proper manner. I will take control as usual.
BOYS: We must take action—before it's too late—these evil zombies—are
walking the streets!
SENTI: Comrades, this thing is very painful to us, I know, but let us do things
in a systematic way.
BOYS: Yes let us kill them—systematically:—five witches—every night.
SENTI: When?
BOYS: Tonight—we will kill them—Tonight—we must go!
KROTCH: Is anyone taking minutes? Is anyone taking minutes?
BOYS: No need for minutes! No need for minutes!
SENTI: Who?
BOYS: That thin ugly black one—there on the corner.
SENTI: Why?
BOYS: She lives alone in a big house!
SENTI: Who?
BOYS: That fatty fatty—.
SENTI: Why?
STEVE: She has a big cat, a big cat, a big black cat!
BOYS: Kill all the suspects. Let's kill all the suspects!
SENTI: Oh! Kubo! Kubo!

*Percussive leap into "Bulala 'bathakathi." Next woman dashes into
circle and is stoned.*

ALL: *Bulala—bulala 'bathakathi!*
Bulala—bulala 'bathakathi!
FIRE: Comrades! Young men of Bhongweni! These cruel mothers are out of
control! Who is the first one? Who is the first one?
BOYS: That Mrs Magudu—she is the first one—she's keeping our brothers—
to be her slaves.
FIRE: Hawu!
BOYS: She has *uhili*—a dwarf—a *tikoloshe!*
FIRE: Hawu!
BOYS: She rides a baboon at night—*borhum! borhum!* (the bark of a baboon)
FIRE: Dammit, the Christians are witches too.

KROTCH: We need evidence, where's the evidence?

BOYS: No need for evidence! No need for evidence!

KROTCH: What about the law! What about the law!

BOYS: We are the law! We are the law!

SENTI: Comrades, let us kill these criminals without delay.

FIRE: Viva the spirit of killing the witches—Viva! Viva!

BOYS: Viva! *Kubo! Kubo! Kubo!*

Percussive leap into "Bulala 'bathakathi." Next woman dashes into
circle and is stoned.

ALL: *Bulala—bulala 'bathakathi*!
Bulala—bulala 'bathakathi!

BOYS wash their hands in a bucket, then crouch in ambush.

THE SACRIFICE

MR MAGUDU and TV REPORTER on the altar. The REPORTER is the devil
with a flaming mic. Dim lights and candles.

WOMEN: [*Crooning gospel song*]
Go away, Devil, go away devil go away
Go away, Devil, go away devil go away
Who is knocking at my door? Who is knocking at my door?
The Devil is knocking at my door . . .

MRS MAGUDU: [*Stepping into centre*] This scene is about a woman who was killed, the first of the women they said were witches. [*Kneels with candle, centre, to pray*]

TV REPORTER: Mr Magudu, your mother was the first to be killed. I do not wish to be insensitive, but—uh, do you think your mother was a witch?

MR MAGUDU: No she was not a witch, I mean every Sunday she was going to church, and I never saw a snake or even a bird living inside her room—I mean there is no proof.

BOYS: [*Encroaching on Mrs Magudu*] *Ziphi izitshixho?* Where are the keys? *Ziphi izitshixho?* Where are the keys?

TV REPORTER: Can you tell our viewers what happened that night, it was the Friday before the funeral for the boys—

MR MAGUDU: I'm still seeing this . . . I can't believe . . . I-I-I don't understand why this thing happened. I mean, we are Christians—

BOYS: *Ziphi izitshixho?* Where are the keys? *Ziphi izitshixho?* Where are the keys?

TV REPORTER: Um, our viewers are very interested in these things, perhaps you could tell them what did happen to your mother . . .

MR MAGUDU: She came from the memorial service for the boys, she was so tired and she was in a rush to cook . . . Actually I was not there at that time, I went to a friend to get a part for the taxi . . . they sent one of the boys to knock at the door, a big crowd, they had a meeting that afternoon . . .

BOYS: *Ziphi izitshixho?* Where are the keys? *Ziphi izitshixho?* Where are the keys?

MR MAGUDU: He knocks on the door and says to her:

ZOL: Where are the children?

WOMEN: Who is knocking at my door? Who is knocking at my door? The Devil is knocking at my door . . . [*Sung in background*]

MRS MAGUDU: What children, *nyana?*

ZOL: Those who were killed, the school children.

MRS MAGUDU: No, I know nothing about those children.

BOYS: *Ziphi izitshixho?* Where are the keys? *Ziphi izitshixho?* Where are the keys?

> BOYS *gather around her as she kneels, clapping into her face,*
> *driving her on with fear.*

MRS MAGUDU: [*Taking a deep breath and then exclaiming in a stream of shrill exhalation*] Then there was a smashing of glass and this gang was coming through the back door, and others coming through the front, breaking the tv and the pictures and everything, and my grandchildren were screaming because they were scared, and the boys were shouting, and the boys were shouting: *Ziphi izitshixho?* Where are the keys?

BOYS: *Ziphi izitshixho?* Where are the keys? *Ziphi izitshixho?* Where are the keys?

MRS MAGUDU: They wanted the keys of my cupboard, and they were checking all the rooms but they couldn't find anything, and I said: "Come and look in the cupboard!"—They were too scared! And I was praying "Oh my God, Oh my God!"

BOYS: *Ziphi izitshixho?* Where are the keys? *Ziphi izitshixho?* Where are the keys?

MRS MAGUDU: They dragged me out and the dog was dead in the garden, they carried me through the streets singing "Kill the witch! Kill the witch!" and I was saying: "Oh my Jesus, help me, forgive them for what they do . . . "

> *Burst of percussion. MRS MAGUDU launches into voodoo dance of fear, ZOL*
> *dancing about her provocatively, then FIRE joins, then SENTI with a knife. They*
> *dance the dance of her death then drag her to the altar, plunge in and bludgeon her,*
> *one woman screaming as the assailants pull back, tries to hold her then collapses in*
> *tears. MRS MAGUDU crawls forward to centre stage and dies. All boys except*
> *SENTI—with a bloody dagger clenched above his head—slink away.*

MR MAGUDU: They cut off all her fingers and stabbed her in the chest, but she still had her clothes on so the intestines could not come out, they carried her to the field on their shoulders, like a soccer champion, and beat her with sticks and crushed her with rocks, these big, big rocks they picked up, when I first heard I just ran in confusion, when I got there I mean if I had a gun I would have blown somebody up—bah-bah-bah—but there were too many police. They arrested seven boys.

MR MAGUDU: You know, if she had been a witch then I would not blame them, but she died saying, "I know nothing." She died saying that.

SENTI: We are cleaning this town, my brother, all of these cockaroaches must go. We want to live in peace. We want our rights, and you want to charge me for murder. Must we all work for these mamas?

MR MAGUDU: You know, if she had been a witch then I would not blame them, but she died saying, "I know nothing." She died saying that.

Exit. SENTI alone with the knife and the body.

SENTI: [*Becoming angry*] Even the police, they do not protect us at all. They just come with their big cars and take all our girlfiends to Chicken Licken while our brothers are murdered by these witches. This thing is not finished, I promise you. I'll go to jail—maybe for twenty-five years. That's how life is. But this thing is not finished. I'll be back. And when I get back I will get those who have sent me to jail. That's how life is. *Bunjalo ubomi.*

SENTI off.

SHAKIN' THE BLUES AWAY

Insect sounds fill the dark night; DEVIL opens cupboard doors. Inside waits a group of white-painted boys, naked but for loin-cloths, arms twisted behind their backs, and wearing long narrow African masks. They throng out onto stage, bobbing like vultures, and gather to feed on MRS MAGUDU, and to menace the audience. A thrill of crackling turn-table sound, the spotlight comes up on INTOMBI 'NYAMA in the cupboard, the zombies glance up as she breaks into an up-tempo and over the top lip-synch of Doris Day's "Shakin' the blues away" by Irving Berlin. The thrilled zombies caper around backing her in fifties musical song and dance. [Editor's note: The song makes reference to "an old superstition way down south" that you can avoid trouble by shaking your body to "a voodoo melody."] Like Dorothy from The Wizard of Oz *she leads the adoring zombies out into the world at large . . .*

THE HACKING

A big bass boom throbs into life. NARRATOR leaps into the arena and throws himself into frenzied dance, then begins his voodoo tirade. Boys return to arena and change into their school attire, and move into positions in a ring around the arena for "hacking dance."

NARRATOR: My friends, this is a true story, you do not believe it. This is a true story of sickness and nobody is knowing how to heal it. Even our ancestors cannot help us as they did in the past—they work fulltime for us day and night, but the people have forgotten them and they have so little power. They come to us in our dreams and say, children of our fathers, we are so hungry . . . This is a story of a big hunger, the hungry ghosts of Africa. This is a story of power! Do you feel it?! Feel it all around you. This is our power! [*Drums*]

INTOMBI 'NYAMA: Look at the evil in this country! Look at the jails full of people! It is destroying this country. People throw away their customs, throw away their respect, throw away their ancestors! What is wrong with the people? What is this sickness? People raping each other, killing each other, young boys carrying guns. You've got to make the Spirit strong in you to fight this evil, got to look inside you and fight it with the strength of our culture!

NARRATOR: This is a story of a big hunger, the hungry ghosts of Africa. This is a story of power! Do you feel it?! Feel it all around you. This is our power! [*Drums crescendo, INTOMBI 'NYAMA and NARRATOR trance dancing*] For six weeks those bodies lay there in the mortuary. Sangomas came, but they could not bring life back to those bodies, they were saying "no, there are too many witches in this place, the witches eat holes in our power. This thing is too strong!" And what can our ancestors do and what can even Jesus do when this thing is eating a community?

Women shriek into "Ababuyanga bantwana bethu" (Our children have not returned)

NARRATOR: This is a hungry story,
INTOMBI 'NYAMA: This story eats people alive,
NARRATOR: Can you feel it, the hunger of this story?
INTOMBI 'NYAMA: It eats us with its jaws,
NARRATOR: It eats us bones and all,
INTOMBI 'NYAMA: The hunger of this story, it has the teeth of the night,
NARRATOR: The hunger of the forest,
INTOMBI 'NYAMA: We are telling you this story, do you see how we die like flies?
NARRATOR: Do you see how it eats us alive?
INTOMBI 'NYAMA: The hunger of evil,
NARRATOR: The hunger of the spirits,
INTOMBI 'NYAMA: The hunger of the night,
NARRATOR: The hunger of the people,
INTOMBI 'NYAMA: The hunger of the roads,
NARRATOR: The hunger of God,
INTOMBI 'NYAMA: The hunger of the mothers,
NARRATOR: Eating us alive . . .

Boys in ring slowly rise up and as NARRATOR cracks his whip at the summit of the altar they launch into the hacking dance around the open coffin while the drums pound and the singers cry. Suddenly they freeze, axes are handed to them and they face the audience in a ring.

BOYS: For two months—it grew fat here—this thing

turning the people against each other
eating the people of our town
until we chopped those bodies—into little pieces.
NARRATOR: Why? [*Cracking his whip*]
BOYS: To drive this thing away.
NARRATOR: Where?
BOYS: Back into the forest
NARRATOR: Where?
BOYS: Back into the night.
NARRATOR: O! Kubo kubo!

They launch back into the manic hacking dance, culminating in FIRE leaping onto the coffin and hacking the body to pieces as the others collapse.

WOMEN: [*Crooning*] Go away, Devil, go away Devil go away
Go away, Devil, go away Devil go away
Who is knocking at my door? Who is knocking at my door?
The Devil is knocking at my door . . .

Cast wrap themselves in blankets and leave the arena singing softly.

NARRATOR: We build our fences up and up and up, even with thorns and with aloes. In the morning they are broken and the mielies are gone. There is something bigger than all of us—something worse than you can imagine. There in the river. There in the veld. We pray to our ancestors and offer them gifts: beer, meat and even money, but this thing is too hungry. You lock your doors at night and close the windows, but it creeps inside, in through the keyhole, and in through the cracks, in while you sleep, in while you breathe. You wake up in the morning and this thing has been inside you and then you are so empty. You wake up too quickly—it is still inside you, and then you are lost . . . Good night. [*Exit with maniacal laughter*]

All break into "Zitshothina, si fela ethongweni" (we die in our dreams) outside the exit, to receive their applause as the audience files out.

A = Afrikaans; *S* = Setswana; *T* = Tsotsitaal; *Z* = isiZulu or isiXhosa

abafana, *Z:* boys, young men

abafazi, *Z:* married women

aikona, *Z:* no

American gang: so called because of their taste for expensive U.S. clothes. Became the most powerful gang in Sophiatown. Numbered about fifteen members.

atjar: a hot pickle or relish made with fruit or vegetables, chilis, and curry spices

Ayesha: sister of the Prophet Mohammed

baas, *A:* boss

Back of the Moon: a famous shebeen

bafana, *Z:* variant of abafana

'bafundisi, *Z:* contraction of abafundisi, priests, teachers

bakkie: small, light truck, mini pickup

Balansky's: the rowdy, run-down cinema in Sophiatown

Bantu: official designation of black South Africans by National Party government. The term is derived from the linguistic designation for the group of languages spoken in southern Africa, but black South Africans dislike it because of its association with apartheid and its grammatical incorrectness—"abantu" means people, "umuntu" means person.

Bantu Education Act of 1953: forced a compulsory, inferior curriculum on the children of the Black majority in all schools whether public or private. The ANC called for a school boycott beginning 1 April 1955. On that date, St. Cyprian's Mission School in Sophiatown closed down rather than teach the required curriculum. "Shebeen schools" and cultural clubs were organized to take the place of official schools.

bioscope: movie house, cinema

Bismillah: "In the name of Allah," a pious expression used by Muslims at the start of any undertaking; "make Bismillah"—"say a prayer and proceed with the task"

bladdy: bloody

blerry: bloody

Blue Train: methylated spirits, so-called because of its color and after the luxury train that runs between Cape Town and Johannesburg

Boere, *A:* Boers, Afrikaners, the National Party government

boet, *A:* brother

boma: stockade in which game animals are kept for protection

bonnet: hood of car

Bop: Television station ran by the Bophuthatswana homeland authority

bra: brother

broe: brother

broer, *A:* brother

Bulala abathakhati, *Z:* "Kill the wizards/witches." Abathakhati are associated with evil magic, in contrast to sangomas, who use magic and divination for healing and helping people. The phrase "Bulala 'bathakhati" was supposedly uttered by Dingane, the Zulu king, when he ordered his troops to kill an unarmed group of Afrikaners who had come to negotiate rights to settle on Zulu land in 1838. The massacre set off a war between the Zulus and Afrikaners. This phrase and its historical reference are well known to most South Africans.

can't-get, *T:* virtuous, well-bred young woman

charf: to say, to tell

codesa-desa: to bargain, to negotiate, after CODESA, the Convention for a Democratic South Africa, multi-party talks 1991–93 to establish a working plan for a government of transition and a new constitution

coevert: O.K., cool; S'coevert—that's cool

Congress: the African National Congress

Congress of the People: 3,000 delegates from the ANC, South African Indian Congress, South African Coloured People's Organization, Congress of Democrats, and South African Congress of Trade Unions met in Kliptown, near Johannesburg, and adopted the Freedom Charter (which called for an end to discrimination and became the central document cited in the struggle against apartheid) on 26 June 1955.

dagga: marijuana

Defiance Campaign: first mass demonstration of passive resistance against the new apartheid laws, organized by ANC and South African Indian Congress. Collective defiance of discriminatory laws began 26 June 1952 and lasted until early 1953. 8,000 arrested.

deurmekaar, *A:* confused

Dikgang tsa gompieno, *S:* News of the day

Dis khuvet onder die korset, *T:* everything's fine, it's cool

doek: a scarf worn over the head

dof, *A:* stupid

dop, *A:* a tot, a shot of liquor

drift: shallow fording point on a river

Drum **magazine:** a popular magazine for urban Black readers. The publisher and editor were English but the journalists were among the most important Black writers and intellectuals of the 1950s. Published exposés of abusive conditions in prisons and was highly respected for its knowledge and treatment of political and cultural issues. Featured some articles on gangs such as the Americans.

fahfee: illegal numbers lottery run by Chinese bookies in Sophiatown

fanakalo (also spelled "fanagalo"): a pidgin used in the mines to communicate between foremen and African workers

Freedom Square: unofficial name. So-called because of rallies held there protesting the government's discriminatory regulations

gaan, *A:* go (the "g" in Afrikaans is a glottal fricative)

gat, *A:* ass, (lit.) hole; in reference to a place, a dingy dive

gatas, *T:* cops

gee pad, *A:* give way, clear out

genuine stuff: pure, imported liquor instead of the homebrew or adulterated liquor commonly available in shebeens

gonee, *T:* knife

haai: exclamation of surprise, hey!

hamba, *Z:* go

hayikhona, *Z:* no

Hillbrow: densely populated residential district in central Johannesburg. By the late 1980s it had become a "grey zone"—although reserved for Whites, few Whites wanted to live in the inner city. Some buildings were abandoned to squatters, many landlords began renting to non-Whites, and authorities did not attempt to enforce the apartheid residential restrictions.

hoendervleis, *T:* white woman, lit. "chicken meat"

hoozit: how is everything?

House of Truth: Can Themba's home, a corrugated iron shack of several rooms, where drinking parties and intense intellectual discussions were held

Huddleston, Father Trevor: Prior of the Anglican Church of Christ the King, champion of urban poor, and critic of apartheid.

Huddleston's Mission: St. Cyprian's Mission School, where Blacks could get a good education before the Bantu Education Act took effect, and which served as a community center.

Immorality Act of 1950: made all sexual relations between Whites and other races illegal, abolished in 1985

ja: yes (pronounced "yah")

jislaaik: common, mild expletive expressing surprise—sheesh, gosh, jeez

jong, *A:* young one, kid

Jozi: Johannesburg

juffrou, *A:* Miss (pronounced "ye-froh")

jungle, *T:* knife

juss-laaik: variant of "jislaaik," more emphatic

kaalgat, *A:* bare-assed

kaffir, *A:* nigger

kak, *A:* shit, crap

kist, *A:* a lidded chest

klap, *A:* slap, smack

kombi: minivan, often used as taxi

Kort Boy: George Mbalweni, leader of the American Gang, which he organized in 1947. Served eighteen years in prison for murder, then settled in Meadowlands, Soweto, where he became a plumber.

kubo: Xhosa war cry

kudu: a large antelope with long curling horns

kwela music: popular urban music of 1950s that combined jazz and African musical forms and emphasized vocals.

larnie, *T:* white person

L.M.: Lourenço Marques, former name of Maputo, the capital of Mozambique

lobola: bride price, a payment, usually in cattle, made by the man to the parents of his prospective bride in some ethnic groups, such as the Zulu.

location: (usually outlying) urban district reserved for non-whites, also called "native township" or simply "township"—notorious for overcrowding, crime, and poor municipal services

lorry: large, heavy-duty truck

luister, *A:* listen

Lut(h)uli, Albert John Mvumbi: elected president-general of the ANC in 1952. Won the Nobel Peace Prize in 1961 for the ANC's nonviolent passive resistance campaign against apartheid in the 1950s.

mahala, *Z:* free of charge

majieta, *T:* young man, dude

makhulu, *Z:* large, big

Maklera, *T:* Newclare, a mixed-race Johannesburg suburb similar to Sophiatown

malaka, *Z:* untidiness, unkemptness, after *mahlakahlaka*

Mandela, Nelson: in the 1950s shared a law practice with Oliver Tambo in Johannesburg, elected national president of the Youth League in 1950 and Deputy-President of the ANC in 1952, volunteer-in-chief of the Defiance Campaign of 1952, exercised his leadership in secret after he was banned from public gatherings and political appointments by the apartheid regime, oversaw the M-plan, became involved in armed resistance in 1961, imprisoned 1962–1990.

Maseru West: district in Maseru, the capital of Lesotho

mashubane, *Z:* revered elder

matara, *T:* lady

mbamba, *T:* home-brewed beer

Meadowlands: a district in Soweto

meneer, *A:* sir

meths: methylated spirits, strained through bread and drunk for a cheap, crazed, sometimes lethal high

mevrou, *A:* Mrs., madam

mfo, *Z:* friend, brother

mielie: corn, cornmeal, the principal staple crop in South Africa

mod cons: modern conveniences, household appliances

Modimo wa khotso, *S:* God of peace

moegoe, *T:* hick, bumpkin, fool

mooch: to hang around, to loiter

Mooi Street: a street in central Johannesburg. "Mooi" means pretty, nice, great

M-plan: "M" for Mandela, an attempt in mid-1950s to build mass membership in the ANC organized in cells at the grass-roots level that would be responsive to direction from a tiered hierarchy of leaders without the need for public meetings.

Mr. Drum: a pseudonym used by various writers for some articles in *Drum* magazine. Henry Nxumalo was the original Mr. Drum, famed for his exposés of prisons and prison farms.

mugu: variant of moegoe

native reserves: homelands, bantustans, rural areas reserved exclusively for Blacks. Under apartheid, all Blacks were assigned "citizenship" in a native reserve, even if they had been born and raised in an urban area and had no connection to the rural area aside from language or remote ancestry

nee, *A:* no

niks, *A:* nothing, nothing doing, no way

nooit, *A:* never

notch, *T:* to understand

nylon, *T:* virtuous, well-bred young woman

Odin Cinema: the cleaner, better-maintained cinema in Sophiatown with a more genteel, well-behaved audience than at Balansky's. Musical concerts and political meetings were also held here.

oke: bloke, guy

Ons dak nie. Ons pola hier!, *T:* We'll never move. We're staying here. (slogan during resistance to Sophiatown removals)

Orlando Pirates: soccer team based in Soweto, also called Buccaneers

ou, *A:* old

ouens, *T:* guys

pack up: to break up in uncontrollable laughter

pap: a stiff cornmeal porridge, staple food of Blacks, eaten with fingers

pasop, *A:* watch out, beware

PE: Port Elizabeth

plek, *A:* place

poephol: fool, idiot, ass

porsie, *A:* apartment, digs; (lit.) portion, allotment

purple haze: methylated spirits

Resha, Robert (Bo) Mweli: became Transvaal President of the ANC's Youth

League in 1953, served as acting national president of the League 1954–55 and as volunteer-in-chief of the ANC's efforts to mobilize resistance to the Sophiatown removals. Left S.A. in 1961 and was a major representative of the ANC in exile.

rubberneck, *T:* loose woman, she turns her head for any man

Sandton: wealthy, exclusive suburb north of Johannesburg

sangoma: witchdoctor, spiritual adviser, diviner, traditional healer, an important figure in Nguni cultures

saracen: armored police van

shebeen queen: owner/proprietor of an illegal bar in one of the non-white townships

shebeen schools: see "Bantu Education Act"

situation, *T:* intellectual

skelm, *A:* thief

skokiaan, *T:* home-brewed liquor served in shebeens made with yeast, sugar, and water, but sometimes fortified with methylated spirits, battery acid, or other unsavory ingredients

skorrie morrie, *T:* good-for-nothing

slegte vrou, *A:* bad woman

Sophiatown: Johannesburg suburb famous for its nightlife and culture where the races could associate freely with one another. One of the few urban areas where Blacks could own land. Only 2 percent of the residents actually owned property; 82 percent were tenants and 16 percent subtenants in very crowded conditions.

steek, *A:* stick, stab

stoep, *A:* raised porch or veranda at front of house

Strydom, Johannes: Prime Minister of South Africa under National Party rule, 1954–58

suka, *Z:* get away!, common expression of distaste or disbelief

Sun City: a gambling resort established in the "independent homeland" of Bophuthatswana, northwest of Johannesburg, in order to avoid the puritanical restrictions of South African laws.

taal, *A:* language

Tambo, Oliver Reginald: helped organize the Youth League of the ANC in 1943. Opened a law practice with Mandela in 1952. Secretary-General of ANC 1954–58 despite being banned from public gatherings in 1954. Deputy-President of ANC 1958–67. Went into exile in 1960. Became Acting President-General in 1967 when Albert Lutuli died.

tante, *A:* aunt

thatha, *Z:* take it (pronounced "tata")

Thembalethu, *Z:* our hope

thula, *Z:* hush, be quiet (pronounced "tula")

tikoloshe, *Z:* small supernatural creature similar to troll, also called Uhili.

tjerrie, *T:* chick, girl

Tobiansky, Herman: real estate developer who laid out Sophiatown. Although he intended the suburb for Whites, when they refused to buy because of nearby sewage facilities, he sold lots to Blacks, Coloureds, and Indians.

torch, *T:* to look at

Triomf: name given the all-White suburb that replaced Sophiatown

tsotsitaal: gangster slang, the street argot of Sophiatown and other urban areas, based on Afrikaans with a liberal mixture of English, various Bantu languages, and free invention; its development was driven by the need for a common urban language and by a desire to distinguish this language from Afrikaans.

tune: to say to. "He tunes me"—he says to me.

ubejane, *Z:* black rhinoceros

uit, *A:* out

Umhlanga Rocks: luxury beach resort area north of Durban

Umkhonto We Sizwe, *Z:* Spear of the Nation. Military wing of the ANC, formed in 1961 due to the failure of nonviolent resistance to stop the advance of apartheid policies.

U.P.: United Party. Held power in S.A. from 1933 to 1948, when the National Party won the election. Remained the official opposition party until the 1980s.

Verwoerd, Hendrik: Minister of Native Affairs 1950–58, Prime Minister 1958–66. The chief architect of apartheid laws.

voetsak, *A:* scram

vuka, vukani, *Z:* wake up

washesha, *Z:* fast

wena, *Z:* you

Westdene: white suburb bordering Sophiatown in 1950s

wiebit, *T:* woman, chick, (lit.) little thing

witgat, *A:* white ass (in Afrikaans the "w" makes a "v" sound)

woza, *Z:* come

Xuma, Dr. Alfred Bitini: President-General of the ANC in the 1940s. Reorganized and strengthened the ANC. Active in protests against pass laws in the 1940s and in defending the rights of Sophiatown property owners in the early 1950s.

yashmak: among Muslims in South Africa, a hood that covers the hair and neck but not the face

Youth League: formed in 1943 to give a voice to young militants within the ANC. Often called for more extreme measures of protest than the ANC leadership. Helped organize a general strike in the Johannesburg area on 1 May 1950 to protest new apartheid laws—rioting broke out and police killed 18 people. Played a key role in the Defiance Campaign of 1952.

zabba-zabba: heavily promoted scratch-card lottery, an evocation of the household appliances and sudden wealth that the lottery promises, a general expletive of enthusiasm, "hey, hey!" Possibly related to tsaba-tsaba, popular music of 1940s and 1950s that mixed African melody and rhythm with elements from jazz and Latin American music, the dance associated with the music in which couples move toward one another and then away without touching.

zetz, *Yiddish:* slap

zol, *T:* marijuana cigarette, joint

Zola Budd: noun—"taxi," a small commercial passenger van, usually unlicensed, working a set route along a main urban road, between city and townships, or on longer routes. Named after the South African Olympic runner because they are white, quick, and accident prone. Verb/adjective—to run quickly/running quickly.

◆

David Graver earned a Ph.D. in comparative literature from Cornell University in 1987. Since then, he has taught drama at Loyola University of Chicago, Stanford University, Columbia University, and the University of Chicago. He is author of The Aesthetics of Disturbance and numerous articles on twentieth-century drama and performance. He has been studying, teaching, and writing on South African drama since 1988. In 1997, he enrolled in the J.D. program at the University of Chicago law school, where he was elected editor-in-chief of the interdisciplinary journal Roundtable for the 1999–2000 academic year.